Jesus Christ
THE
RISEN
LORD

Jesus Christ
THE
RISEN
LORD

FLOYD V. FILSON

ABINGDON PRESS
New York ⨍ Nashville

JESUS CHRIST THE RISEN LORD

Copyright © MCMLVI by Pierce & Washabaugh

Library of Congress Catalog Card Number: 56-8740

Scripture quotations unless otherwise noted are from the
Revised Standard Version of the Bible and are copyright
1946 and 1952 by the Division of Christian Education of the
National Council of the Churches of Christ in the U. S. A.

SET UP, PRINTED, AND BOUND BY THE
PARTHENON PRESS, AT NASHVILLE,
TENNESSEE, UNITED STATES OF AMERICA

PREFACE

SINCE THE OPENING CHAPTER EXPLAINS MY POINT OF VIEW, there is no need to discuss or defend it here. The second chapter presents the essentials of the common New Testament preaching. This chapter is therefore basic for all that follows; the remaining chapters develop in more detail the points that appear in the outline of the basic Apostolic Gospel.

Such a method involves some repetition, but it has the advantage of giving first in general survey the basic message of the Apostolic Church, and then providing a more detailed discussion of each major topic in that outline.

My thanks go to the many students at McCormick Theological Seminary with whom I have discussed biblical theology. They have heard me try more than one pattern of presentation and finally come to the one used in this book. I also recall with pleasure the six summer weeks of 1952 which I spent teaching New Testament theology in the Perkins School of Theology at Southern Methodist University. I found there another opportunity to test the outline here presented.

In the preparation of this book, as in so many other undertakings, I have been greatly helped by the kindly criticism and competent typing of my wife.

FLOYD V. FILSON

CONTENTS

CHAPTER I

Biblical Theology
BASIS AND METHOD

THIS BOOK IS AN ESSAY IN BIBLICAL THEOLOGY. NOT MANY DECADES ago numerous scholars joined in emphatic rejection of the phrase "biblical theology," and there still are those who consider it outmoded. Such scholars assert that biblical theology fails to do justice to the diverse nature of the biblical writings, which offer only fragmentary doctrinal discussions and are unsystematic in content. They further declare that scholarship can speak only of human experience and ideas, and that therefore the term theology, which takes God seriously, is not a proper term for historians, who deal with man's life and thought. They also insist that it is artificial and unscientific to separate the Bible from other Jewish and Christian literature of ancient times; indeed, they regard it as partisan and distorting to study the canonical Jewish-Christian writings apart from the full stream of ancient life and religion.

Moved by these views, such scholars prefer to speak of the history of religion; they study the history of religious ideas. At the most, they are willing to speak of the religion or the thought of the Bible, or of the Old or New Testament.[1] In all this they express their honest conviction that the scholar's task is to be objective. He studies, speaks, and writes as a conscientious neutral, whose one purpose is to determine the truth and state it without partisan bias. Those who hold this view of the task of biblical scholarship are neither atheists nor cynics. The ones whom I know are men of faith, and I respect their honesty of mind and vigor of conscience. They are convinced that the method of study which can advance the interests of both scholarship and faith is

[1] A strong presentation of this viewpoint is made by E. W. Parsons, *The Religion of the New Testament* (New York: Harper & Bros., 1939).

the rigidly objective method which they champion, and they hold that biblical theology violates basic demands of that method.

For more than a generation, however, there has been a strong tendency to return to the use of the term biblical theology.[2] The conviction has grown among many Christian scholars that we cannot do justice either to historical truth or to Christian concern without using the approach which biblical theology supplies. This conviction I fully share, and in this book I try to give it persuasive expression.

It is not my aim nor would it serve my present purpose to carry on extended debate with those who hold a different view. By far the best thing is to state as clearly as possible the point of view and basic convictions which shape my thought, and then let the strength or weakness of that position come to light in the actual presentation of the biblical message. The viewpoint which underlies this presentation may best be summarized in eight points.

I. God the Central Axiom and Actor

Biblical theology takes seriously the fact of God. If we limit our presentation of biblical content to the purely human and natural scene, we cannot deal with God as anything more than an idea or interest of mankind. There are, of course, many scholars who insist that neither in general historical study, nor in the history of ideas, can we do more than deal with what men have thought about God, or what they have done to establish relations with the God whom they make the object of their faith and thought and cult practice. In this view, God is an idea. Men may think that he is real, and the historian therefore may say that men think so, but he is simply describing the attitude of men; he is not asserting or denying the existence or action of God. That is outside his field.

The biblical writers would be utterly unable to understand this point

[2] For surveys which show this trend, see Otto J. Baab, "Old Testament Theology: Its Possibility," and Amos N. Wilder, "New Testament Theology in Transition," both found in The Study of the Bible Today and Tomorrow, ed. H. R. Willoughby (Chicago: University of Chicago Press, 1947), pp. 401-18 and 419-36. See also in The Interpreter's Bible the essay of G. Ernest Wright, "The Faith of Israel" (New York and Nashville: Abingdon Press, 1952), I, 349-89, and R. H. Strachen, "The Gospel in the New Testament" (1951), VII, 3-31.

of view. For them God was a fact; indeed, he was the central fact of all life and history. The whole story made sense to them only because they could trace, at least in part, the presence and working of God. They were gladly committed to worship and serve him. They knew that "the fool says in his heart, 'There is no God'" (Pss. 14:1; 53:1), but they could not understand how any sensible man could say such a thing, and they almost never felt the need to argue for the existence or crucial importance of their God. They spoke as committed believers. Any presentation of the biblical content that breathes a neutral or detached air is a radical distortion of their message.

Moreover, in their faith they did not regard God as an impersonal ideal, or as a remote or passive being, or as one whose relation to human history is merely past or future. They had an idea of history quite different from that which we derive from the usual high-school or college course in history. Modern writing of history deals essentially with human experience in the natural world. To the biblical writers this would be worse than a kingdom without a king, a home without parents, a ship without a pilot. They thought of history as the scene of God's holy, powerful, and purposeful action. Without that central actor the movements on the human scene made no sense. With him at the center there was meaning and hope for those who allied themselves with the purpose of God.

To take this outlook seriously shatters the entire method of objective study. Therefore, biblical theology confronts us with a crucial issue at the very outset. Theology, as the root meaning of the word makes clear, is the doctrine of God, the living God, the God men know by faith. He who turns to God is no longer neutral. Biblical theology, properly understood, must break with the method of neutral historical study.

But it is not only the biblical theologian who finds it necessary to abandon the pose of rigid neutrality. More and more it has become clear that all our grasp and writing of history involves a vigorous element of interpretation. To make sense of all these billions upon billions of endless details, the student of history consciously or unconsciously must seek a clue which enables him to put together a picture that satisfies

11

his mind and appeals to his readers. As a matter of fact, the work of every great historian, including those of the critical and liberal viewpoint, reveals on close study a rather definite philosophical basis. The Hegelianism of Ferdinand Christian Baur is only one example. But if every historian actually has a point of view and a set of philosophical or theological presuppositions, it is far better to face and admit this fact openly, and it is no longer fair or proper to belittle biblical theology because the note of faith and commitment shines through its presentation. The crucial question is simply this: Which viewpoint is true? Which is capable of presenting with the greatest faithfulness and clarity the message which the Bible contains? And it is hard to see how this biblical message of faith can ever be presented clearly and fairly without taking seriously the fact of God as the unquestioned axiom and central actor of the whole biblical story.

This position does not sacrifice either intelligence or honesty. If God not only exists, but also acts and controls the course of history, the intelligent and honest thing is to live and think and write our account of the biblical message in the light of that fact. Such a fact is too basic and dominant to ignore. We must study, think, and write in the presence of God and in the light of his action and demand.[3]

It is hard to see how this can rightly lead to intellectual laziness or to dishonest warping of facts discerned in study. The biblical God claims the whole life of man. The loyal response to that claim will include the dedication of the mind to God. And it will offer not a weaker but a stronger impulse to honesty. How did the idea ever originate that academic duty and neutral scholarship will guarantee honesty, but that faith and loyalty to God will warp the mind, weaken the conscience, and lead to distortion of facts? It may be true that Christian scholars have often sinned by not facing squarely all the facts or by letting pious profession substitute for hard study. It no doubt is true that Christians—like many others—find it difficult to shake themselves free from inherited ideas. Furthermore, we need not belittle scholars who maintain integrity out of a sense of duty to their profes-

[3] See my essay, "The Central Problem Concerning Christian Origins," *The Study of the Bible Today and Tomorrow*, ed. H. R. Willoughby (Chicago: University of Chicago Press, 1947), pp. 329-44.

12

sional task and standards. But we certainly have no reason to admit that faith is the inevitable foe of honest study. He who believes in God, the holy God of truth, has the highest motive for rigorous scholarly method and honest presentation of facts. How could anything but facts and truth and persistent, intensive study honor the God of righteousness and truth?

The crucial question is whether there is such a living God. To those who are convinced that he both exists, acts, and claims man's loyalty, it is only natural to present biblical theology upon this frankly theological basis.

II. God's Redemptive Work in History

Biblical theology finds in God's special work in history the characteristic form and content of the biblical message. It never belittles the religious experience and thinking of individual men, and it recognizes that God speaks to individuals in specific situations. But the unique thing about the biblical message is found not in its system of ideas, for the Bible is not a closely knit thought system, but rather in the ongoing working of God in history.

The Bible does not define God in a formal way. It does not codify its content into a formal theology. Its human actors are not unrelated individuals. They are links in a human chain, actors in a succession of events in which the "eyes of faith" have seen the connected and purposeful working of God.[4] This chain of events, spokesmen, and workmen of God reaches far back; it points back to the eternal purpose and creative working of God in giving life to man. It also points forward to the fulfillment of God's purpose, the completion of his plan. And it traces a thread of divine action and guidance that leads from the origins of this world to the full realization of God's purpose.

Along the pathway through the centuries appear many great and striking individuals, who speak and act for God with earnestness and power. There is compelling evidence that faith in God enriched the lives of these individuals as well as of multitudes of less prominent people. But they are never hermits, without relation to God's people

[4] Paul S. Minear, *Eyes of Faith: A Study in the Biblical Point of View* (Philadelphia: Westminster Press, 1946).

and ongoing plan. They are members of God's people; they serve his purposes.

This is, as we have noted, a special kind of history. Attention centers on the special group and individuals whom God used to advance his purpose. Even among the special people who had the opportunity and privilege of serving God, there were many—indeed, they were evidently the majority—who failed to sense their privilege and do their part. But this slender line of faithful servants of God, imperfect as they were and inadequate as they knew themselves to be, did God's work in their day, and they handed on their heritage and task to the chosen minority who were willing to accept the trust. The biblical writers find the essential meaning of all human life and history in this special thread of history, this special group who represent and serve God's purpose.

The importance of this fact is not merely that God's people have had a history. This might be true, and yet the message might conceivably be of such a kind that it could be stated in quite other forms and still lose nothing essential. But that is not the case in the biblical message. God has made himself known to men, he has given his help to men, he has provided the redemption they need, precisely by his working in history.[5]

When we present the biblical message, therefore, we do not outline a system of ideas. We rather tell a story, a story of God's special dealings with men to judge and save them. Inherent in this story is the assertion that God is working out his purpose in history; what he has done has led to where we are now, and this points on to what he will do to complete his purpose. History, and more specifically God's working in history, is therefore the indispensable form of biblical theology. If we ever forget that our task is to tell a history and show where each biblical figure and each later Christian fits into that history, we have not only abandoned the biblical framework of the gospel, but we have als abandoned a vital essential of that gospel. We cannot substitute for this history a philosophical formulation of Christianity, or offer in its place

[5] The relation of "salvation history" to world history is discussed by E. C. Rust, *The Christian Understanding of History* (London: Lutterworth Press, 1947).

an outline of spiritual and moral principles, without losing the very nature of the Christian message.

This accent on history is never presented in the Bible with major focus on the past. It always directs attention to the present and points on into the future. What God has done and will do is vitally related to what he is doing. His dealings with other generations yield their meaning only as the reader or hearer of the biblical story knows that the message lays claim to his life; he must belong to God's people and take his place in the stream of God's historical action. It is his own heritage and history and hope. An inherent claim thus reaches out from this historical message to challenge the hearer to acknowledge that through this history, God speaks to him and his generation. This is a conception of history which excludes, as the full realization of the fact of God always excludes, any idea of neutrality. The story is the vehicle of God's claim upon him who hears it. The human figures in the story speak and act for God; the meaning of their lives in both success and failure is found in their relation to the ongoing work of God; and they are the spiritual ancestors of all those who later hear the story with spiritual discernment and respond to it in faith.

III. *The Human Factor*

Biblical theology takes seriously the human factor, which plays its part in both the biblical history and the writing of the biblical books. There have been non-Christian religious leaders, and even misguided Christians, who have held a different view. They claim that they or their accepted leaders are but the passive mouthpieces of God. They insist that God so controls his human agents that no human element enters into their words or decisions. We read of prophets who think that the very inactivity of their own minds is the guarantee that their message has a divine origin. And we find people who think that the writers of the biblical books were nothing more than animated pens, through which God wrote his revelation without the active participation of any human mind.

Such a view finds pictorial expression in a frontispiece which precedes the Gospel of John in some medieval Greek manuscripts. This full-page illustration pictures an explicit view of direct and verbal divine inspiration. The apostle John stands in the center. From a small cloud in an upper corner of the illustration a hand extends downward and rays of light flash forth, to indicate that God is speaking to the listening apostle. At the apostle's feet sits Prochorus, his scribe. With one hand cupped to his ear, John listens intently as God tells him what the Gospel is to say. With the other hand John gestures downward to the seated scribe, to indicate that he is dictating exactly what the voice of God has spoken. The picture assumes clear hearing, clear speech, and accurate writing, but its essential meaning is that the Gospel of John is dictated by God. The mind and Christian experience of John have no direct role in this process.

We have only to read and compare the two gospels of Matthew and John, the two letters Galatians and James, the two prophetic books Isaiah and Ezekiel, to know that this illustration is misleading. In every biblical book, and especially the ones which most often grip the imagination and the minds of men, the vibrant personality of the human servant of God makes its powerful impact upon us. God did not use dictaphones or tape recorders; he used men, and each man was an individual unlike any other biblical figure or writer.[6]

Since this is what the sovereign God has thought it wise to do, we his creatures are in no strategic position to object. His method may complicate our historical and theological study, for we can never weave together into a neatly harmonious whole all the details of content and emphasis which we get from these spokesmen of God. But it nevertheless clarifies the truth that life is a scene where God so uses different people with their varying gifts that the story has a rewarding richness and opens a way of usefulness to every individual. We can learn from people of varied backgrounds and capacities; we can find those who speak with the greatest power and helpfulness to us; and we can take heart in knowing that every type of person, and every gift man has, can find its place in the total work of God. We therefore accept the biblical variety of personality and expression, and do not resent that this sometimes makes it difficult to grasp the oneness of the biblical story. The oneness is in God, in his purpose, in his working through

---

[6] Andrew C. Zenos made use of this fact in his book on New Testament theology, *The Plastic Age of the Gospel* (New York: The Macmillan Co., 1927).

16

successive stages of history; he blends into complementary harmony the varied gifts and service of the many imperfect men and women whom he calls to do and voice his will.

To recognize the human factor means to recognize that all aspects of human life have their place in the biblical picture of life. When we write about the biblical message, and try to grasp and state its guiding ideas, we may slip into an intellectualism which loses the richness of human life and Christian experience. Biblical theology is not concerned simply with the mind. It sees man in his need and failure, his repentance and faith, his worship and fellowship, his work and his kinship both with nature and with God's life and purpose. The Bible is concerned with the whole man in his total need, and with the full answer to that need in the gospel of God.

To recognize the human factor in the Bible is also to recognize the difference between the men of the Bible and the modern man. Those ancient servants of God lived in a quite different intellectual, social, scientific, and political setting than the one we know.[7] Biblical theology must try to recapture living touch with the setting of their life; it must seek to understand what they faced and how their needs were met. Thus it can never be a mere duplication of the systematic theology of present-day church thought. It is content to let the ancient people have the world view they really had; it is concerned to find out how they worshiped, lived, and thought in that setting.

Two dangers beset those who pursue such study. We may succumb to pride as we think of the improved scientific and technical setting of our life today. We may regard our situation as the adequate standard by which to judge all previous generations. We may forget that we have tremendous limitations, and that each year we have to give up ideas which we have firmly held for what we hope are better interpretations of the nature of the world and man. We too are fallible; our mental and social framework is fragile and rapidly changes.

[7] The most noted statement of this difference comes from Rudolf Bultmann in his essay on *Neues Testament und Mythologie*, which is most conveniently found in *Kerygma und Mythos*, ed. Hans Werner Bartsch, Hamburg, 1948, pp. 13-53 (Eng. tr., *Kerygma and Myth*, London, 1952). He insists that we must strip away all ancient mythology and restate the gospel in existentialist terms. For a recent defense of the main aim of Bultmann, see F. Gogarten, *Demythologizing and History*, Eng. tr. from the German (New York: Charles Scribner's Sons, 1955).

We may also overlook the essential oneness of our situation with that of ancient man. In the deep things of faith, moral discernment, and intellectual vigor, we are not essentially different from those earlier generations. The human factor is basically what it has been through the centuries; man in his failure and need must look to God for the help and power to become what he was meant to be. In this crucial area we are but men and not gods; we share the need of the biblical generations, and we can learn from the history and message of the biblical writers. They do not suffer by comparison with our time.

IV. *The Setting in the Church*

Biblical theology implies the church as the setting of its work.[8] This may alarm some who remember the history of Christian scholarship. In a real sense, the rise of biblical theology was a revolt against rigid ecclesiastical control of biblical study. For a long time the study of the Bible was dominated by dogmatic theology, which the church used as a norm by which to judge historical questions. A revolt against such suppression of free historical study had to come. Courageous scholars had to insist that such dogmatic systems, constructed in later times, were secondary; the primary thing was to go back to the biblical documents and let them speak directly to the competent student.

This step was not merely an emancipation for scholarship; it was likewise a great benefit to the church, for it gave a truer and more vital expression to what the biblical documents had to say. It would be a fatal step to put biblical study back under the ecclesiastical control of post-biblical doctrinal statements. These creedal statements, which claim to present the message of the Bible, must be subject to correction from the Bible wherever the biblical evidence indicates that they need it.

This conclusion, however, does not mean that we wish to banish the church from all contact with biblical theology. Once we take God as the central axiom and actor of the biblical story, once we accept the biblical history as the unique redemptive working of God, who thereby brings together those who hear and respond to this message, we are not only willing but eager to enter into the stream of that history

[8] Frederick C. Grant recognizes this fact. See *An Introduction to New Testament Thought* (New York and Nashville: Abingdon Press, 1950), p. 28.

18

and count it our history. We know that we are not related to God as isolated individuals, but are rather able to find our full life only in living relation to God's people and God's ongoing purpose. We belong in the church, the fellowship of believers who gratefully share the Christian heritage and respond to the gifts and demands of the gospel. We cannot and do not wish to work in any other setting than that which the church provides us. This is not slavery; it is responsible freedom in fellowship. This is no limitation on intellectual activity; it is the full use of our God-given abilities in the setting of the community life of faith and worship which makes the biblical message live.

There is still another way in which biblical theology finds its home and setting in the church. It is so important that it deserves separate statement.

V. The Existence of the Canon

Biblical theology is possible only because the canon of Scripture exists.[9] It is of importance only to those who regard the formation of the canon as a wise and justified step.

Whenever we use the word Bible to designate the books of our Old and New Testaments, we really imply the acceptance of the canon. We recall that these writings have been gathered together in one collection and given unique standing in the church. The canon ultimately exists because of God's gracious redemptive action, but historically it exists only because of church action, for the church by a gradual process collected and set apart these books. Every reference to the canon implies also the existence and action of the church. This gives added force to our insistence that biblical theology always implies the church as its setting, for it deals with the Bible, and the church defines the canon and gives us the Bible. We therefore work in a church setting, with a canon created by the church to preserve and protect in its original form the basic gospel message. The extent of this canon is fixed by the Christian fellowship of which we are a part; it is not a decision subject to personal preference.

[9] On the formation of the New Testament canon and its relation to the Old Testament, see Adolf von Harnack, *The Origin of the New Testament and the Most Important Consequences of the New Creation*, tr. J. R. Wilkinson (New York: The Macmillan Co., 1925).

It is possible, of course, to accept the canon as a historical fact, and stop there. Whether a scholar is a Christian or an atheist, he must accept the fact that to preserve its heritage and serve its needs, the church set these books apart, gave them unique status, and henceforth accepted the collection as its Bible. A non-Christian who accepts this process as a fact but sees nothing uniquely authoritative in this collection may speak of it as the Bible, but he will have no conviction that the canon was a necessary and vital step in God's plan. Its formation happened, but without theological justification.

Those who hold such a view naturally will not be bound in their studies by the idea of the canon. They may consider the Book of Enoch or First Clement to be as important as the biblical books for the study of human experience and thought. Their aim will not be to grasp and set forth with convincing clarity the special biblical message about God, his acts and his claim.

To those who respond in faith to the living God and accept the gospel message of redemptive history, the situation appears quite different. Something unique took place in the biblical history. It did not just happen; it was the work of the living God. The writing of the books which enable us to learn that story and grasp its meaning was the most important literary process that ever occurred. The collection of those books has preserved the basic story, and given all later generations of the church the basis by which to judge the later developments in its life. The real reason for biblical theology is not to satisfy curiosity about past history, but to grasp with honesty and clarity the message that gave life to the church and gives reason for later church growth and thought. It was a sound and wise step to tie all future generations of the church to these basic documents. The canon is not only a fact of history but a fact of theological significance, and biblical theology works in the light of this fact.

VI. *The Unity of the Bible*

Biblical theology accepts as a sound working basis the unity of the Bible.[10] To be sure, the immediate effect of the rise of biblical theology

[10] A symposium on the unity of the Bible appeared in *Interpretation*, V (1951), pp. 131-202, with contributions by G. Ernest Wright, Floyd V. Filson, Robert C. Dentan, Paul E.

was to call attention to the diversities in these books. The former artificial dogmatic unity was replaced by a vigorous emphasis on the differences between the writers and books of the Bible. This was a necessary and fruitful insight. No longer can anyone assert that monotonous identity marks the approach and messages of these various writers. What we said above as to the constant presence of the human factor in the history and writing of the Bible should be sufficient to exclude so gross a misunderstanding. The diversities are obvious.

These writers differ in the time in which they lived; they appear in a series that covers over a thousand years, and we could not expect men to think, speak, and act in identical patterns through so long a period. Even the relatively brief New Testament period presents a remarkable series of varying life situations. These biblical writers vary in literary skill and in choice of literary form; they range from the prosaic plodder to the imaginative, poetic, penetrating creator of magnificent literature. They vary in the degree of their grasp of God's purpose and will, and they accent now one aspect and now another. They offer a wide range of psychological types, and therefore differ in depth and in approach to truth. They are divided into two distinctive groups by the fact that part of them wrote before the coming of Jesus Christ, while the others wrote after that event had given a new center of faith and thought and action. We not only admit the rich variety of the Bible; we insist upon it.

Yet if exact uniformity were the only basis for unity, all families would break up, communities would dissolve in chaos, and not only the church but all other social organizations would be wrecked on the rocks of disunity. Unity can be a real fact where there is variety; in fact, living unity exists on no other basis. To expect the Bible to show monotonous uniformity, to require the biblical writers to show unity by being identical in personal type and expression, would be to ask the impossible; it would be to ask what never occurs in any other area of life. Unity is always unity in diversity; it is a shared variety, a mutually enriching and mutually complementary uniting of elements that otherwise would be fragmentary and ineffective. This is the unity of the

Davies, and Robert M. Grant. See also H. H. Rowley, *The Unity of the Bible* (London: Carey Kingsgate Press, 1953).

21

Bible, and it is real. Its existence is implied in the very conception of the canon. It is acknowledged by the church. It is a fact to which we must do justice in biblical theology.

This unity is a unity centered in God and in his working in Israel and Christ and the church. It is a unity discerned in a history which, though never monotonous, moves in the line of God's purpose. It is a unity that grows out of a life understanding and a thought world which has no real parallel in the history of the rest of the world. Parallels by the thousands there certainly are, but they are parallels to this or that aspect of the biblical message. They help understand the Bible, and biblical study can never ignore any such contribution, but when the entire picture is surveyed, the Old and New Testaments stand apart— their message about God and history and life is unique.[11] No ingenuity of scholarship will ever fit all the diverse features of the Bible into one neat and flawlessly consistent pattern, but no skepticism can justly deny the deep-flowing, continuous unity which holds together this story of the living God who works in history for the correction, salvation, and guidance of mankind.

The task of biblical theology is to discern and state this unity. It will note faithfully the varied ways in which the biblical writers share this common position. It will have no nervous fear that the variety may destroy the unity that dominates the whole. It will let two clashing passages state two sides of a paradoxical pattern; faith and mature thought will know that they have a deeper unity and that neither can be omitted from the total picture. But it will not forget its main task. Biblical theology exists to state the central biblical message with clarity and vigor, and with a balance in which each human witness and each separate testimony of faith receives a fair hearing and emphasis.

VII. *The Central Role of the Christian Gospel*

Biblical theology so states the unity of the Bible that the New Testament gospel of Christ controls the presentation. Yet it recognizes the indispensable and permanent role of the Old Testament, and it so presents the New Testament gospel that the Old Testament is clearly

---

[11] This is the thesis of two complementary studies, one by G. Ernest Wright, *The Old Testament Against Its Environment* (London: SCM Press, 1950), and the other by myself, *The New Testament Against Its Environment* (London: SCM Press, 1950).

seen to provide a necessary preparation and a permanent, integral part of the Christian message.[12]

At least two reasons make it imperative to clarify the relation between the two Testaments. In the first place, the Old Testament was written before the time of Jesus. It may seem astonishing that the Old Testament, which can give no direct witness to the central gospel story, was kept by the church as an integral part of the Scripture. The importance of the Gospels is immediately apparent. It is almost as clear that the work and witness of the apostles of Jesus are necessary to give the full Christian witness about Jesus Christ. But it may seem far less important to unite the Old Testament with the New Testament to form one Scripture. Whoever has a vivid sense of the radically new work of God in Christ needs to think carefully about the permanent role of the Old Testament, whose latest writing must be dated nearly two centuries before the career of Jesus.

In the second place, the sheer bulk of the Old Testament will create a problem for the unwary. It is more than three times as long as the New Testament. Unless biblical study retains a clear sense of where the center lies, it may unconsciously subordinate the Apostolic Witness to Old Testament threads of thought. Primitive, legalistic, or sacerdotal areas of the Old Testament can then become dominant and shape interpretation of the gospel.

For this reason, it is urgent to understand why the church kept the Old Testament. But let us note first of all that the church did keep it from the first. There never was a time when the church was without a Bible. Jesus accepted and used our Old Testament as his Scripture. So did the apostles. Even when, in the second century, Marcion and the Gnostics discarded it, the church rejected Marcion and the Gnostics and kept the Old Testament. This is clear.

But it is important to understand why the church thus accepted and preserved the Old Testament as Scripture. To put the reason in one sentence, the church kept the Old Testament because it contained the divinely given witness to Christ. Only when we keep this fact in mind can we understand and state the unity of the Bible.

---

[12] Harnack clearly sees this, but he is not happy about all of its results (op. cit.); and see also his book on Marcion (2nd ed., Leipzig: Hinrichs, 1924), p. 217.

If the Old Testament is an independent collection of writings, historically important for the history of religion and throwing light on the origin of Christianity, but forming no integral part of the Christian witness, it must certainly be denied a place in the Christian canon. But the church has always seen in the Old Testament not only the indispensable background and preparation for the gospel, but also a permanent and integral witness to Christ.[13] For this reason, it has accepted the Old Testament as authoritative Scripture, and has given it a vital place in the worship and teaching of the church. To justify its place in the canon, therefore, the Old Testament must continue to be interpreted as a phase of the Christian witness to Christ, and as a permanent witness to that redemptive will and work of God to which Christians answer in faith.

The concern for the interpretation of the Bible as a whole is not new to biblical theology. When biblical theology as distinct from dogmatic theology first became an object of intensive study, the Bible was treated as a whole. Before long the practice prevailed of studying each Testament separately, and it became the custom to state separately the message of each Testament. This had its advantages. Increasing complexity in the task of scholarship meant that the scholar had all he could do to master the problems of one Testament. Realization of the differences between the Testaments promoted this tendency to division of labor. Co-operation between Christian and Jewish scholars in Old Testament study, and between Christian scholars and students of the Greco-Roman world in New Testament study, accentuated the separation. But the end product of such compartmental treatment of the Bible is not good. It tends to loosen the bond of the Old Testament with the church. It also tends to deprive the New Testament of the Old Testament foundation on which the New Testament itself insists.[14]

While, therefore, co-operation between scholars of all faiths and interests is wholesome and fruitful, and the intensive study of individual sections of the Bible material yields many good results, the church

---

[13] A valuable statement of this point is given by G. E. Phillips, The Old Testament in the World Church (London: Lutterworth Press, 1942).

[14] For the New Testament use of the Old Testament see R. V. G. Tasker, The Old Testament in the New Testament (2nd rev. ed.; London: SCM Press, 1954).

must set limits to overspecialization and continued fragmentation. The final result would be fatal both to a clear grasp of the biblical message and to the interests of the church. The aim of the study of both Testaments is to find and state the message they give to the church. Christian scholarship is convinced of two things: neither Testament can be properly and fully understood without taking into account its integral relation to the other; and in this integral relation the gospel message of the New Testament gives the center from which the whole must be understood and placed in perspective.

VIII. *The Interpreting Role of the Resurrection*

Biblical theology finds its clearest starting point and interpreting clue in the resurrection of Jesus Christ.[15]

When we undertake to state the biblical message in proper framework and proportion, the choice of a starting point, and of the initial fact which will most clearly illuminate the nature of the task, is a crucial decision. We might start with an analysis of man's need, and on the basis of our results go to the Bible to see what it has to say. This would keep the discussion relevant, but it would lack a trustworthy standard by which to interpret the spiritual and moral situation of our time. The Bible finds that standard not in what man now is, but in God—in God's purpose for man and God's work for man. Therefore, man as we know him cannot be the basis on which Christians understand life or the Bible.

We therefore might take the general theistic position, the widely accepted fact of God, as the starting point of biblical theology. This would have the advantage of recognizing that God is the axiom and chief actor of the entire biblical story. It would make it seem easier to deal with the Old Testament, where Christ does not come directly into the picture. But so general a starting point could easily make Christ appear to be a secondary and late feature of the total message, and this would completely contradict both the whole tenor of the New Testa-

[15] I have stated the following argument in "The Focus of History," *Interpretation*, II (1948), 24-38. Maurice Goguel, *The Birth of Christianity*, tr. H. C. Snape (New York: The Macmillan Co., 1953), pp. 69 ff., gives essential recognition to the controlling role of the Resurrection.

ment and the early Christian understanding of the Old Testament. Therefore, it cannot be accepted.

God is always central in biblical theology, but not in a way that any other religious message can parallel. He is always present in the Christian message in his relation to Christ, and the earliest Christian message will not permit us to give Christ a secondary or intermittent role in the gospel. To catch the distinctive flavor of the biblical message, therefore, we must find a starting point more characteristic of the original gospel message. God is the axiom, actor, and constant reference point of the entire story, but we must find a focal center that will bring out the unique character of that story.

For this reason it will not do to start with the Old Testament. We must recognize clearly that at every stage the Old Testament is the background and accompanying guide for Christian preaching and thought. Yet, from the beginning of the Christian church it was the new decisive action of God which determined the church's understanding and use of the Old Testament. The Old Testament receives its interpretation from a central event. Christian faith, worship, and thinking find their center and interpreting clue in that event. To do justice to the Bible itself, our starting point must be Jesus Christ.

Yet even here we still face a choice. How do we gain the understanding of Christ which the Old Testament foreshadows and the New Testament presents? It may occur to us to begin with the birth of Jesus, and so center attention upon the Incarnation. But that would put in the center what is decidedly not the central New Testament point. Two of the four Gospels do not even find it necessary to tell the story of the birth of Jesus. No other book of the New Testament except Matthew and Luke contains any narrative of his birth and infancy. The idea of incarnation is not the dominant and controlling theme of the New Testament. If we seek to understand and state the gospel message as the New Testament writers themselves did, we must look for a feature which they all regarded as central. We cannot make the birth of Jesus the starting point and interpreting clue.

It would suit a widespread modern interest to begin with the public ministry and teaching of Jesus of Nazareth. This would make a prompt appeal and call attention to important facts; the ministry and teaching

26

of Jesus have an importance which we must not undervalue. We dare not lose sight of the reality of the human career of Jesus, his natural friendliness, his human sympathy and helpfulness, and his penetrating presentation of the urgent claim of God on man's daily life. Without these facts the figure of Jesus would not be real, the Incarnation would be a mere phantasmal appearance, the ground of his challenge to men and the tragedy of his rejection by men would not be clear, and the meaning of the Cross would elude us. A Christian faith that belittles or ignores the essential role of Jesus' teaching, healing, and friendship lacks solid foundation. It cannot command the loyalty of men. The Christ of its worship lacks definite character and appeal.

Nevertheless, the unity of the Bible and the nature of the gospel cannot be properly grasped by taking the teaching and public ministry as the basic interpreting clue. Certainly the New Testament writers did not proceed in that way. Only three of the twenty-seven books of the New Testament deal in any full and concrete way with the teaching of Jesus.

Even the Gospel of John concentrates on the person of Christ and the need of love among believers; it contains no details of Jesus' teaching about the varied phases of daily life. If we had only the Gospel of John, Jesus would not be the real figure that he is to us; this Gospel has its powerful influence only because we always think of the Christ it portrays in the light of the more detailed portraits which the Synoptic Gospels provide.

The other twenty-three books have even less material about the teaching and public ministry. Consider the Book of Acts. Its author knew all the teaching which he had already recorded in the Gospel of Luke. Nevertheless, he does not quote a single saying of that Gospel, and he gives only one new saying, "It is more blessed to give than to receive" (Acts 20:35). The rest of the New Testament, like the sermons in Acts, gives no presentation of the sayings and ministering acts of Jesus in Galilee. If we seek a starting point which will be common to the entire New Testament and explain its unity, it cannot be the teaching and public acts of Jesus. The fact that at least a quarter of each Gospel deals with the events immediately preceding and following the death of Jesus is a better clue.

27

This may seem to point to the Cross as the central fact upon which to base our presentation of the biblical message. If we were to judge by modern Christian art, hymns, and devotional usage, this would seem the certain answer. Indeed, the elaborate presentation of the Passion Story in the Gospels, and the frequency with which the rest of the New Testament mentions the Cross and its meaning, appear to clinch this conclusion. Yet the conclusion is completely false. None of the New Testament books, none of the New Testament sermons, none of New Testament thinking was centered in the Cross.

This assertion will shock many Christians, but a specific example will clearly establish its soundness. There is one great leader who for a time built his thinking and action upon the fact of Jesus' crucifixion. That was Saul of Tarsus—before his conversion. The Crucifixion proved to him that God had disowned Jesus, that Jesus was a fraud, that his claim was therefore false, and his followers deluded. Therefore, Saul persecuted the church and denounced Jesus. Then he changed. Why? Not because he had thought more clearly about the meaning of the Cross. It was because a new fact became real to him. A new fact *interpreted* the Cross. Christians are Christians and speak with conviction of the immense meaning of the Cross solely because another fact has come into the picture, a fact which reverses the apparent meaning of the Cross and enables the believer to see its real place in God's redemptive work.

That central interpreting fact is the resurrection of Jesus.[16] This is the climactic message to which each of the Gospels moves. This was what the apostles knew they were to preach—they were to witness to the Resurrection (Acts 1:22).[17] This was the fact which the unbeliever found incredible, but the Christians knew was true. In the light of this fact the Crucifixion found its Christian interpretation; the ministry, its climax; the plan of God, its interpreting clue; and the future, its way to power and victory.

It may seem to some that to begin with the Resurrection is to borrow

[16] On this subject see A. Michael Ramsey, *The Resurrection of Christ* (Philadelphia: Westminster Press, 1946).

[17] For two historical studies of the importance of the resurrection faith see Johannes Weiss, *The History of Primitive Christianity*, Eng. tr. from the German (New York: Wilson-Erickson, 1937), I, 14-31; Maurice Goguel, op. cit., pp. 29-86.

trouble. After all, other aspects of the Christian message are important, and many of them arouse less antagonism today than the Resurrection. It could seem expedient and congenial to begin with a less controversial area of the gospel message, link Jesus with his background and his time, and show his likeness to other great leaders and thinking of mankind, and then hope to lead the interested hearer on to appreciate the vital role which the Resurrection plays in the total biblical message.

Two objections discredit this cautious diplomatic approach. For one thing, it is by no means clear that the most effective way to present the gospel is to find a noncontroversial starting point or a common denominator which Christians share with other people. To begin on the periphery, or with a feature which is not the interpreting center of the message, will necessitate a later transfer of perspective which may be a rude jolt to the hearer and so prove a source of resentment. The person who hears the biblical message has the right to hear it with the perspective and interpreting focus which that message itself contains.

This lays bare the basic objection to the search for an inoffensive approach. It is false at the outset to the nature and emphasis of the biblical presentation. The entire early church moved out from the realization that Jesus Christ had risen. It shaped all its faith, worship, life, and thought in the light of this fact.

The entire New Testament was written from the post-resurrection viewpoint. Even when the writers do not mention the Resurrection, they speak from the life outlook of a church that lives in the glow of the resurrection faith. Even when interpreting the Old Testament, they do so in the light of this faith, and in its writings they find clues which point ahead to the career of Christ, and especially to its climax in the Cross and Resurrection. Modern scholarship has looked in many places for the central fact which explains the basic oneness in spirit and message which we sense in the New Testament. That central fact should now be clear. The interpreting clue and the organizing fact of biblical theology is the resurrection of Jesus.

We therefore think that the way to present the biblical message is to accept this clue, take seriously this fact, recognize it as the illuminating center of New Testament thinking, and move out from this tremendous witness of faith to state what the biblical gospel is. We begin with the earliest preaching, which had this resurrection emphasis. We try from this starting point to state and understand the basic preaching of the earliest gospel witnesses. We then move out in every direction to trace God's work, and discern the picture of faith and life which results from this basic message. For biblical theology is essentially the message of Jesus Christ, the risen Lord of his church.

CHAPTER II

Christt the Risen Lord

THE ENTIRE NEW TESTAMENT WAS WRITTEN IN THE LIGHT OF the resurrection fact. To all of its writers, Jesus is the central figure of history, and they understand and interpret his career in the light of his Resurrection. They regard this resurrection not merely as a possibility or even as a probability; it is for them the one rock-bottom fact upon which the solid structure of Christian faith and life is built. This does not mean that the first believers considered all other facts unimportant. But they interpreted the other facts in the light of the decisive fact that God had raised Jesus from the dead, and that chosen witnesses could testify that they had seen him. The gospel which the apostles preached and the New Testament writers recorded was the gospel of Jesus Christ the risen Lord.

The Earliest Preaching

Back of the New Testament lie years of Christian faith, worship, life, and thought. These vital documents do not originate the basic witness of the first Christians. They rather record and develop it. Each writer is, of course, a distinct individual, whose personality, interests, and style emerge in what he writes. But they all write in the setting of the church. Their purpose is not to devise some new message which their fellow Christians will regard as a fresh and startling discovery. It is rather to state truly and effectively the one message on which their common faith is founded.

In other words, they are presenting and applying the basic message that first took form in the oral preaching and teaching of the church.[1]

---

[1] So Martin Dibelius, From Tradition to Gospel, tr. Bertram Lee Woolf (New York: Charles Scribner's Sons, 1935), pp. 14-15: "I describe preaching as the original seat of all

31

The hearers of Jesus were not a class in school who eagerly wrote down in notebooks the lectures Jesus gave. On various occasions—most of them informal—they heard his words about faith and life and saw his acts and manner of living. They lived among a people who preserved much of their heritage in the form of oral tradition, and at first they preserved and spread their gospel story in oral form.[2] They spoke to groups and individuals about the career of Jesus and God's whole work for men, and interpreted it all in the light of the resurrection story. If we wish to know the basic message which underlies the entire New Testament, the best path we can follow is to seek out the earliest preaching of these disciples, who were fervent with enthusiasm born of the knowledge that Jesus had been raised from the dead by the power of God.

This preaching was a witness to Christ. It testified to what God had done and was doing through Christ. The disciples were never neutral reporters; they were dedicated followers of the risen Christ, sent out to tell their story on the basis of their own assurance of the Resurrection (Acts 1:8, 22). Their purpose in giving their personal witness was to win others to follow Christ; their message was vigorously evangelistic. At first their activity was local, but their horizons soon expanded and they saw their task in broad terms; their message was missionary in character. They could not complete their work, however, merely by presenting a simple message and then leaving the hearers to shift for themselves. On the contrary, they had to inform these hearers in some detail concerning the content and meaning of their message. They had to answer questions and apply their gospel to life. They had to foster a sense of common helpfulness and build an effective brotherhood. All this required patience and persistence. Their mission included teaching.

It is important to keep clearly in mind the form of this basic preaching. It took the form of historical recital, a recital of crucial facts interwoven with the interpretation of their meaning which the disciples had gained

---

tradition about Jesus . . . mission preaching, preaching during worship, and catechumen instruction."

[2] C. C. Torrey argued that the Gospel material was given written shape "almost immediately after the death of Jesus." The Four Gospels (New York: Harper & Bros., 1933), p. 255. E. J. Goodspeed seems right in saying that "the story of Jesus and his teaching first circulated" in the form of "oral tradition." Introduction to the New Testament (Chicago: University of Chicago Press, 1937), p. 126.

from the resurrection of Jesus. The message was essentially interpreted history.

To those who knew the Old Testament, it was nothing new to cast the message in the form of historical recital. As G. Ernest Wright has pointed out, "theology as recital" is a form of theological presentation familiar from the Old Testament.[3] The Book of Deuteronomy will serve as an example. It recalls the great acts of God which preceded and accompanied the Exodus and the wilderness wandering; it claims the obedience of Israel on the basis of this decisive action of God for his people. Throughout both the Pentateuch, the prophetic account of Israel's history, and the great prophetic books, we encounter this unique form of theology—"theology as recital." It states what God has done, is doing, and will do in history; it confronts Israel with the duty they owe as a result. Thus the pattern of New Testament preaching echoes, in a new and powerful way, a method of teaching long known in Israel.

How clearly can we determine the content and tone of the earliest Christian preaching? Our search is for the basic message, the earliest evangelistic witness from which sprang the church and its further teaching. In seeking out this earliest message, C. H. Dodd has played a notable role. His study of *The Apostolic Preaching and Its Developments* [4] is one of the most significant books of the last generation in the field of New Testament study. In it he makes a basic distinction which deserves our attention.

Dodd distinguishes between the preaching (or *Kerygma*, which is the Greek word for the message proclaimed) and the teaching (or *Didache*, which is the Greek word for teaching content). The evangelistic preaching, he says, would naturally come first; later the more detailed teaching would be given either to those who were interested in considering Christianity further, or to those who had believed and needed further instruction on how to worship and live.

This distinction between preaching and teaching contains much truth. The evangelistic preachers had first to challenge attention, then tell the basic facts of God's action, Christ's career, and man's duty, and finally appeal for the decision to believe in and follow Christ. People who

[3] *God Who Acts: Biblical Theology as Recital* (London: SCM Press, 1952).
[4] (Chicago: Willett, Clark & Co., 1937.)

wished to inquire further, or believers who needed to grow in understanding and usefulness, called for different treatment. They had to be given further facts; they needed details concerning the life of Jesus and the teaching of Scripture (our Old Testament) as well as guidance concerning what it means in daily life to be a Christian.

With this general difference in situation would often go a difference in the gifts of leaders. One type of leader could capture the attention and imagination, strike home to the will, and win converts for Christ. He was the preacher, the evangelist. Another could more effectively and patiently answer questions, interpret Scripture, explain the teachings of Jesus, and make clear the meaning of Jesus' life, death, and resurrection. He was the teacher, the pastor, the Christian friend who could aid the slow maturing of faith and character.

Yet this distinction can be greatly overdone, and it sometimes is pushed beyond reason. No preacher could win converts with a bare list of assertions about God's plan and his action in Christ. He had to give examples and details. In other words, he had to teach as he preached. The preacher of any message that roots in history must inform and win the mind as well as stir the imagination; he must continually teach. So every New Testament preacher was inevitably a teacher.

This simple fact is often obscured because the sermons we find in the Gospels and Acts are so brief. The longest sermon in Acts can be read in less than ten minutes. Most of them are no more than three minutes long. We should recall that Paul once prolonged his speech until midnight, so that a young man fell asleep and fell out the window in which he was sitting (Acts 20:7-9). The Apostle obviously was not in the habit of preaching three-minute sermons. These sermons in Acts are but summaries of what the Apostles said at much greater length and with much more detail. Their summary nature conceals the fact that illustration and detail must have marked every sermon. Every Christian preacher taught as he preached.

Similarly, every Christian teacher was seeking, as was the evangelistic preacher, to awaken Christian faith and loyalty. These early Christian teachers were not neutrals; their interest was not limited to stimulating intellectual curiosity or encouraging an active mind. Their aim was to

34

win men to faith in Christ and to promote Christian living. We thus recognize that while there was a general difference between the initial evangelistic preaching and the continuing, more thorough teaching, the two methods always overlapped. The preacher was a teaching evangelist, and the teacher was an evangelistic teacher.

Where Do We Find the Earliest Preaching?

If then we accept, with the qualification just stated, the difference between preaching and teaching, we must determine where we can find in clearest form the original preaching message. The best clue lies in the sermons in the first half of Acts.

Quite plainly the New Testament letters cannot be our basic source for this purpose. They presuppose the basic preaching, but they are written to churches which have heard that preaching, accepted it, and now need guidance in the ongoing situations of Christian life. They occasionally give valuable clues to what the earliest preaching included. For example, in First Corinthians Paul repeats the tradition about the Lord's Supper that he had received in the early days of the church (11:23-26). A little later he recalls another central portion of the gospel tradition, which he had been taught within a very few years of the events concerned:

That Christ died for our sins in accordance with the scriptures, that he was buried, that he was raised on the third day in accordance with the scriptures, and that he appeared to Cephas, . . . to the twelve. . . . to more than five hundred brethren . . . to James . . . to all the apostles . . . also to me. (15:3-8.)

Thus the letters may reflect the content of the original gospel tradition and indicate important points in the earliest preaching, but their purpose is to give Christians needed teaching, exhortation, rebuke, and guidance in personal and congregational problems of worship, doctrine, and life. So we cannot hope to get from the letters the full content or outline of the earliest preaching. If we can discover such an outline elsewhere, we then can compare it with the letters, which include the earliest writings of the New Testament, and see whether fundamental agreement appears.

Neither can we get the outline of the original preaching from the Book of Revelation. It speaks to the church in a day of persecution. It undertakes to nerve a sorely tried church to hold fast in view of the certain and imminent triumph of the cause of Christ. It gives only a few brief flashbacks to the previous acts of God through Christ, and it does this to foster confidence in the coming triumph. We may check our results with the content of the Book of Revelation, but this book will not give us the outline we seek.

The Gospels come closer to giving us what we want. They tell us the story of Jesus in detail and in order, although the order is not always chronological.[5] Here we are near the content of the earliest preaching. We cannot rate too highly the contribution which the Gospels make to our understanding of the message of the Apostolic Church. To see this, we need only to ask how much of an outline and how many details of the life, ministry, and teaching of Jesus we could derive from the letters of the New Testament, or even from the Book of Acts, which quotes but one saying of Jesus and reports not a single event of his public ministry. Without these Gospels the Christian message would suffer from a fatal vagueness. Yet even the Gospels are not our best source for the earliest preaching of the church. Their orderliness and detail show that they were directed largely to the teaching side of the church's task. The picture we form of the earliest preaching must square with the content of the Gospels, but we must derive that picture elsewhere.

The best source for the outline and essential content of the earliest apostolic preaching is in the sermons of the first half of Acts. Of the importance of these sermons in the mind of Luke, the writer of Acts, there can be no doubt.[6] They occupy about a fifth of the total space of

[5] Form Criticism has stressed the use of the gospel in the life of the Church. See M. Dibelius, op. cit. in Note 1; K. L. Schmidt, Der Rahmen der Geschichte Jesu (Berlin, 1919); R. Bultmann, Die Geschichte der synoptischen Tradition (2nd ed., Göttingen, 1931); Vincent Taylor, The Formation of the Gospel Tradition (London: Macmillan & Co., 1933); L. J. McGinley, Form-Criticism of the Synoptic Healing Narratives (Woodstock: Woodstock College Press, 1944); and for a recent survey A. H. McNeile, Introduction to the Study of the New Testament, 2nd ed. revised by C. S. C. Williams (Oxford, 1953), pp. 46-58.

[6] The Lucan authorship of Acts seems to me highly probable. I recall hearing Martin Dibelius and Edgar J. Goodspeed discuss the subject. They agreed that such a work as Luke-Acts, with its claim to literary standing, must have borne the name of its author from the first.

that book, and this indicates their importance for Luke.[7] They claim
to present what Peter, Stephen, and Paul said in their evangelistic preaching. If they are essentially reliable, we possess in them the basic message
of the Apostolic Age.

Are the Sermons of Acts Authentic?

The genuineness of these sermons, however, has been vigorously denied
by many scholars. One reason is that ancient historians were notoriously
free in the composition of speeches, which they wrote to enliven and
dramatize their story. Our modern standards require exact reproduction
of speeches made at crucial moments in history, but ancient writers of
history had no such standards; they aimed at literary effectiveness rather
than word-for-word quotation. We can understand this; there were no
word-for-word accounts of such significant speeches. The ordinary practice in historical writing of the Hellenistic period was to express freely,
in the writer's own style, the thoughts which the author considered
appropriate to the occasion and suited to show the reader the significance
of the event.[8]

One question remains. Did these historians know the substance
of what had been said on such occasions, or were they governed entirely
by their own imagination and their view of the meaning of events? Many
scholars think that the frank statement of Thucydides gives the answer:
the writers composed freely with no solid basis of tradition. This conclusion has been accepted so widely, and applied to Luke's method so
confidently, that we may well quote and examine the crucial passage of
Thucydides.

In Bk. I, sec. 22, of his *History of the Peloponnesian War* Thucydides
explains his method:

As to the speeches that were made by different men, either when they
were about to begin the war or when they were already engaged therein, it
has been difficult to recall with strict accuracy the words actually spoken,

---

[7] On the speeches of Acts see H. J. Cadbury, *The Making of Luke-Acts* (New York:
The Macmillan Co., 1927), ch. xiv, and his extended note in *The Beginnings of Christianity*, Part I, *The Acts of the Apostles*, Vol. V (London, 1933), pp. 402-27. For a
more favorable view of the speeches see F. F. Bruce, *The Acts of the Apostles* (London:
Tyndale Press, 1951), pp. 18-21, and B. Gärtner, *The Areopagus Speech and Natural
Revelation* (Uppsala, 1955), pp. 26-36.
[8] There seems no doubt that the Jewish historian Josephus did just that.

both for me as regards that which I myself heard, and for those who from various other sources have brought me reports. Therefore the speeches are given in the language in which, as it seemed to me, the several speakers would express, on the subjects under consideration, the sentiments most befitting the occasion, though at the same time I have adhered as closely as possible to the general sense of what was actually said.[9]

To conclude from this famous passage that Thucydides' speeches were a free literary creation uncontrolled by historical fact is to misread and misrepresent what he says. He claims to know when speeches were made. He himself was present at some of the events, and had reports from other persons concerning speeches made on other occasions. He states clearly that he has kept as close as possible to "the general sense of what was actually said." He says honestly that neither he nor his reporters could give the exact words of any of the speeches, and therefore he has put their substance in his own words and in the literary form he thought most effective. But in spite of what some scholars have alleged, he does *not* say that his speeches are mere fiction.

What Thucydides says of the speeches he writes is what we should say about the sermons and speeches of Acts. They are written in the characteristic style of Luke. There have been attempts to show that they contain the known language and style of the speakers in question. The speeches of Peter, it is argued, resemble in vocabulary, style, and ideas the epistles of Peter, and the speeches of Paul show a similar resemblance to the letters of Paul. A number of such resemblances can be listed, and they deserve attention, but they often deal with points which occur also in other parts of the New Testament, and so are common usage; and they do not cancel the fact that the distinctive style of Luke appears in these speeches. The exact *literary form* of these sermons is due to the pen of Luke.

But it is futile to try to ascribe to Luke the origin of all the *ideas* in these sermons and speeches. He had unusual opportunities to learn from leaders of the Apostolic Church what had been done and said on crucial occasions, and the speeches contain unmistakable marks of coming from just such sources. The theology of these sermons, as recent study has shown, is early and relatively undeveloped. They do not reflect the

[9] As cited in Cadbury, *The Making of Luke-Acts*, p. 185.

peculiarities of Luke's gentile background or of Paul's missionary message to the gentile churches. They are essentially pre-Pauline, and contain features, such as the reference to Jesus as the "Servant" (Acts 3:13, 26; 4:27, 30), which never reappear in such explicit form in the later part of Acts or in the New Testament letters. Luke has put in his own style an early tradition concerning the preaching of the earliest Christian generation. We need not argue, as C. C. Torrey does, that these early chapters of Acts were originally written in Aramaic and only later translated into Greek.[10] That theory cannot be proved, and is highly improbable. But we have solid reason to conclude that the sermons of the first half of Acts provide a substantially trustworthy summary of the earliest Christian preaching.

Which Sermons Reflect the Common Gospel?

The sermons of main value for our present purpose are the sermons of Peter and the early sermons of Paul. The defenses which Paul later made before the Jerusalem mob and the Roman governors (Acts 22:1-21; 24:10-21; 26:2-23) have too personal and autobiographical a focus to serve as primary sources for our purpose. They also come from a time later than the earliest generation in which we now are interested. Other speeches in the latter part of Acts are too sketchy to provide an outline of Paul's missionary preaching. The speeches at Lystra and Athens have limited scope, and help us little. At Lystra Paul confronts a unique situation (Acts 14:8-18). A pagan priest, having falsely concluded that Paul and Barnabas are gods come down to earth, is on the point of offering sacrifice to them. Paul's one immediate aim is to stop this blasphemous practice, and make it clear that a right faith in the one true God would stop such ridiculous mummery. The passage does not pretend to be a full statement of Paul's evangelistic preaching. It certainly does not intend to praise "natural theology," as some modern theologians eagerly assume; it seeks to correct error and lead to repentance rather than to confirm the hearers in any ideas they already have.

Similarly, at Athens Paul does not give his full message (Acts 17:22-31). The famous speech on Mars' Hill is often considered the complete

---

[10] In *The Composition and Date of Acts* (Cambridge, 1916). A more balanced view of the Aramaic background of the Gospels and Acts is found in M. Black, *An Aramaic Approach to the Gospels and Acts* (2nd ed.; New York: Oxford University Press, 1954).

statement of what Paul wanted to say to the Athenians. It is hard to understand how this delusion arose. Paul here attempts an unparalleled conciliatory approach. But he knows where he is going. He moves straight to a judgment on the idolatry and polytheism of Athens; the past was a time of ignorance, he concedes, but it was a time not free from guilt, and so he demands repentance. He supports that demand by warning of the last judgment by "a man," appointed by God and raised from the dead. At the end he is ready to give a clear statement of what God has done through Jesus Christ, but he is interrupted when he mentions the Resurrection. As soon as he refers to that un-Greek idea, some openly mock him, while others courteously cease listening with a promise to hear him again at some other time. He had not finished what he had to say. When he came to his central message of the risen Christ, he lost his crowd, and few believed. This speech cannot be used as a typical sermon of Paul, or as a complete report of all that he wanted to say at Athens.

One other great speech in Acts fails to give us the characteristic outline of the earliest preaching. The defense which Stephen made to the enraged crowd at Jerusalem is the longest speech in Acts (7:2-53), but it is in part a defense, even more an indictment and rebuke, and not at all a characteristic evangelistic sermon.

His opponents charged that Stephen was not loyal to his ancestral Jewish faith. They charged him with speaking against the Law and the Temple, and so against God. They claimed that it was Jesus' teaching which prompted him to this blasphemy. In his reply he uses the characteristic biblical form of religious speech; his defense and rebuke take the form of a historical survey. Here he shows that God had dealt with his chosen representatives both in and outside of Palestine, and at times and in places where no temple was available. He shows how Israel had habitually been rebellious against God's spokesmen. He indicts his hearers for failing to keep the very Law which they so angrily accuse him of undermining. Thus he deals with the immediate controversial situation and does not give an outline of the gospel message of the church.

For that outline we turn to the sermons of Peter in Acts 2:14-40; 3:12-26; 4:8-12; 10:34-43, and to Paul's sermon in Acts 13:16-41. They

40

are at best but brief summaries of what was said on these occasions, and the actual literary form is the work of Luke, the author of Acts. We cannot expect every point of the message to appear in every sermon. But we note the common pattern and the use of historical survey to show how God has acted to save men. We gain a good general picture of what the earliest preachers said when, impelled by their faith in the risen Christ, they began to preach to others to win them to share the speaker's faith. We now state the main points of that common gospel.[11]

The Essential Message

1. God has begun to fulfill his promises (Acts 2:16; 3:18, 24; 10:43; 13:32-33). In detail there is much, much more to come. But the decisive fulfillment has already come in Christ. It gives the solid assurance that God will certainly fulfill every promise which still awaits fulfillment.

This theme of fulfillment ties the Christian message to the heritage of Israel. The gospel does not reject that heritage. It proclaims that now its climax and fulfillment have come. Therefore the gospel's tie with the Old Testament is unbreakable. For the Old Testament records the former works of God and promises his new and greater work. Now that Israel is entering a new era in the history of God's dealings with her, the Old Testament is kept and studied with new zeal, and its words are seen in new dimensions. The interpreting clue is the Resurrection, which has sharpened the church's eye to see in the Old Testament the clues which point forward to Jesus Christ and the church.

These first Christians were Jews. They followed a Jew, Jesus of Nazareth. They knew that he was more than a mere heir of Judaism, but they knew him and thought of him in the framework of Judaism. They knew that he had accepted, used, and interpreted with authority the Jewish Scriptures, so they in turn accepted them without question, studied them with renewed interest, and interpreted them in the light of what God had done for them in Jesus Christ. They presented their message to fellow Jews, for they regarded that message as the crown and fulfillment of their Scripture and their Jewish heritage.

[11] Cf. Dodd, op. cit., ch. i, and Bo Reicke, "A Synopsis of Early Christian Preaching," in The Root of the Vine: Essays in Biblical Theology, by A. Fridrichsen and others (New York: Philosophical Library, Inc., 1953), pp. 128-60. See also E. Stauffer, New Testament Theology, tr. John Marsh (London: SCM Press, 1955), part 2.

From the beginning the Christian faith was preached not as the repudiation, but as the fulfillment of the Old Testament and its promises.

2. The promised new age of God's effective rule has begun (Acts 2: 17 ff., 33, 36; 10:38; 13:38-39). Among the Jews of that time the widespread faith existed that God would not permit the tangled confusion of life to continue indefinitely, nor would he let his loyal people continue to suffer without judging the evil and vindicating those who had trusted in him. Dominated by a foreign totalitarian power, ground down by excessive taxes, widely ridiculed and restricted in rights, the Jews had reasons to long for better times.[12] The Old Testament faith in God as the Lord of history forbade them to surrender either to despair or uncertainty. God would act; he would fulfill his purpose, establish his righteous order, and care for his people.

Because this hope had so little prospect of fulfillment by any human means, multitudes looked to God to intervene in some remarkable way. They pictured their hope in vivid language. They developed an "eschatology," a message about the end of the world and the final realization of God's purpose. Some of their writings were apocalyptic, depicting the coming triumph as near at hand, soon to be miraculously wrought by the sudden, dramatic intervention of God. The atmosphere of first-century Judaism contained much of this vivid expectation.

Jesus had shared its basic spiritual conviction that God's decisive action was at hand, and had even declared that the kingdom or rule of God was beginning. The first preachers, moved especially by the tremendous meaning of the Resurrection, had added reason to say that the decisive actions of history were already in process.

To us, those events seem long ago and far away. We find it hard to think of them as the beginning of God's final and perfect order. But our task is to understand how the first generations of Christians believed and thought. They had thrilled to the beginnings of God's new work in Jesus' ministry. Then they had passed through the dark hours of his arrest, condemnation, death, and burial. But they had been lifted to heights of wonder and enthusiasm by the realization that God had raised Jesus from the dead. They saw at work a divine power, even more

[12] Frederick C. Grant, *The Economic Background of the Gospels* (New York and London: Oxford University Press, 1926).

clearly victorious than the power they had seen in the ministry of Jesus. These were events of immeasurable import. Nothing would ever again be the same. God was working out his will, and the crucial events, the manifest beginning of God's great victory over all hostility and sin, had happened in their own day and community. What could they say but that the new age had begun?

It is greatly to the credit of C. H. Dodd that he has seen so clearly this apostolic witness to the coming of the new age.[13] Albert Schweitzer had shattered the complacent evolutionism of an earlier generation of New Testament interpreters, and had demonstrated that Jesus announced, and the early preachers preached, that the coming of God's kingdom was imminent.[14] But he had made one mistake; he missed the dominating sense of wonder, gratitude, and urgency which gripped the first disciples because they knew without question that in the work of the crucified and risen Christ, the fulfillment had *already begun*. It was not merely a vivid hope; in essence and in large part the gift had already been received.

This realization of the eschatological hope Dodd has seen and stressed. But he has failed to give adequate place to the early Christian conviction that this fulfillment is thus far but partial, and awaits the time when the full and final Kingdom will come.[15] Dodd is quite clear that the first disciples had this hope for a future completion of God's plan, but it is not quite congenial to him that they thought in this way. With his Platonic leanings he would have preferred to have them all say only that, "The age to come has come." [16] But the first disciples were not Platonists: they were Jews who had the biblical sense that God was working out his purpose in history. Therefore, although they spoke with complete confidence of the beginning of the final age in Christ, they

[13] *Op. cit.*, also in his *Parables of the Kingdom* (New York: Charles Scribner's Sons, 1936).

[14] *The Quest of the Historical Jesus*, Eng. tr. from the German (2nd ed.; London: Macmillan & Co., 1911).

[15] Dodd speaks with more recognition of the limitations of the term "realized eschatology" in his recent work, *The Interpretation of the Fourth Gospel* (London: Cambridge University Press, 1953), p. 447, n. 1. He there says that he likes the phrase of Joachim Jeremias, "sich realisierende Eschatologie."

[16] These words occur in Dodd's *The Apostolic Preaching* (Chicago: Willett, Clark & Co., 1937), p. 147.

still looked to the future for the complete establishment of God's ever-lasting order.

Like Dodd, Rudolph Bultmann has personal difficulty with the eschatological expectancy of the Apostolic Age. He honestly intends to take history seriously, but his existentialist pattern of thought drives him to seek the essential meaning and content of the gospel in the present situation.[17] He does not do justice to the vivid sense of coming victory which marks the earliest Christian faith and preaching. He knows that faith is openness to the future, and is able to walk unafraid toward whatever may come; and this is a great insight. But for him, things to come fade into a non-biblical vagueness. He realizes that the apostles looked for a future triumph, but he has to rethink this hope into other patterns in order to get from it a living meaning. He thereby loses much of the depth and power of the original Christian conviction that the new and final age of God's effective rule has just begun and is moving certainly and rapidly to its full realization. And the Resurrection, which Bultmann explains as the disciples' realization of the meaning of the Cross, is the chief factor which impels the first Christians to give this vivid eschatological emphasis to their preaching.

3. This fulfillment has come, and this new age has begun through the work of God in the historical Jesus. The preaching centers in this story of God's work for men in Jesus Christ.

a) The historicity of Jesus is essential. (Acts 2:22; 4:10; 10:38.) To those who are interested in Jesus only as a teacher, his ideas are all that matter. Others have considered him merely the outstanding embodiment of an ideal; given the ideal, Jesus is no longer of permanent importance, and may be regarded as merely the animated scaffolding which is better removed when the ideal truth is clearly grasped. Still others have considered Jesus only the greatest or one of the greatest of the prophets and religious geniuses of mankind.

None of these three groups has been greatly disturbed by the assertion of some radical scholars that Jesus never lived. They have the teaching and the ideal; they can look for help to other prophets and can watch the historical figure of Jesus fade and vanish without dismay. They feel

[17] See his essay on "Mythology and the New Testament" in *Kerygma and Myth*.

44

no great loss when Jesus is called "the god made man," [18] or is interpreted as the symbolic personalization of a social process.

Not so the disciples of Jesus. Not so the earliest preachers. Not so the church. The entire Christian gospel disintegrates when deprived of the historical existence of Jesus as a real human figure. Beyond all doubt, the story of Jesus the man and leader came into circulation in the years immediately following the time of his alleged career. If no such man lived, fraud or delusion is involved, and the gospel depends on untrustworthy witnesses. But the matter is even more serious. By its very nature, the gospel stands or falls with the historicity of Jesus. It tells of the unique and central action of God in a historical person, Jesus Christ. If the historicity of Jesus fades away, the whole content of the gospel vanishes with it. In this gospel God is the one God, the Lord of history, who acts in history and through his chosen agents. Jesus is his central and unique agent, whose historical career is the instrument of achieving the eternal purposes of God. The historicity of Jesus is therefore essential to the truth of the entire gospel message.

This necessity need not alarm us. The historical existence and career of Jesus is attested by Paul, whose conversion cannot be dated more than half a dozen years after the death of Jesus. It is unassailably present in a gospel tradition which rests upon eyewitnesses. It is supported by sermons in Acts, whose primitive character must be admitted. It has strong attestation in hostile Jewish tradition, which would instantly have denied the existence of Jesus if the Christian movement could thus have been dealt a deathblow. It receives minor confirmation from Roman historians whose witness is early enough to be important. We have not the slightest reason to hesitate in stating that Jesus of Nazareth lived, worked, taught, and died as the gospel tradition says. The Christian has no less reason to say that he rose as that tradition tells us. The historicity question is settled; it is puerile to try to keep it alive.

b) Jesus was born of the line of David. (Acts 2:29-31; 13:22-23.) He therefore was qualified to be the Son of David, the Messiah expected by

---

[18] This phrase occurs in the title of a book by P. L. Couchoud (1937). On the historicity of Jesus see M. Goguel, *Jesus the Nazarene: Myth or History?* Eng. tr. from the French (New York, 1926); H. G. Wood, *Did Christ Really Live?* (New York: The Macmillan Co., 1938); and C. C. McCown, *The Search for the Real Jesus* (New York: Charles Scribner's Sons, 1940), ch. v.

great numbers of his fellow Jews. In him the Jews could find the fulfillment of the best and truest of their people's hopes; in him God's
promises to Israel came to realization.

The earliest preaching contained no reference to the Virgin Birth,
and no account of the infancy and childhood of Jesus. This does not
bar the way to acceptance of the doctrine of the Virgin Birth once it
is found to fit the total content and doctrine of the gospel, but it points
out anew where that earliest message placed its accent. Its focus was on
the Resurrection rather than on the birth of Jesus, and it began its
account of his historical career with the opening of his public ministry.

c) The preparatory work of John the Baptist was probably a common
feature of the earliest preaching. (Acts 10:37; 13:24-25.) John's importance for the earliest preachers as well as for later Christians was
that he set the stage for the appearance of Jesus and called him onto the
scene. He announced the imminent coming of God's decisive action.
He summoned Israel to face the righteous claim of God, and to repent
in view of the coming of God's judgment and new order. He pointed
to the *Other One* who should become the center of attention to those
who were listening to John.

d) The fact of Jesus' public ministry was presented and to some
extent described. (Acts 2:22; 10:38-39.) To our modern minds, one of
the most astonishing things in the Bible is that the sermons of Acts are
so meager in references to Jesus' ministry and teaching. The situation is
the reverse of what large numbers of Christians would prefer to find.
So it is of the greatest importance to understand the logic of the sermons
of Acts; perhaps no other point can do more to give us a clear understanding of New Testament theology.

Let us look for a moment at the position of the writer of Acts. Luke
is not ignorant of the teaching of Jesus, nor does he lack information
about the acts of Jesus during his public ministry. He has already given
in his Gospel an abundance of specific incidents and concrete teachings.
Yet when he comes to Acts, he is content with sermon summaries which
pass lightly over that abundant material, and concentrate upon other
features of God's work in Jesus Christ.

This can only be because Luke knows that the early sermons had the
emphasis he gives. And it can only be because he was satisfied with that

emphasis. When he must give a brief summary of what the great evangelistic preachers of the Apostolic Church said, he puts the emphasis on the death and resurrection of Jesus and on the work of the Holy Spirit in the church. He knows that Jesus did not achieve his purpose, and therefore God did not achieve his purpose, merely through the teaching and public acts of Jesus. The effective achievement of God's saving purpose came through the climactic events of the death and resurrection of Jesus, and the gift and work of the Holy Spirit. He does not despise the teaching and the ministry; the masterly Gospel of Luke sufficiently demonstrates this. But he puts the center of the sermons elsewhere, and he knows that the church did so from the start.

Such is the explanation of the fact that the sermons of Acts do not relate even one healing miracle of Jesus' ministry, do not describe even one specific event of the public career between baptism and arrest, and cite only one saying of the teaching of Jesus (Acts 20:35), a verse not found in any of the Gospels. Jesus did preach; he was the great expected prophet; his character was above reproach, and so his crucifixion was entirely unjustified; he exercised divine power in miraculously healing the sick—the sermons of Acts state all this. Luke knows it is true. He knows it is important. But he knows decisive events, more central and crucial for men's salvation—the death and resurrection of Jesus, and the gift and work of the Holy Spirit. So he leaves aside the details of the acts and teachings of Jesus, and sets these pivotal facts in clearest focus.

e) The death of Jesus was from the beginning an unfailing item in all Christian preaching (Acts 2:23; 3:15; 4:10; 10:39; 13:27-29). More than one reason prompted this inclusion. It was necessary for apologetic reasons; the preachers had to make clear that the criminal's death which Jesus suffered was not due to any fault of his, but was a crying injustice to a noble and innocent man. It was also necessary in the course of the gospel story. It gave the background for the resurrection toward which the story moved. It was further necessary to show the purpose of God; from the first some explanation of the death, some theology of the Cross, was indispensable.

It is sometimes thought that Paul began the theological development of the Christian message. This implies the curious, amazing idea that the pre-Pauline preachers could talk about the Cross without considering

47

or stating its meaning. It should be obvious that Christians could never refer without interpretation to so central an event. Indeed, the Christian message is inherently an interpretation of events, and has been from the start. Paul did not begin the process of explaining why Jesus died on the cross. Heartbroken disciples, puzzled believers, had to have some answer at once.

We need not and should not assume that the first explanations were complete or adequate. We should rather regard it as certain that they were tentative and fragmentary. But one thing we know: the starting point of interpretation was the resurrection fact. This showed that the death did not mark the defeat or the end of the work of Jesus. It proved that God had not disowned his Son, but had vindicated him. It sharpened attention to passages of Scripture which suggested that this had all happened in the plan of God; there was a purpose of God working out in it, even if that purpose was mysterious and not yet clear to human thought.

Jesus' death expressed his complete obedience and his concern for God's will and God's people. As the disciples looked at the contrast between the steadfastness of Jesus and their own defection, they were able to recall clues that Jesus gave, and moved toward the clear statement, soon attested in the tradition, that "Christ died for our sins in accordance with the scriptures" (I Cor. 15:3). We cannot trace in detail the earliest explanations of the death of Jesus; but along such lines as we have sketched, reverent thought moved to conclusions which conformed to Scripture, satisfied the mind, and claimed the faith of the disciples.

f) The resurrection of Jesus was the central fact of the gospel message. (Acts 2:24; 3:15; 4:10; 10:40; 13:30.) It formed the climax and interpreting center of the account of what God had done for men through Jesus. It was the key fact. The several occasions when the risen Christ made his presence known to his disciples led to a confident witness which the entire group, after some initial cases of hesitation, accepted without question (Matt. 28:17; Luke 24:41; John 20:25).

The New Testament narratives about the Resurrection are hard to harmonize. Did the first appearances occur in Jerusalem or Galilee? Did Jesus appear in physical form, or in a transformed body or form of existence which has no real parallel in our present human life, and so cannot be clearly described? We can never solve all these problems with certainty. Most likely the first appearances to the apostles were in Galilee, and this led to a rallying of the believers in Jerusalem where such appearances continued. Paul seems to be the best guide to the nature of the appearances; Jesus' form of life after the Resurrection was not the physical form of life we know; it was a higher, freer form.

The essential fact is that Jesus came back and was personally present with his disciples; he was able to make his presence known and his will understood. Nothing but such a real appearance, which the disciples naturally apprehended in forms conditioned by their past experience with Jesus, will explain the new start, the amazing vigor, the continued life and growth, and the intensive theological development of the church. The Christian faith is essentially a resurrection faith. Christian theology is essentially resurrection theology. The Resurrection was the climax of the apostolic preaching, and when the center is moved to other events in order to provide a more easily acceptable message or a more common ground of faith, the Christian faith and message cannot but begin to disintegrate. It can only be what it has always been from the first day of the Apostolic Church by remaining the good news of the risen Christ.

Certainly to the first disciples, the Resurrection was indubitable fact. It was the answer to all slander of Jesus and to all those who would reject him. It was the basis for all future faith, worship, thought, and witness.

g) The risen Christ is the exalted Lord of the church (Acts 2:33, 36; 4:11; 10:36). There is a fatal weakness in our modern emphasis on Easter. That emphasis is of course true to the gospel message; the Resurrection is central. But too many Christians begin to look to a long summer vacation once they have had a "big Easter." For the first Christians, the Resurrection was not the end of the story; it was the climax which leads on to further momentous developments. Jesus was "exalted at the right hand of God." (Acts 2:33.)

The frequency and importance of this aspect of early preaching is often obscured because we speak of the Ascension rather than of the Exaltation. The ascension story occurs only in Acts 1:9-11, and in a textually very uncertain statement in Luke 24:51. This could lead us to say that the Ascension is only a special idea of Luke. But that would be radically wrong. Luke's pictorial account of the Ascension is matched by numerous references to the exaltation of Jesus to the right hand of God. They occur in the early sermons of Acts; indeed, eleven New Testament books, by at least seven different writers, refer clearly to this Exaltation.[19] It obviously was a constant feature of early Christian preaching and teaching.

This is not just a bit of outmoded celestial geography. We know, as the pre-Copernican generations did not, that we cannot literally describe heaven as located straight up from where we stand. We know, as John Calvin saw,[20] that God does not have a right hand, and we may add that it is figurative language to say that either he or Christ is now sitting down. But we express the honor God gives to Christ, the transcendent greatness of Christ and his unique and authoritative position, by this language which New Testament preachers and writers use. We use symbols and figurative language in both science and philosophy, as well as in common speech, and we need feel no qualms or hesitation about using it in the immense outreach of Christian worship and thought. We can reach into the immensities of reality only with such figurative language; we would have to stop living if we could not do so. The magnificent description of Christ as triumphantly exalted at the right hand of God is not a mere antique frill of the apostolic preaching; it carries living truth.

Coupled with this reference to the exaltation of the risen Christ is the reference to Jesus as Lord. Modern Christians often use this title without thought or definite content. In the usual New Testament use it implies the Resurrection and Exaltation. The Greek word *kyrios* was at first an adjective, meaning "having power or authority." It described anyone who had such power or authority. Then it came to be used as a descriptive noun to designate those with special power or position—husbands (!), slaveowners, kings, gods. A Hebrew word *Adonai* spoke of God as Lord, and this view was characteristic of the faith and thinking of Israel. The Greek-speaking Jews naturally used the Greek word for

---

[19] Oscar Cullmann, *Christ and Time*, Eng. tr. from the German (Philadelphia: Westminster Press, 1950), p. 151.

[20] "We must not imagine to ourselves any one place, since *the right hand* is a metaphor which denotes the power that is next to God." *Commentary on a Harmony of the Evangelists Matthew, Mark, and Luke* (Eng. tr.), III, 393.

Lord to refer to their God. Thus, it is not surprising that when the Christians wanted to give the highest honor to the risen Christ, they spoke of him in obedient reverence as their Lord. Both the Aramaic-speaking and the Greek-speaking Jewish Christians promptly recognized Jesus as Lord. The use of the word in early sermons in Acts (e.g., 2:36), and the transliterated Aramaic word for "our Lord," *Maran*, in I Cor. 16:22, show that from the earliest days the church hailed Jesus as the exalted Lord of his people. The fact that the title Lord is given to Jesus in every New Testament book except the epistles of John proves that the early practice continued without interruption. It had preparation in the usage of Jesus himself (Mark 12:35-37), but its common New Testament use is to refer to the risen, exalted Christ.

What do these references to Exaltation and lordship mean? They imply and result from the Resurrection. They recognize that for his earthly work Jesus has been uniquely honored by the Father. But this does not mean that Jesus is now taking a long heavenly vacation, without active interest in the life of the church. He has a central role in the continuing life of his people. As his position at the right hand of God implies, he acts with authority as God's supreme and central agent in the carrying out of God's will. The idea that once Easter is over, we are through with Jesus until the last judgment (if there is one), completely misunderstands New Testament faith and preaching. Jesus is the effective and active Lord of his church. Absence from sight does not prevent actual lordship.

h) The risen and exalted Lord continues his work through the Spirit. Peter says to the Pentecost crowd that Jesus, exalted, "has poured out this" manifest evidence of the gift of the Spirit (Acts 2:33). He tells the hearers that those who are baptized "in the name of Jesus Christ" will receive the Holy Spirit. To accept the lordship of Jesus Christ is to receive from him the Holy Spirit.

Apart from Acts 2:33, we find few specific statements that the risen Christ gives the Holy Spirit. The Gospel of John, to make it clear that it is the risen Christ who gives the Divine Spirit, tells how Jesus breathed upon the disciples on the evening of the resurrection day and said, "Receive the Holy Spirit" (John 20:22). All four Gospels promise the gift of the Spirit through the greater one who will follow John (Matt.

51

3:11; Mark 1:8; Luke 3:16; John 1:33), and the fact that they state this expectation so confidently reflects their knowledge that the promise has been fulfilled. The Book of Revelation speaks of the seven eyes of the Lamb as "the seven spirits of God sent out into all the earth" (5:6). This is a symbolic way of saying that the risen Christ, of whom the book is speaking, sends into the world the divine Spirit (probably described as sevenfold to indicate the fullness of the gift). The passages in Paul's letters which speak of the work of the living Christ and the Holy Spirit in almost interchangeable terms (Rom. 8:9-11; II Cor. 3:17-18) have puzzled interpreters, but they show that the presence of the Spirit is indissolubly linked with the interest and activity of the risen Christ in his church. The risen Christ and the Holy Spirit are neither separable nor completely identifiable, which is precisely what the trinitarian doctrine of the church is meant to say. The risen Christ continues his work as Lord through the gift and work of the Holy Spirit.

i) The risen Lord will return to complete the work of God (Acts 3:20; 10:42). He will save God's people, judge all evil, do away with all that hurts men and thwarts the full realization of God's will, and establish the perfect, eternal divine order. The disciples, few in number, might have seemed to the casual observer hopelessly outnumbered and certain to be overwhelmed in the course of time. But these disciples themselves had no such defeatist attitude. God had revealed his purpose to his spokesmen in Israel and preserved that revelation in Scripture. He had acted decisively in Christ to redeem men and give ground for hope. He had made Christ the Lord of the church. He could be counted on to complete through Christ what he had so graciously and powerfully begun.

The anchor of this hope was not in despair or frustration. It was rather in what had already been done by God; it was based on facts which faith saw were the authentic clues to the meaning of all history. The victory was certain because God had promised it, because God's work in Christ guaranteed and began it, and because faith could see that it would surely come—and in the not too distant future.

5. This message of God's gracious and powerful action in history is an offer of forgiveness, and it leads to a call to repent and believe. (Acts 2:38-41; 3:19; 10:43; 13:38-39.)

Back of all the apostolic preaching is the frank recognition of the fact of sin. This divine redemptive action has been necessary because the sin of man puts him in a desperate situation. Nor is it only the outsiders, those who have not heard the earlier story of God's work in Israel, who need to face their failure. Even God's favored people have sinned and need a message of help. We sometimes hear that the apostle Paul fastened a morbid sense of sin upon a previously blithe and optimistic church. This idea is pure imagination. Apart from the fact that Jesus himself spoke of man's sin and need of repentance (Matt. 6:12; 7:11; Mark 1:15), the preachers of the church from the first set forth the same message. Conscious as they were that they had failed their Master and betrayed his trust in them (Mark 14:37, 50), they knew that they took up the task of the church only as forgiven men. Out of their own experience the fact of sin became real, and this awareness was supported by Scripture, by the teaching of Jesus, and by social observation, and it was sharpened by their sense of the holiness of God.

For this sin against God, man cannot make reparation. That is beyond his ability. Only God can open the way to restored fellowship and new life. And the message of the gospel story is that this is just what God has done through Christ. So this story is told with an evangelistic purpose. The aim of the preachers is to win men to accept the offered message for themselves. This requires sincere regret, deep repentance, honest recognition of failure and need. The preaching leads to a call to repentance.

But this is only part of the call. The call is to faith. The hearers must receive this message, acknowledge that it is true, see that it applies to them and brings them under God's judgment, acknowledge their need, put their faith in Christ as sent of God for their salvation, and enter into a life of faith, worship, and obedience. The preaching is never for information only. It does not speak in neutral tones. This story comes to each hearer, as it already has come to the preacher, with a demand for decision and commitment. It aims to show man's need and reach his will. It seeks not to satisfy mental curiosity, or even to answer speculative problems, but to solve an urgent life situation. It will answer man's questions—his deepest questions—but it will do so by relating him to

God's offer and demand, and by giving him the setting of faith in which alone he can gain the true understanding of life's meaning.

The Common New Testament Message

We have thus derived the outline of the earliest preaching from the sermons of Acts, and at times have confirmed it by side glances at other New Testament passages. This outline is the common core of the New Testament. To be sure, even in the sermons we find the unworried variety and the lack of concern for systematic unity which mark the entire New Testament. We do not expect to find every point in every writing, or to always find it stated in the same way. This message grips men of all kinds; it can be held and stated in various forms. But amid the variety which exists and the healthy development which takes place, there persists this common core, this basic outline, this testimony to the historical action of God which fulfills his promises, carries forward his purpose, inaugurates the new age in Christ, and opens out through the Resurrection into the exalted lordship of Christ. He exercises this lordship through the Holy Spirit, and so leads men toward the sure final victory which God will achieve through Christ's triumphant action at the last day.

The letters of Paul reflect this basic message. Since they are written to churches which have already heard the gospel and accepted it in faith, Paul does not go over it in order and in detail; he turns in each case to the fact or feature of the story which throws light on the situation with which he is dealing. But he keeps echoing the points which we have covered in our outline.[21] This is the more significant when we remember that Paul's letters were written to churches which were mainly Gentile in membership. The earliest sermons were addressed to Jews. But what Paul says to the Gentiles agrees in substance with what the church had said from the first to the Jews. The common core message was from the first this gospel centered in Jesus Christ, the risen Lord.

The other letters of the New Testament give general support to this conclusion. They are less detailed writings, and illustrate the wholesome variety of leadership and thought in one great church; but there is no

---

[21] See C. H. Dodd, *The Apostolic Preaching*, ch. iii.

sign that they depart in any essential form from the message we have found in the early sermons. The Epistle of James is the least charac-teristic of these writings. It is important for the church to recognize this, for many Christians are tempted to cut all the other New Testa-ment writings to fit the pattern which they think they find in this Epistle. It would be misguided, however, to let this one rather short Epistle dictate the interpretation of the other twenty-six writings, espe-cially since it is probably one of the later writings of the New Testa-ment. Moreover, this attempt to discredit the common core message even fails to do justice to the Epistle of James itself. Its references to Jesus as the Lord (1:1; 2:1; 5:8) imply the resurrection and continued authority of Christ, and the references to the coming judgment give him a decisive role in the climax of history (5:9). Even this Epistle cannot be interpreted as merely a body of helpful religious teaching; it assumes that the risen Christ is the object of faith.

Now that we have found the common outline of the earliest preach-ing, we likewise see the relation of the Gospels to this basic message. They assume and expand the common outline, and show that the min-istry and work of Jesus were prominent in it. Their emphasis on scrip-tural fulfillment, on God's action in history, and on Jesus as the central figure of history and the key actor in God's redemptive drama; their accent on the Cross and Resurrection, as shown by the large proportion of each Gospel which deals with the final events of Jesus' career; their hints of the coming exaltation, lordship, and rule of Jesus by the gift of the Spirit; and their repeated insistence upon the decisive role of Jesus in the final judgment—all these points show that the Gospels are an expansion and support of the essential points of the common preach-ing, with particular attention to the details of the Ministry, Death, and Resurrection. They give an indispensable expansion in these respects, but they do not shatter or discard the common outline.

Two recent developments of gospel study support this conclusion. The view of C. C. Torrey that all four of our Gospels, as well as Acts 1:1-15:35, were originally written in Aramaic, and only later translated into Greek,[22] has failed to win general recognition, and we can hardly

[22] Set forth in *The Composition and Date of Acts* (Cambridge, 1916); *The Four Gospels* (New York, 1933); *Our Translated Gospels* (New York: Harper & Bros., 1936); *Documents of the Primitive Church* (New York: Harper & Bros., 1941).

accept it. But it has underlined the fact that Semitic atmosphere and linguistic features mark these writings, and that they derive their material from sources not too far removed from the date of the events which they report.

Torrey's view has its negative aspects. He supports his theory mainly by alleged mistranslations which he finds in our Greek form of the Gospels and Acts, and so holds that our Gospels are open to correction at these points. Moreover, he does not accept the Christology of the Gospels as authentic. But the logic of his theory is that our Gospels and the first half of Acts rest on very early tradition and agree with the early preaching of the church. Indeed, Torrey definitely holds this view; he claims that the distortion in Christology which he finds was injected into the tradition at the very beginning of the Apostolic Age, in a practically instantaneous transformation of the original facts. Such radical, immediate, and universal transformation of central facts is impossible to document or defend. But Torrey has to recognize that the essentials of New Testament theology go back to the very beginning of the New Testament Church.

Form Criticism is another form of study which has produced some radical conclusions which do not necessarily follow from this method.[23] It is a study of the early, oral, preliterary form of the gospel tradition. It assumes—and rightly—that the background of the Gospels was not some research-scholar's library, but rather the worship, teaching, preaching, and controversy of the church. It holds that the gospel material was used in living connection with the life and work of the church. In other words, the tradition was used in the preaching and teaching of the apostles and other first-generation Christian leaders. It supported the preaching, illustrated the points of the common outline, and provided material for more detailed instruction of those whose attention and interest had been attracted by the basic evangelistic message. Both the theory of Aramaic originals and that of Form Criticism tie the Gospels back to the preaching and teaching activity of the earliest church, and it is not surprising that the Gospels fit in with the common core of the Christian message.

Indeed, the very form of the Gospels reflects their relation to the

[23] For important books in this field, see n. 5 of this chapter.

preaching. The Gospels are not biography or history in the usual sense. They tell a story which has meaning for the faith and life of those who hear it, and lay claim to the life of their readers or hearers. They aim to support and enforce the preaching, to clarify its basis and meaning, and to claim the personal response and decision of those who receive their message.

Thus, in the common core of the early Christian preaching we have laid hold of the unity which marks the New Testament. The points of this outline underlie the whole New Testament and continually bind the New Testament together into a common witness to God's past, present, and future work in Jesus Christ.

Such a message, consistently Christocentric and centered in the resurrection of Jesus, may seem to divorce the New from the Old Testament. To avoid this mistaken idea, we need only recall why the Christians kept the Old Testament as Scripture. They found in it the background of the story of God's work in Jesus Christ. They recognized God's work in Israel as a part of the one continuous historical work of God which has its center in Jesus Christ. They found in the Old Testament the divine promise of that unique and central figure, the coming prophet, servant of God, and king. In the light of the Resurrection they found the Old Testament to be at its deepest level a Christ-related book, which supports the total witness of the Apostolic Church. They kept it because its divine revelation, demand, judgment, and promise constituted for them an integral and essential part of the gospel message of Jesus Christ the risen Lord. We must study with care this relation of Christ to Israel and the Old Testament.

CHAPTER III

The Christ of Israel

WE TURN TO THE QUESTION OF THE RELATION OF JESUS CHRIST to Israel. Up to this point I have presented the viewpoint which underlies the study of biblical theology, and have given in outline the basic message upon which the New Testament Church was founded and developed. We shall now examine more in detail, and in a mainly chronological order, the redemptive work of God which finds its interpreting center in the Resurrection. We therefore turn our attention to the beginnings of the biblical story, and examine their relation to Jesus Christ. This is essentially the story of Israel and the Old Testament.

Before we begin the study of the place of Israel and its Scriptures in the gospel message, however, it must be noted that the biblical story reaches back to the beginnings of human life and history. The Bible is the story of God's dealings with the world; therefore, it begins with the creation story, and by the use of primitive traditions, sketches as a prelude God's dealings with men prior to his selection of Abraham and Israel for his special purpose.[1] The first eleven chapters of Genesis have an essential role in the full biblical narrative.

In fact, these primal events would claim a larger part in New Testament preaching and thought were it not for three limiting factors:

1. The church had these things recorded in the Scriptures, and since its interest centered in the message of redemption, it felt no need to repeat and restate the story of creation and the beginnings of human life. Christian leaders referred to these things on occasion, but did not make them the focus of interest.

---

[1] See H. Wheeler Robinson, *Inspiration and Revelation in the Old Testament* (New York: Oxford University Press, 1946), pp. 17-23.

2. In early Christian thought the backward glance was predominantly toward the dealings of God with Israel. The church was vividly conscious of its close tie with Israel; its backward look was directed chiefly to God's dealings with Israel and to her connection with Christ and the church.

3. New Testament interest and thought concentrated strongly on the present situation. The real concern of the early Christians was their relation with the Israel of the time of Jesus and the apostles. They looked backward only to throw light on present issues, for they had no merely historical or speculative interest. These three factors kept the church from extended discussion of creation and the earliest history of mankind.

Yet it is certain that for the New Testament Christians God is the Creator of the world and human life (Acts 17:24; Heb. 1:2). And what he made was good (Gen. 1:31; I Cor. 10:26). The blame for man's sin is not his. It was due to man's guilty choice. Because God created man as a responsible creature—made in the very image of God—sin creates a desperate problem, and man faces ruin and death. The need of divine help thus goes back to the beginnings of human history, and God's first steps to meet human need reach back to those early days. That God is the creator of all men, that sin is the problem of all men, and that the remedy must have a world outreach, are background facts for understanding God's election of Israel and his covenant with this one people. The universalism implied in the doctrine of creation and in the world-wide problem of sin throws light on the role of Israel and the scope of the gospel. The first eleven chapters of Genesis prevent special attention to Israel from becoming a narrow nationalistic eclipse of the world rule of the one God.

In still another way the story of creation and of God's dealings with the whole of earliest mankind is connected with the gospel story of Jesus Christ. As the church grew in its grasp of the full meaning of Christ's work, it could not limit its thought of him to one brief period of history. He was not merely a man whose origin it could trace to the day of his birth. His unique relation to God was no late supplementary addition to the divine plan and purpose. In this human life the eternal Son of God had become incarnate in history and had done his central work, but his full role was no late or transient one. He who was the active agent of the Father in redemption had been likewise his active agent in creation.[2] In this the Son paralleled the relation of the Father himself to human history. The God and Father of Jesus Christ was both Creator and Redeemer, and his Son was his active agent in both respects.

This ascription to the Son of the active role in creation does not appear often in the New Testament. There is good reason for this. To these Christians the new act of God in Jesus Christ was so central, the epoch-making significance of the entrance of the Son of God into human life was so clear, and the new era of the lordship of Christ opened up by the Resurrection was so fruitful, that they could not give equal prominence to that earlier work. Their historical sense was too strong to permit them to emphasize the time before Christ as much as they did his earthly career. So the role of the Son in creating and upholding the created order plays no central role in the New Testament.

Yet this view is early. It is stated by Paul, the earliest New Testament writer, not only in explicit words in Col. 1:16, but also in I Cor. 8:6, whose brief statement is clear when compared with Colossians. It appears again in the Epistle to the Hebrews (1:1-3). The Gospel of John ascribes the same creative and world-supporting role to the Divine Word or Logos (1:1-18). In the Book of Revelation Jesus Christ is "the Alpha and the Omega, the first and the last" (22:13; cf. 1:17). This less explicit reference also points to the history-embracing role of the Son.

We need not say that this cosmic role of the Son was clearly understood and stated from the very first days of the church. But it is clear that it soon was affirmed, and that there was no objection to it in Christian circles. The original message accented the ministry, death, resurrection, and active lordship of Christ. But with remarkable swiftness the conviction soon attained clarity that his full role reached back to the beginning; he is the active agent of the Father throughout history. Only a quarter of a century after the death of Jesus, within the

[2] On "The Pre-existent Christ" see Elias Andrews, *The Meaning of Christ for Paul* (New York and Nashville: Abingdon Press, 1949), ch. xi. On creation through Christ, see Gösta Lindeskog, *Studien zum neutestamentlichen Schöpfungsgedanken* (Uppsala, 1952), I, especially pp. 207-16.

lifetime of eyewitnesses and personal disciples of the Galilean ministry, Paul could state this conviction as a settled conclusion of Christian thinking, and there is no evidence that other Christian leaders challenged his Christology. Here is a striking proof of the rapid and early maturing of the classic convictions of the church concerning the role of Jesus Christ.[3]

The main interest of the New Testament, however, is not directed toward the general history of mankind. Neither the early history before the choice of Israel nor the later centuries of gentile history receive prominent attention. We find references to the wide scope of God's work (e.g., John 1:4, 9), and to the universal knowledge of God (Acts 14:17; Rom. 1:20; 2:15), but these are not used to vindicate a natural theology which would lessen the need of the gospel. On the contrary, the few passages which look at the wider work of God are used to show that the Gentiles have knowledge and are responsible for their sin, and so should repent. The chief concern with the world at large is with the nations as a field of mission work. All men need Christ.

In keeping with this lack of speculative interest and this concern with the gentile world as a present mission field, the backward look is almost entirely confined to Israel. There the story of God's special redemptive working began, the story that led directly to its climax in Jesus Christ. It was in Israel that Jesus was born, lived, and worked. The burning question that faced the newborn church was its relation to the people among whom it had emerged.

God had chosen Abraham and given him great promises (Gen. 12:1-3). He had chosen the descendants of Abraham, particularly the people of Israel, as his special people.[4] His divine purpose was linked with their history. It was not because of their numbers or their inherent goodness or superior wisdom that he chose them (Deut. 7:7; 9:4-6). Nor was it merely for their selfish enjoyment that God chose them and made his covenant with them. Though they often failed to grasp the fact, he chose them to serve him and witness to his will and pur-

---

[3] That these convictions had their source in the career and nature of the historical Jesus is the contention of J. Gresham Machen, *The Origin of Paul's Religion* (New York: The Macmillan Co., 1921).

[4] On God's election of Israel and his covenant with her see H. W. Robinson, op. cit., ch. xi, and G. Ernest Wright, "The Faith of Israel," in *The Interpreter's Bible* (New York and Nashville: Abingdon Press, 1952), I, especially pp. 352-57.

pose. Nor was continuance of this special relation with Israel due to their steadfast faithfulness, for they were often "stubborn and rebellious" (Ps. 78:8), and drew divine judgment on themselves. But he did not withdraw his mercy; he persisted in his purpose to work out his plan through them.

This conviction that Israel has a special relation to God and a special role in history runs through the Old Testament, and the New Testament likewise accepts it as the way God works out his purpose with men. A clear statement of the gospel message calls for a study of Jesus as the Christ of Israel.

The Heir of Israel

It should not be necessary to emphasize that Jesus was a Jew. But misguided attempts to demonstrate that he was basically dependent on Egypt or India, the recent Nazi attempt to show that he was an Aryan, and the tendency of recurrent anti-Semitism to discount his Jewish blood and indebtedness,[5] make it worth while to point out that in race and religious heritage Jesus was a Jew. He was first of all the heir of Israel.

In one respect this truth may need to be qualified. Jesus grew up in Galilee, a region which some first-century Jews despised. It had never been the center of the life of the chosen people. In times of war and invasion it had suffered severely. Indeed, in the days of the Maccabean War it was a largely pagan region, and Simon rescued and took to Judea the loyal Jewish minority (I Macc. 5:20-23). Even in the days of Jesus, it seems, there still was more gentile influence in Galilee than in Judea. So, in Galilee Jesus may have been more open to the influence of the Greek language and ideas, and more exposed to gentile contacts, than if he had been reared in some Judean town.[6]

It is quite likely that Jesus heard Greek spoken, could speak it some--what, and knew some Gentiles. But this we cannot prove, and the evidence that exists shows decisively that in any case he was a Jew who regularly spoke Aramaic,[7] and lived faithfully within the Jewish frame-

[5] Such views are exposed by Eugene S. Tanner, *The Nazi Christ* (Tulsa: University of Tulsa Press, 1942).

[6] See Ch. Guignebert, *The Jewish World in the Time of Jesus*, tr. S. H. Hooke (New York: E. P. Dutton & Co., 1939), pp. 7-11.

[7] On Aramaic as Jesus' mother tongue see Gustaf Dalman, *Jesus-Jeshua*, tr. Paul P. Levertoff (New York: The Macmillan Co., 1929), pp. 1-16.

work of his town and country. The faithful worship and religious instruction of a Jewish home had been his preparation from early years. The worship and religious thinking which he shared in the synagogue, and the occasional visits he made to the temple in Jerusalem, gave him further ties with his heritage (Luke 2:46; 4:16). From his early years, he developed that remarkable knowledge of Scripture and deep penetration into its deeper meaning which form so striking a feature of his ministry and teaching. He was the grateful heir of Israel.

Jesus was further indebted to Israel for the religious framework of his ministry. The synagogue provided the setting for much of his teaching, especially in his early ministry. The Scripture which he read on occasion in the synagogue gave him a basis for teaching about his role and his message (Luke 4:16).

The temple at Jerusalem was not the center of his ministry, for the Synoptic Gospels are undoubtedly correct in locating the main portion of his public ministry in Galilee. But as the symbol of the unity of God's people, it drew the imagination of every loyal Israelite, and Jesus shared the common view that it was in a special sense the house of God (Mark 11:17). He could not endure the profanation of what every Jew should regard as a sacred place. And when he was in Jerusalem, the outer courts—the only areas into which he as a layman could go—became the scene of teaching sessions with his disciples and other listeners.

How often Jesus visited the temple is not certain. The Gospel of John reports that he went to Jerusalem for a series of feasts, so that the yearly cycle of religious festivals becomes the framework of his ministry. We need not deny that such visits did occur; but the impression we receive from the Gospel of John when read by itself, that the ministry of Jesus centered in Jerusalem and to a lesser extent in Judea, must yield to the clear testimony of the Synoptic Gospels that Jesus worked chiefly in Galilee. The fact that the Twelve—and indeed the entire group to whom the Spirit came on the day of Pentecost—were Galileans (Acts 2:7) shows where the center of the ministry really was. This Galilean center of Jesus' ministry makes it clear that his interest was not in priestly or sacrificial rites, but in a prophetic message and ministry.

Jesus was likewise indebted to Israel for the immediate stimulus to take up his own ministry. Some find this background in a circle of poor but pious Jews who in humble life cherished the best of the heritage of Israel and helped to shape the life and thought of Jesus.[8] The existence and influence of such a special circle is possible, but cannot be proved. It would not be theologically troublesome if true, for if the incarnation has real meaning, it permits the healthy development of spiritual life in the setting of favorable social conditions. And we must remember that through his mother and local community Jesus did receive and profit by the heritage of his people. He could have received the same benefit from others as well.

The spectacular discovery of ancient Jewish documents at Qumrân and neighboring points near the west bank of the Dead Sea will add to our knowledge of first-century Judaism.[9] These documents come from a sect which was at least closely allied to and probably was identical with the Essenes. Their geographical location at a distance from Galilee and their withdrawal from normal Jewish life make it unlikely that they directly influenced the boyhood and early manhood of Jesus; the possibility of indirect influence remains. Certainly the immediate stimulus to Jesus' ministry did not come from this sect.

The real background of the ministry of Jesus is the preaching and influence of John the Baptist. All four of the Gospels regard the Baptist's work as the prelude to Jesus' ministry, and the apostolic preaching began its account of Jesus' ministry with a brief sketch of the preparatory work of John.

This is a little surprising. Reasons of strategy might have led the church to keep silent about the importance of John the Baptist. It is clear from the Gospels that his reputation persisted (Mark 11:30-32). Many of his disciples continued loyal to him even after his death. The

---

[8] See M. Goguel, *The Life of Jesus*, tr. Olive Wyon (New York: The Macmillan Co., 1933), p. 262.

[9] The literature on this subject is extensive. For surveys see H. H. Rowley, *The Zadokite Fragments and the Dead Sea Scrolls* (Oxford: Basil Blackwell & Mott, Ltd., 1952); A. Dupont-Sommer, *The Dead Sea Scrolls*, tr. E. Margaret Rowley (New York: The Macmillan Co., 1952), and *The Jewish Sect of Qumrân and the Essenes*, tr. R. D. Barnett (London: Vallentine, Mitchell & Co., Ltd., 1954); M. Burrows, *The Dead Sea Scrolls* (New York: The Viking Press, 1955). The *Bulletin* of the American Schools of Oriental Research and *The Biblical Archaeologist* offer opportunity to keep up with developments in this field.

Gospel of John denies the central place to the Baptist so explicitly as to show that, for some, John was a rival to Jesus (1:6-8, 15, 19-23, 29, 35-36; 3:25-30). The Book of Acts confirms this. As late as the latter part of Paul's ministry, we find disciples of John the Baptist at Ephesus, where the Gospel of John most likely was written (Acts 18:25; 19:3). The fact that chronologically Jesus followed John, and that John baptized Jesus, might easily be used to show that John was the superior and Jesus only a follower with no independent significance.[10]

If nevertheless the church faithfully and continually began its story of Jesus' work with a reference to the ministry of the Baptist, this constitutes convincing testimony to the importance of John. It was in response to John's preaching that Jesus came to the Jordan to hear and be baptized. The fact that the Spirit drove Jesus into the wilderness immediately after the baptism (Mark 1:12) may be intended to show that he henceforth was independent of John. The Baptist nevertheless was a major figure in the background of Jesus' ministry. He had prepared the way by his stirring preaching; he had stirred Jesus to leave his home and give his life to the special service of God.

To understand how greatly Jesus was indebted to his Jewish heritage, we must survey some basic convictions which he inherited and shared.[11] He did not accept them without criticism and development; but this freedom need not obscure the great extent of agreement.

1. God is the central fact of life. We often take this point for granted, and it seems irreverent to suggest that Jesus ever doubted it. As a matter of fact, he did not. There is no evidence that he ever questioned the infinite importance of God as the Lord of life both for the people and for the individual. One God, holy, righteous, gracious, faithful, the Creator and the active Lord of history, working out his purpose in his-

[10] An able recent study of John's career is given by Carl H. Kraeling, *John the Baptist* (New York: Charles Scribner's Sons, 1951). On possible connections of John with the (Essene) Qumrân sect, see M. Burrows, *op. cit.*, ch. xv.

[11] On the basic Old Testament faith and thought see, in addition to H. W. Robinson, *op. cit.*, and H. H. Rowley, *op. cit.*, the following: W. F. Albright, *From the Stone Age to Christianity* (Baltimore: Johns Hopkins Press, 1940); Otto J. Baab, *The Theology of the Old Testament* (New York and Nashville: Abingdon Press, 1949); W. Eichrodt, *Theologie des Alten Testaments* (Leipzig, 1933-39); William A. Irwin on "The Hebrews" in *The Intellectual Adventure of Ancient Man* (Chicago: University of Chicago Press, 1946), pp. 223-360; Norman H. Snaith, *The Distinctive Ideas of the Old Testament* (Philadelphia: Westminster Press, 1946); and G. Ernest Wright, *The Challenge of Israel's Faith* (Chicago: University of Chicago Press, 1944).

tory, and rightly claiming the grateful faith and wholehearted loyalty of his people—this common biblical faith was a heritage of immense meaning (Deut. 6:4 ff.; Isa. 44:6). We should not take it for granted. It was no commonplace of ancient times. It has no real parallel in non-Jewish circles, even though partial parallels appear in many places. The full message of the one God stands out in the Old Testament and in the gospel of Jesus and the apostles with a purity and power that has not been equaled.

2. God reveals himself and his will for men. In the relation between God and man, the initiative is with God. It is not possible for man by searching to find out God; he may search, but he does not surprise and discover God by unaided human genius. God makes himself known, and man's essential role is to respond in faith. This does not reduce man to an automaton or machine. He has his freedom and responsibility, but he has it within the setting of God's overarching initiative and sovereignty, for God is the Lord, and he makes himself known.

"The heavens are telling the glory of God" (Ps. 19:1), and to men of faith, nature spoke its message of revelation, but this was never the center of Israelite religion. Man is made in the image of God (Gen. 1:27), and it is through human agents that God's revelation finds its characteristic biblical expression. The scriptural account of God's dealings with men becomes the instrument of revelation; and those who—like Jesus—responded in faith to God, acknowledged that in the Scriptures God had made his ways and purpose known and had given men a priceless record of his revelation.

3. This revelation took place in history and through men who played their role in history. The revelation was not basically a code of law, though portions of the Pentateuch particularly collected and arranged rules of life. Nor was it a set of principles, although many great guiding principles emerge. It was essentially a revelation of God's presence and will through history, and through the interpretation given to that history. In this revelation, God used many nameless servants as well as agents of special prominence who emerged at crucial times and played a vital role in carrying forward God's purpose and stating his demand. Jesus knew that he was taking his significant place in this revelation

history, and so he could say as he began his work: "The time is fulfilled" (Mark 1:15).

4. The covenant was the historical framework of God's dealings with Israel. The election of special individuals for special roles took place in connection with the covenant. God chose a special people, and made a covenant with them. This was not a contract on equal terms, such as men make. God is the superior; he graciously offers a mutual relation in which man receives rich blessings if only he proves true to his trust and promises. God made such a covenant with Abraham (Gen. 15). He made what may be regarded as the key covenant with Israel at Sinai (Exod. 24).

Both the righteousness and the grace of God come to light in the sequel to these covenants. Israel does not fulfill her part, and if God were not God he could cancel the covenant and abandon Israel. But while he must punish and chasten his sinful people, he cannot give them up. His steadfast love works on to win them to true loyalty and constant obedience. So we find a series of renewed covenants in the Old Testament, leading on to the promise of a new covenant in which the law and demand of God will be written in the hearts of men, and they will do gladly what their people have so often failed to do (Jer. 31:31-34).

This covenant idea Jesus retains. Perhaps one of the worst blunders of certain recent study was its view that Jesus had thought in individualistic terms. He never gave up the thought of the covenant; he interpreted his death as the means of establishing a new covenant with his people (I Cor. 11:25). And this covenant, whatever its capacity to expand in outreach, was with Israel.

5. The covenant, as we have implied, is with the community of the covenant people. Man's relation to God is set in a community pattern. His worship, obedience, and service take place with the people of God. Thus, election and covenant have a social as well as a religious setting. A bare individualism never existed in Israel. Those who speak of the individualism of Jeremiah and Ezekiel overstress one aspect of their thought. Jeremiah, as shown by the above quoted promise of a new covenant, thought of his people as the setting of man's relation to God.

Ezekiel describes the worship of the privileged time to come as a community worship centered in the rebuilt temple (37, 40 ff.).

This community pattern continues in the ministry and thought of Jesus. He lived in the setting of Israel, and shared its community worship and life.[12] He never withdrew from that community life, and he never told his disciples to do so. Hence the disciples, after his resurrection, gather in Jerusalem, go to the temple, join in the religious life of their people, and take up their witness as ministers to Israel.

6. The divine revelation contains an inherent moral demand. Part of the durable strength of the Old Testament revelation was its clear insistence on the holiness of God and his moral demand on men. The primitive numinous and ceremonial sense of holiness took on the meaning of God's unfailing moral integrity. He made this world a moral order. The true life of man is in obedience to him; no other way of life has a future. This sturdy prophetic note keeps religious loyalty from degenerating into mere emotion or external form. The heart of it is obedient response to the righteous will of God both in reverent worship and in moral action. This dominant prophetic note runs through the Old Testament and marks it off from other faiths.

It is just this quality which recurs so prominently in the message of Jesus. In his initial call to repentance, and in his repeated insistence that men must do God's will in daily life and even accept the costly way of self-sacrifice to serve God's cause, Jesus presents God's moral demand as imperative for all who agree to serve God (Mark 1:15; 8:34; 12:29-31).

7. This feature of the heritage of Jesus helps us to understand the central role of faith in human life. The faith which emerges continually throughout the Old Testament story is an act of the will and not merely a mental assent or a volatile emotion. It is a personal choice within the covenant people, a decision to serve God and his purpose, and to trust in him. Faith by nature finds active expression; it is not real without giving the will to God. This note of faith which involves loyalty and dedication marks all that Jesus did and taught.

8. In his clear recognition of the seriousness of sin, Jesus accepts and deepens his ancestral heritage. Some have thought that Jesus shook

[12] See Joseph Klausner, *Jesus of Nazareth*, tr. Herbert Danby (New York: The Macmillan Co., 1925), pp. 363-68.

himself free from all pessimistic thoughts about mankind, and lived with sunny optimism about the healthy ability of man to deal with all moral problems and failures by the simple act of the human will. Had he done so, it would have set him off from his Jewish background. From the early forms of sacrifice, which still suggest something of a primitive sense of uncleanness, to the higher expressions of man's moral wrong as disobedience to God, the Old Testament shows us a religious people conscious of their faults and of their need for restored fellowship with God. Not every sacrifice, of course, was considered an offering for sin. But vaguely at first, and later more explicitly, it was felt that something was needed to bring man and God together. Certainly in the period of the Old Testament writings, sin was of concern to the people of God as a whole, and so to all of its members.

Jesus fully shared this concern for the moral need of his people. He came preaching repentance (Mark 1:15), and spoke of men as evil (Matt. 7:11). He taught his disciples to pray regularly for forgiveness and to recognize that others fail and need forgiveness too (Matt. 6:12; 18:21-35). He agreed with his Jewish heritage in taking seriously the fact of sin. Believing as he did in the holiness and judgment of God, he had to take seriously whatever marred the moral quality of men.

9. The idea of history as moral conflict was common to the Old Testament and to Jesus. The sin of man was not merely a matter of individual expression and concern. It poisoned the relations of men and came to vicious expression in group perversion. Families, groups, and nations were affected by this taint. It led not merely to passive resistance to God's righteous will, but to active hostility and attack on God's cause and people. In the Law we find recognition of social solidarity in sin; in the Prophets we observe that the nation may fall into wrong, and peoples may fight against God's cause and people.

Jesus reflects this view; he sees Chorazin, Bethsaida, Capernaum, and Jerusalem uniting in unbelief and sin (Matt. 11:21-24; 23:37). But he also reflects a continued development of thought in Israel, according to which the forces of evil are active not merely among men but also in superhuman realms (e.g., Matt. 12:25-28). Life is not a neutral area but a battleground. Evil is not passive but actively hostile. Man is not helpless, for God and his hosts are active for good, and powerful to triumph. But the struggle is real, and it is far more than a conflict within the soul of the individual man. It is a conflict on the scene of history and in the cosmic scene, where God's rule will prevail only through active warfare against evil. It is this idea which later finds meaning in the thought of Christ as the active Lord and the effective leader of the battle against powerful forces of evil.

10. Because God is the active Lord of history and is concerned about helping his people, the note of hope continually recurs in the Old Testament. We find numerous stern passages in the Old Testament, as we do in the words of Jesus; indeed, some of the sternest passages in the Bible come to us in the words of Jesus himself. But the idea that the prophets spoke only doom, and that all pictures of hope were later additions by weakhearted successors, does violence to the Bible and artificially divides the one prophetic message. No doubt on specific occasions a prophet spoke only stern words, but back of the sternness was a faith in God which looked for a realization of God's will, even if the prophet could not say how this would come. The Old Testament has a hope—for Israel, at times for mankind (Isa. 19:24-25), and in a few late passages for the resurrection of the individual (Isa. 26:19; Dan. 12:2). This note of hope crystallized into a strong message in the ministry and words of Jesus, with his promise and initial gifts of physical healing, spiritual renewal, resurrection, and permanent salvation.

Taken as a whole, the above series of points shows the deep kinship between Jesus and his ancestral heritage. They combine into a distinctive religious position which has no full parallel in the world of his time. Compared with every other religious environment of that time, Jesus and his heritage show a unity, and between them and all pagan forms of faith and life there exists a noteworthy difference.

Jesus was a Jew, and he lived as a Jew until the end of his life. At the end of his career, even though opposition and danger loomed before him, he went to Jerusalem to present his final challenge and appeal. (Luke 9:51.) He spoke with deep emotion of his concern for the spiritual welfare of Jerusalem (Matt. 23:37; Luke 13:34); and he was roused to indignation by the callous commercialism which defiled the sacred precincts of the temple (Mark 11:17). His whole ministry was

70

carried out in the Jewish framework. He was no neutral cosmopolitan who lacked racial and national attachment; he never sought any other environment than the Jewish one in which he was born.[13] To be sure, he was no blind slave to his heritage. He could criticize both his people and their teachings on certain points; but he was the heir of Israel, he accepted in its essentials her heritage, and worked to the end of his life within that heritage.

The Christ of Israel

The word Christ is to us a proper name, and the Christian church has become so gentile that we often wrongly think of the Jews as outsiders. It takes an effort of mind and imagination to recapture the deeply Jewish meaning and feeling embedded in the word Christ. But since it is one of the basic titles given to Jesus in the New Testament, and because it can take us deep into Jewish thinking and the mind of Christ, it deserves special study.[14]

This word Christ is a Greek word, *Christos*, which is identical in meaning with the Hebrew word *Messiah* (John 1:41; 4:25). Both mean "anointed." As a descriptive adjective the early use of the word varied. It was used of priests, who were literally anointed with oil to set them apart for their ministry (Exod. 29:7; Lev. 8:12). It was used of kings, who likewise were literally anointed to consecrate them to their office under God (I Sam. 2:10; 10:1; Ps. 2:2; 89:20). This usage was confined almost entirely to the anointing of the kings of Israel, but when a pagan king was used as God's instrument in carrying out the divine purpose—as was Cyrus, king of Persia—he too was called figuratively the Lord's anointed (Isa. 45:1). That the word could be used in a figurative way, with no reference to the literal use of oil, is clear also from Ps. 105:15, where the patriarchs are called "my anointed ones" and "prophets."

In time the hard experience of subjection to foreign powers gave rise in Israel to the expectation of a great divinely sent leader who

[13] When he withdrew into the regions of Tyre and Sidon or of Caesarea Philippi, it was for a time of withdrawal rather than for a public ministry to Gentiles. Cf. Mark 7:24.
[14] For brief studies of this and other titles of Jesus see Vincent Taylor, *The Names of Jesus* (London: St. Martin's Press, 1953). On Jesus as Messiah see also B. S. Easton, *Christ in the Gospels* (New York: Charles Scribner's Sons, 1930), pp. 164-73, and Wm. Manson, *Jesus the Messiah* (London: Hodder & Stoughton, Ltd., 1943).

would achieve God's purpose for his chosen people. The use of the word anointed to describe such a leader almost never occurs in the Old Testament. The word is used in Dan. 9:25 with reference to an expected leader, in an apocalyptic passage which is writing past and present history in the form of prophecy. Without this specific word, however, the expectation of a great leader sent of God recurs in many passages. In them the emphasis is on the Davidic descent of the coming ruler; the basic passage is II Sam. 7:11-16, but the same promise occurs in the prophets (Isa. 11:1-5; Jer. 33:15; Ezek. 34:23-24).

The use of the word anointed to describe the great coming leader of God's people appears in a number of the Pseudepigrapha. For example, Ethiopic Enoch 48:10; 52:4 reflects this use, as do IV Ezra 7:29; 12:32 and Psalm of Solomon 17:36. Such passages support the clear indications of the New Testament that this expectation of a coming anointed ruler of God was current among the Jews at the time of Jesus. It was not held by all, and there are Jewish writings of that general period which contain no reference to such a messianic expectation. However, the failure of a writer to refer to it does not prove in every case that he did not know or share this hope.

According to the New Testament, Jesus was conscious that he fulfilled this messianic expectation, and the Apostolic Church was certain that he had done so.[15] But since the number of modern scholars have asserted that he never thought of himself as the expected Messiah, the issue calls for careful discussion.

We may begin by examining the New Testament writings and the apostolic preaching. Every New Testament writer accepted the message that Jesus had fulfilled the messianic expectations of the Jews. The belief was so unquestioned and needed such little emphasis among Christians that the very title Christ could soon become a proper name. Our modern use of "Christ" as a proper noun occurs in the earliest New Testament writings; it arose before the middle of the first century. That use obviously was preceded by a period of unquestioned acceptance of the messianic role of Jesus.

This means that not only every New Testament writer, but also every early preacher of the church, accepted this view. There never was

[15] See also on this point ch. vii.

72

a time in the Apostolic Church when the gospel lacked the confident announcement that Jesus was the expected Messiah. The church had a Christology from its very beginning. The only question is whether it instantaneously and universally, with no sign of hesitation, ascribed to Jesus a role which he himself had never claimed or accepted. C. C. Torrey has actually affirmed that this happened.[16] But unless strong evidence forces us to accept such an amazing distortion of historical fact, both logic and the earliest Christian testimony argue that Jesus' own thought and statements led his disciples to speak so confidently of his messianic role.

The problem arises from the remarkable reticence of Jesus. He did not come forward with an open messianic claim.

On this point we unhesitatingly accept the Synoptic account, for the Gospel of John is concerned not with the historical development of ideas, but with the total Christian witness to Jesus, and so it presents that full witness clearly from the first chapter. In the opening chapter this Gospel calls Jesus the Logos or Word, God, Light, Son of God, the Lamb of God, Rabbi, Messiah or Christ, the King of Israel, and the Son of Man. John the Baptist and other men state the full and eternal significance of Jesus before his ministry has really begun. This is dramatic method, which from the beginning to the end placards the full Christian witness so that the reader of the Gospel cannot mistake the meaning. It disregards the chronological stages by which Jesus' followers reached this understanding; its one aim is to make clear to the reader the full meaning of this human life.

For the chronological stages we must turn to the Synoptic Gospels. They show that Jesus made no public claim to messiahship. Even when Peter, near Caesarea Philippi, led the disciples in identifying Jesus as the expected Messiah, Jesus told them not to tell others (Mark 8:27-30). In the outline of Mark, it is only at the triumphal entry into Jerusalem, in the last week of his life, that Jesus gave a strong clue to those who could remember Zech. 9:9 and interpret an acted parable; and only before the high priest at the trial did Jesus openly state that he is the expected Messiah of the Jews (Mark 11:1-10; 14:62). The other Synop-

---

[16] Our Translated Gospels, pp. xli-xlix.

tic Gospels are not so clear even here; but we shall find that their more cautious phrasing has an explanation.

The clue to the hesitant attitude of Jesus is in the nature of popular thought about the coming Messiah. The messianic hope included varied aspects. That he would be the spiritual leader of his people, no good Jew would deny. But to people ground down under foreign rule, forced to pay enormous taxes,[17] and chagrined that God's chosen people were subject to gentile domination, political liberty and national dominance in the world scene loomed large. They wanted a leader who would defeat the Romans, liberate the Jews from financial and political oppression, and make their people the regnant power of the world.

Jesus had to face this expectation. But he could not accept it nor did he try to fulfill it. He knew the history of his people. No doubt he knew what had happened under the Maccabean family's leadership. This family rose in revolt against the attempt by the Syrian ruler Antiochus Epiphanes to stamp out the Jewish faith (168 B.C.). They achieved religious freedom, and went on to seek the political liberty they thought necessary to protect their religious freedom. Within less than a century these Maccabeans had become so corrupt, so weakened by luxury and civil strife, that Pompey could seize Palestine for Rome without a battle.

What Israel needed most of all was not political liberation, but a right relation with God. The meaning of the temptation story in the Gospels is that Jesus rejected military and political programs and deliberately turned to preaching and teaching (Matt. 4:1-11; Luke 4:1-13). He determined to call Israel to repentance and faith as the conditions of entering the coming kingdom of God. His method may seem futile. It certainly was slow. It depended on winning the people of God to a voluntary response to God's call. It emphasized the spiritual and moral aspects of the expected Messiah's leadership, and discarded the idea that organization, force, and political dominance were the keys to spiritual victory. The principle of the Cross was implicit in this decision reached at the threshold of the ministry.

This decision made, Jesus could not speak of himself as Messiah, for

[17] F. C. Grant, *Economic Background of the Gospels* (New York: Oxford University Press, 1926), pp. 87-104, lists the varied Roman taxes and religious dues.

what people would hear in such a statement would be a claim to political kingship. In addition, the claim would expose him to arrest and execution as a rebel by Rome. This was no imaginary danger; it was on that very charge that he finally was put to death upon the cross (Mark 15: 26). To avoid intervention by the Romans, to avoid misunderstanding of his purpose by the people, to concentrate upon his prophetic message, and win the voluntary allegiance of men to the will of God, Jesus said nothing of his conviction—which had come to vivid consciousness at his baptism by John—that he was chosen by God to be Israel's Messiah (Mark 1:11).

Even when Peter discerned the secret, Jesus did not want it noised abroad. It would still be misunderstood; as the sequel proved, even his own disciples did not yet understand him. Jesus had penetrated into the secret of spiritual victory; he had to look forward to the Cross. The victory God would win, the only victory to which Jesus could look forward, would come by the path of willingly accepted suffering.

When on his final visit Jesus entered Jerusalem with a mute reference to the humble scene described in Zech. 9:9, he showed that he was ready for those who had insight to learn his secret, but he did not force it upon them. Even when he told the high priest who he was, the non-committal manner of answering first the high priest and later Pilate may have been the actual form he chose (Matt. 26:64; 27:11). He meant what Mark 14:62 says: he knew that he was the God-sent Messiah of his people. But he was not the kind of leader whom the high priest and Pilate had in mind. So he may have said in effect: "That is your word; I cannot accept it in the sense you give it; but if I could use it and give it the spiritual and moral content which it has for me, I would accept it, for I am Israel's Messiah."

The certainty that the word Christ would be misunderstood if he used it openly in his ministry, the desire to put God's claim before men free from distracting features, and the political danger involved in using the term of himself sufficiently explain the reticence of Jesus. But the early church understood from the first that he was the Messiah and had known himself to be such. The gospel writers all know that he held this view. The placard on the Cross shows that the Jewish leaders charged him with claiming messianic kingship, and Pilate condemned

Jesus on the pretext that he had made that claim. When we consider the witness of the early church in which eyewitnesses held a prominent role, the witness of the Gospels—which have eyewitness testimony as a basis—and the charge of the high priests and the decision of Pilate, we can only conclude that Jesus held himself to fulfill the messianic expectation. He was the source of the view of the Apostolic Church. This is the only natural explanation of their prompt and unhesitating identification of the crucified and risen Jesus as the Christ of Israel.

The gospel message, then, is that Jesus was divinely sent to Israel and held a unique role among them. His ministry was almost entirely confined to Israel. He almost never left their native land, and although there were numerous Gentiles and gentile cities in Palestine, it was only by urgent request that he ministered to them (Matt. 8:5-13; Luke 7:1-10; John 4:46-54). He went to his people and claimed their loyalty. He was the rightful claimant to their ear and following. He fulfilled the expectation that God would send an anointed leader.

This concern for his fellow Jews was reflected by his disciples. They gathered in Jerusalem after the Resurrection, and directed their preaching solely to the Jews until persecution drove them out and taught them that the gospel was a world message which the Gentiles also would hear and accept.

The undoubted Jewishness of Jesus has led some scholars to say that the only difference between Jesus and other Jewish leaders was that he held himself to be, or his followers held him to be, the Messiah.[18] But this difference is crucial. It would have transformed the Judaism that then existed. If the leaders and people had accepted the claim of Jesus, he would have become the center of their life and thinking. In every aspect of their life his leadership and lordship would have given new form to their worship and community life. It may be futile to speak in his way. He was not accepted, and we cannot change past history. But to speak thus may call attention to the fact that the messianic claim of Jesus was tremendous. The Messiah was to be the central figure of the Jewish people, dominant in all Jewish thought and life. The life of

[18] E.g., R. Travers Herford, *The Pharisees* (New York: The Macmillan Co., 1924), p. 212.

Israel under him would be a Messiah-centered, or as we may say with the use of the Greek word, a Christ-centered life.

Israel was wrong in rejecting the leadership of Jesus, their Christ. This point needs clear statement because of the unhappy situation of our day. Christians have often condemned Jews of later generations to social disgrace, economic oppression, and political subjection because most—but not all—of the Jews of Jesus' day rejected him. This sinful action of Christians has brought shame on Christ himself. In a generous attempt to right this wrong, some recent Christians have conceded that Jews need not face the claim of Jesus to be their rightful leader. Thus both by hostile and by friendly feelings for the Jews the Christian church has tended to become a purely gentile movement. It cannot do so and be Christ's church. Because of the claim of Jesus and the apostles that he is the expected Messiah of Israel, the Jews have an honored place in his church.

The view just expressed is branded by some Christians as anti-Semitism. They think we have no right to present the claims of Jesus to the Jews. But they are wrong. Jesus was a Jew; he came to the Jews with a message and a claim for loyalty; he claimed, the apostles asserted, and the church ever since has claimed that he is the Messiah of Israel. It is not anti-Semitism to keep this aspect of the gospel clearly in focus in the total biblical message.

The matter must be put even more strongly. It is anti-Semitism to exclude the Jews from the evangelistic and missionary interest of the church. It is anti-Semitism to regard the gospel as the one pearl of great price to which all other nations should respond in faith, while the Jews alone are left outside the range of the gospel which the church believes offers the words of eternal life. If I were a Jew, I think I would say: "These Christians say they have the one universal and indispensable gospel; they go to great lengths to carry it to all other nations and peoples, but they leave me out; that is anti-Semitic."

The gospel is for the Gentiles; of that we shall speak in more detail later. But prior to that fact, and even clearer in the New Testament, Jesus is the Christ of the Jews. The gospel appeal includes them.

CHAPTER IV

Christ and the Old Testament

THE NEW TESTAMENT IS A CHRISTOCENTRIC BOOK. IT IS ALSO theocentric, but God's relation to man is through Christ. The career of Jesus Christ, and the message of what God does for men through him, give unity to the New Testament.

It is just this Christocentric note which seems to separate the New Testament from the Old Testament, which was written before the time of Christ and therefore lacks explicit Christian content. Yet the church has always held that the Old Testament is the church's book, and that it has a vital link with Jesus Christ and therefore with the New Testament. We must examine this issue.

Recent events have renewed the interest in this problem. Seminaries and other schools tend to study the two Testaments separately. This raises the question whether there exists an indissoluble unity between them. The violent attempt of Nazis to remove the Old Testament from the Bible and to deny the Jewish origin of Jesus is not forgotten.[1] The question arises on the mission field.[2] Is it necessary to follow the Old Testament story to find the way to Christ? May we not take people directly to Christ from their native religions, which would then be regarded as providential preparation for Christ? Why not ignore the Old Testament?

This is no new issue. In the second quarter of the second century, Marcion rejected the Old Testament.[3] He asserted that its tone and

---

[1] See Eugene S. Tanner, op. cit.
[2] See G. E. Phillips, op. cit.
[3] Among the important books on Marcion are Adolf von Harnack, Marcion: Das Evangelium vom fremden Gott (2nd ed.; Leipzig, 1924); John Knox, Marcion and the New Testament (Chicago: University of Chicago Press, 1942); E. Blackman, Marcion and His Influence (London: Macmillan & Co., 1950).

message differed from the gospel. Therefore, he ascribed the Old Testament to the Demiurge, the inferior, just god to whom creation was due; Christ and the gospel message came from the true God of grace.

The fallacy of this view is easy to discern. The New Testament will not permit such rejection of the Old Testament. Throughout the New Testament, citations appear which accept the Old Testament as authoritative Scripture. The repeated fulfillment theme shows the early Christian conviction that the gospel story carries to its climax the divine revelation and story which the Old Testament began. We find continual use of the Old Testament history, prophecy, language, and ways of thinking. To give up the Old Testament would be to disown a basic feature of the New Testament; the Christian writings would be discredited as misguided and based upon error.

Nor is this view of unity between the Testaments confined to the New Testament writers. Both Jesus and the apostles accepted the Old Testament as Scripture and used it in their teaching. The church can neither discard the Old Testament nor regard it as merely temporary, preparatory scaffolding. It is part of the Christian Bible.

Christ the Key to Unity

But this is true only when the Old Testament is interpreted in relation to Christ. Jesus found guidance for his ministry and preaching in the Scriptures of his people. The earliest preachers used the Old Testament to show God's purpose in Christ, and interpreted the Christian faith as the divinely given fulfillment of the faith of Israel.[4] If Christianity is true, the Christian interpretation of the Old Testament is the true interpretation. Other interpretations are either limited or erroneous; for Paul says of the veil which kept the Jews from full and true understanding of the Old Testament's ultimate meaning for faith, "only through Christ is it taken away" (II Cor. 3:14). The Old Testament is the church's book, one with the New Testament as Scripture and guide for Christian faith and life.

How then is this unity to be understood? Not simply in the sharing

[4] B. P. W. Stather Hunt, *Primitive Gospel Sources* (New York: Philosophical Library, Inc., 1951), emphasizes the importance of Christian interpretation of the Old Testament as the initial stage in the production of the Gospels.

of common ideas. There is such a common fund of basic ideas. We have already noted how many central ideas Jesus shared with the Old Testament. The same kinship occurs in the apostolic preachers and in all the New Testament writings. This alone, however, would not give a Christian message. It would rather mean that the Old Testament is the normative part of Scripture, by which Jesus and the New Testament are controlled. But this reverses the true relation between the Testaments. The New Testament and the apostolic preaching have a new note and center. They give to the work of Jesus Christ too central a place for him to be but an echo or dependent of the Old Testament. The controlling center of the entire Bible is the New Testament message of Christ and the Spirit.

Nor is the unity merely one of agreement as to the nature and will of God. There is deep unity in these matters. The idea that the Old Testament is a book of law and the New Testament a book of grace is a caricature of both Testaments. There is a strong accent on the righteousness and moral demand of God in both Testaments, and the notes of grace and faith are likewise found in both. Paul, for example, can say that his gospel message upholds the Law and that love fulfills the Law (Rom. 3:31; 13:10; Gal. 5:14); he can also say that Abraham and David lived in faith, and that David spoke of forgiveness and grace (Rom. 4:3, 6-8).

The unity between the Testaments is found mainly in a special history in which God acts.[5] He acts to carry out his sovereign and gracious purpose, to make himself and his will known to men, to judge and condemn evil, and to give salvation to all who will respond in faith and love. This is a history where God provides the cement of unity by his consistent purpose and working, and Christ is the center and interpreting guide by whom we understand the entire story. This understanding finds its effective starting point in the Resurrection, grasps thereby the full meaning of the career of Christ, and so with Christ as the focus, discerns the unity of the entire biblical story. We must note three aspects of this unity.

[5] This is the basic assumption in the common gospel message, as we saw in ch. ii.

Unity Free From Dominant Legalism

The Christ-centered view of the unity of the Bible subordinates the legal framework which grew out of the legal aspects of the Old Testament and marked the Judaism of New Testament times. What to do about the Law was a burning issue for Jesus and his followers. As a movement arising in Judaism, the Christian group had to determine the role and permanent importance of the Law. In the debate over this question at least four solutions were offered:

1. Some followers of Jesus claimed that the Law, since it was given by God, is permanently valid and obligatory. They held that every disciple of Jesus must accept the Law, including its ceremonial pre-scriptions, and observe it faithfully. Man's relation to God, they argued, depends upon observance of it.

Two apparently strong reasons support their position. In the first place, certain Old Testament passages indicate that the Law is perma-nently in force. The Judaizers, as we call those early Christian partisans of Jewish legal observance, must often have quoted Gen. 17:9-14. Here God tells Abraham what his descendants in the covenant must do; they must circumcise every male child "throughout your generations." The tie with the covenant is broken if this law is not observed.

Words of Jesus also could be cited to support this position.[6] In a Q saying, found both in Matt. 5:18 and in Luke 16:17,[7] Jesus declares that not a single point of the Law has been or will be canceled. We may see in these words a strong figurative statement that Jesus' aim was merely to promote faithful obedience to the will of God; the Judaizers, whom some accuse of inventing this saying, would say that this saying of Jesus proves their case: the Law remains in force—all of it. Even Paul could say that he does not abolish the Law, but rather upholds it (Rom. 3:31), and that love fulfills the Law (Gal. 5:14). Obviously neither Jesus nor Paul intended to break with the Law or despise it.

Yet Jesus was critical both of the Law and of the oral tradition which to the Pharisees was equally valid. He rejected decisively the oral tradition; it had no binding authority for him. (Mark 7:5-13.) But he also

---

[6] For a careful study of Jesus' relation to the Law, see Bennett Harvie Branscomb, *Jesus and the Law of Moses* (New York: Harper & Bros., 1930).

[7] Since this saying apparently stood in Q, it has a strong claim to be authentic.

sat loose to ritual aspects of the Law, disregarding laws of clean and unclean when he wanted to reach and help a needy person. (Mark 1:41.) He even nullified details of the Law; he said flatly that divorce, which the Law allowed (Deut. 24:1), has no place in a life really lived under God's will (Mark 10:2-12; Luke 16:18; I Cor. 7:10-11),[8] and he declared that the taking of oaths, which the Law permitted and regulated (Num. 30:2), should be avoided (Matt. 5:33-37). On occasion Jesus could appeal from one portion of the Law to another to justify his words; this was so in the case of divorce, where he appealed to the purpose of God as revealed in creation (Mark 10:6) to cancel the concession to human weakness found in Deut. 24:1. But on such matters as the discarding of oaths and the radical denial of the distinction between clean and unclean foods (Mark 7:15-19), he acted in direct conflict with explicit prescriptions of the Law.

Paul went even further in open refusal to practice the Law in literal detail. Christ was the end of the Law for believers (Rom. 10:4), and Gentiles were not bound to observe it; they were saved solely by God's grace received in faith and expressed in love. Even Jews must not count on the Law for any part of their salvation, and while they might live by it as a regular practice, they had no right to insist on it when to do so would break the unity of the church (Gal. 2:14). On this point Marcion was right; the message of Jesus contains a deep note, made explicit in the teaching of Paul, which requires the Christian to reject the Law as the binding control of life and to center in Jesus Christ all faith and obedience to God.

For a time the early church weighed the suggestion that Jewish believers in Christ could live by the Law while gentile Christians remained free from it. The conference at Jerusalem, at which the freedom of gentile Christians from the full observance of the Law was conceded (Acts 15), came close to this "denominational" division of the church into two parts. The incident at Antioch in Syria, when Peter and even Barnabas separated from their gentile fellow Christians

[8] Matt. 5:32 and 19:9 differ from Mark, Luke, and Paul in giving unchastity as the one legitimate ground for divorce. It appears that Jesus mentioned no exception; the will of God is for a permanent monogamous union; any failure to realize such a union falls short of the divine will. Matthew adjusts the teaching to church conditions and agrees essentially with the rabbinical school of Shammai in contrast to the more lax school of Hillel.

(Gal. 2:11-14), looked in the same direction. Even Paul could live with Jews according to Jewish law and custom and take a Jewish vow when no theological issue was at stake (I Cor. 9:19-23). But this did not satisfy the Judaizers. It was cultural accommodation rather than recognition of their claim that every Christian must observe the Mosaic Law. As soon as the interests of the church demanded it, Paul could and did drop the Jewish legal mode of living.

In meeting actual crises the church attained clarity on this issue. Jesus was critical of aspects of the Law and was not rigidly observant of its details. Stephen sensed this free position, but did not develop it to full clarity. Barnabas sensed the universal range of the gospel and its freedom from legal framework, even if he wavered in his view at Antioch. Paul clearly stated and defended the logic implicit in the attitude and teaching of Jesus. The Jerusalem conference was not so clear, but in principle its decision agreed with Paul (Acts 15:23-29).[9] The Law was not basic to salvation; the gentile Christians need not observe it to share the covenant and receive salvation. The few prescriptions they were asked to observe, to facilitate free association between Jewish and gentile Christians (Acts 15:29), were a concession such as practical church life often requires. The Law was not the basis of the church.

The term Judaizer is not used of Christians today. But the issue recurs. Whenever the Bible is treated as a literal law, whenever a legalistic and literalistic interpretation governs the church's use of Scripture, the essential standpoint of the Judaizers persists. A legalistic use of the Old Testament is a perversion of the intent of Jesus and the New Testament.

2. Some Christians used allegorical interpretation to get rid of legal rules and relate the Old Testament to the Christian gospel. This view claims that the real message of the Old Testament is not in its literal historical meaning, but in a second (and even a third) sense—a hidden sense which allegorical interpretation brings to light. This allegorical sense then becomes the real meaning; the literal meaning is ignored or regarded as unimportant.

[9] It is possible that the decree was formulated by the Jerusalem leaders sometime later than the conference of Gal. 2:1-10 and prior to Paul's last visit to Jerusalem (Acts 21:25). For our present purpose the point is that the Jerusalem leaders conceded that gentile Christians did not need to practice circumcision and keep the Jewish law to be saved. For a study of "The Apostolic Council of Jerusalem," see Foakes-Jackson and K. Lake, The Beginnings of Christianity (New York: The Macmillan Co., 1925), V, 195-212.

This method enabled later generations to get rid of many primitive or troublesome Old Testament passages. Outworn ritual could be interpreted to carry a high spiritual message; questionable moral acts could become a symbolic expression of respectable truths; primitive stages could be eliminated as sources of embarrassment and made the vehicle of noble ideas; historical problems could have the sting taken from them because the story was considered important only as teaching some allegorical truth.

This allegorical method could be used in one of two ways. In its extreme form it could claim that the Old Testament was never meant literally. The ancient writings only expressed in cryptic form the Christian gospel, and with the coming of Christ the true meaning became clear. The so-called Epistle of Barnabas, in the first half of the second century, asserted this view on occasion (9:4), but the method was rarely used in this extreme form. Christians were too aware of the essential place of the history of God's working in the Old Testament period to let that history dissolve into a set of cryptic references to Christian events and truth. In their way they were alive to the fact that in spite of the problems involved, the literal, historical meaning of the Old Testament was essential to the gospel of Christ.

The other and much more usual way to use the allegorical method was to give the literal meaning a secondary and perhaps temporary significance, so that the allegorical meaning is the important and permanent one. Paul on rare occasions can drop into allegorical interpretations of Old Testament persons and passages to extract a meaning from material not literally congenial to his argument. Sarah then becomes typical of the Christians, and Hagar, though not literally the mother of Israel, becomes the spiritual ancestor of that people. Sarah represents the new and heavenly Jerusalem, while Hagar represents Mt. Sinai and the earthly Jerusalem and the worship and legal practices that center there (Gal. 4:21-31).

Such allegorical interpretation, while it reflects the conviction that the Old Testament must be related to Christ, is inevitably subjective, and is important primarily in showing the convictions and thinking of those who use it. Its content is *not* in the Old Testament, but is read into the earlier record. Sound interpretation of the Old Testament must start from and always respect the literal, historical meaning. This does not exclude imaginative writing or deny that an Old Testament writer may play with double meanings of words, but it insists that our first and constant task is to grasp the writer's intent and build upon that. Allegory is a broken reed.[10]

3. Another view was that the Old Testament Law was a valid but temporary framework of life for God's chosen people. This is a part of the New Testament view. Jesus showed respect for the Law, but recognized that aspects of it were no longer binding. He could not tolerate a legal regulation that stood in the way of human kindness. The early church usually combined the same respect and critical outlook. The charge made against Stephen by foes of the church was that an anti-legal principle was inherent in his gospel (Acts 6:11, 14). The Jewish Christians who offered the gospel to Gentiles at Antioch in Syria, and Barnabas and other Jewish Christians who accepted this new development, implicitly continued the same trend (Acts 11:19-26). Even if they themselves continued to observe the Law, they did not expect Gentiles to do so. The Jerusalem conference, whether or not it passed the decree recorded in Acts 15:23-29, agreed that Gentiles did not need to keep the Law to be saved. God's plan had entered a new phase. Whether the Jews had the same freedom as the Gentiles was not always clear, but the legal framework no longer controlled the church as it had the synagogue.

It was Paul who vigorously stated and defended the basic fact: Christ is the end of the law to the Christian (Rom. 10:4). Perhaps Jesus' death on the cross influenced this development in a way not often noted. Before his conversion Paul had taunted Christians with the charge that death on the cross brought Jesus under the curse of God. He could quote the Law to show this (Deut. 21:23; cf. Gal. 3:13). As a Christian he could no longer regard Jesus as being under a curse; God

[10] Closely related to allegory is typology, which finds in Old Testament persons and events types which are matched by New Testament persons and events. Outstanding works along this line are L. Goppelt, *Die typologische Deutung des Alten Testaments im Neuen* (Gütersloh, 1939); Wilhelm Vischer, *Das Christuszeugnis des Alten Testaments*, 2 vols., Zollikon-Zürich, 1942-43 (tr., of vol. I, A. B. Crabtree, *The Witness of the Old Testament to Christ*, London: Lutterworth Press, 1949); and A. G. Hebert, *The Throne of David* (London: Faber & Faber, 1941). Typology certainly plays a minor role in the New Testament.

had vindicated his Son. So it must be the Law which was discredited. It no longer could be accepted as the framework of God's dealings with men. Christ was the end of the Law.

Paul never thought of denying that the Old Testament contained the revelation of God's will as well as of his goodness and grace. But the Law as a system of life, especially in its ritual aspects, was no longer in force. And the demand which Paul—with all early Christians—still heard in the Law centered in the spiritual and moral aspects whose fulfill- ment did not come by legal observance, but by the guidance and power of the Spirit of God.

4. The deepest Christian insight, however, was that the Law itself, and the entire Old Testament Scripture, contained a thread of revela- tion and life deeper than legal prescription. This was the thread of faith. This was the deep exegetical insight of Paul in Gal. 3:6-9 and Rom. 4. From Abraham on, Paul could discern this thread of faith running through the story of God's dealings with Israel. And with it went the note of forgiveness and grace. The Old Testament in its truest meaning was not a lawbook; it was not in violent contrast with the New Testament message of grace; it announced in an earlier form but in emphatic confidence the same message of grace that Paul was to preach with such power. The message of grace has meaning only when man knows God's righteous will and recognizes his own sin and need of divine forgiveness. But it is the word of grace and man's answering faith, not the code of law, which is the central word of the Old Testament revelation and Scripture.

The Dominant Prophetic Note

The Christ-centered unity of the Bible subordinates the legal aspect of the Old Testament and recognizes as dominant the prophetic aspect. The word prophetic here does not mean mere prediction of future events, although the Old Testament contains such predictions; leaders aware of God's will and man's sin declared God's judgment on man's willfulness and also promised God's redemptive action. The real char- acter of prophetic utterance appears in its tremendous certainty of God, its firm confidence in his purpose and power, and its penetrating judg- ment of all persons and events in the light of God's lordship and man's responsibility to him. Interpretation of all life in the light of God's clear claim on men, fearless weighing of all human life in the light of its response to or rejection of God's will, cutting through the externals of religious observance to judge life by the standard of active obedience to the righteous God—this is what we mean by the prophetic note.

It is this note which is the chief glory and the distinctive mark of the Old Testament.[11] We do wrong to think of the Old Testament primarily as a lawbook. Even in the Pentateuch this prophetic note emerges repeatedly. For example, it is present in the ritualistic book of Leviticus, in the demand to love one's neighbor as one's self and to care for the sojourner in the land. (19:18, 34.) Moses himself was considered a prophet (Deut. 18:15, 18).

The primary importance of the so-called historical books is not that they tell historical facts. They do this, but they bring all this history to the bar of judgment and ask what Israel and her leaders have done in the sight of God. The Jews call these books the "Former Prophets," and this grasps the true character of these writings. They interpret what happened in the light of God's will and Israel's responsibility to him.

The writings of Israel's great prophetic figures and their disciples continue this prophetic note which constitutes the unifying thread of the Old Testament. Part of the greatness of Israel was that they produced these fearless rebuking prophets, and then respected their words and writings enough to preserve for later generations those stern rebukes which superficial patriotism might have been quick to suppress.

But this same prophetic note marks the New Testament. John the Baptist continued the prophetic tradition. The crowds often described Jesus as a prophet (Mark 8:28; Matt. 21:11); they felt his deep kinship with the Old Testament prophetic message, which he took up, clarified, and deepened.[12] Several apostolic leaders, and many unnamed leaders, are called prophets (Acts 11:27-28; 13:1; I Cor. 12:28). This is one prominent way in which the unity of the two Testaments emerges.

Later church theology has continually referred to Jesus as prophet,

[11] Martin Buber traces this note back to the earliest Hebrew writings in *The Prophetic Faith,* tr. Carlyle Wilton-Davies (New York: The Macmillan Co., 1949).
[12] The identification of John as Elijah is implied in the description of his dress (Mark 1:6) and is clearly intended in Mark 9:13. The idea has its roots in Mal. 4:5.

priest, and king. Of this trio the title prophet usually receives least attention. That Jesus Christ is Lord and King is generally asserted, and that he is the great high priest is likewise emphasized, especially among those who stress the atonement and sacrificial ideas. But in church circles the repeated evidence of the Gospels and early Christian teaching that Jesus was a prophet, that he was indeed *the* great prophet who fulfilled the expectation of Deut. 18:15, 18, too often falls into the background. The result is to obscure the fact that the same rugged type of ministry and the same ringing presentation of God's claim marked both the Old Testament and the New Testament line of preachers. To be sure, Jesus must be described in terms which express his uniqueness; the New Testament demands that. But this need not conceal the fact that he was the climax of the magnificent line of prophets which constitutes the glory of biblical history.

Promise and Fulfillment

The Christ-centered unity of the Bible is expressed in the theme of promise and fulfillment.[13] Christians often express this truth—too simply—by saying that the Old Testament prophecy finds its fulfillment in the New Testament. At times this theme receives a mechanical expression that obscures its real strength. Examples of strained interpretation occur. Because the writer of Matthew did not take into account the parallelism in the poetic passage of Zech. 9:9, where only one animal was in mind, he described Jesus as riding into Jerusalem on two animals (Matt. 21:1-7). Paul, although he knew that the word "seed" or "offspring" in Gen. 12:7 is a collective noun, and so used it in Gal. 3:29, takes the same word in verse 16 of the same chapter to have a singular reference to Christ alone.

Such examples are not frequent, and their appearance is not surprising, since such methods of using Scripture were common in the first century. But they neglect the historical meaning of these Old Testament passages, and it is gratifying that such artificial use of the fulfillment theme is not characteristic of the New Testament. The basic

[13] See Emil Brunner, *Revelation and Reason*, tr. Olive Wyon (Philadelphia: Westminster Press, 1946), part I.

claim is that the continual message of promise given by God in the Old Testament has come to its fulfillment in the gospel story.

Underlying this claim is the deep conviction that God is working out his purpose in history. There is a continuity in his actions. The earlier stages point ahead to his continued work and the fuller realization of his plan. This plan reaches its climax and center in Jesus Christ and the rise of the church. Therefore the Old Testament is incomplete without Christ, and at the same time it is the necessary preparation for Christ. It shows God working out his purpose and moving to the central act and revelation in Christ his Son.

In the earlier stages God's leaders were given a sense of a great work of God moving forward to realization. They also saw clearly the challenge to God's work in their day. They saw that whatever great victories had been won, the full and decisive action of God was still needed to achieve his will. They looked forward to those later stages. We do not need to think that they saw in detail all that was to come. They saw "in a mirror dimly." (I Cor. 13:12.) But they spoke in hope. They spoke God's promise.

From the later stages of God's working, the church could look back and see that in Christ and the rise of the church, God had in part fulfilled those promises. The church did not claim complete fulfillment. The decisive action had occurred in Christ, but the full results of that victory had not yet been achieved. They would come; what God had done in Christ guaranteed this to men of faith, and the working of the Holy Spirit steadied and supported this confident conviction. The decisive stage of fulfillment, however, had begun.

From its post-resurrection vantage point, the church could see more meaning in the Old Testament history and promises than the Old Testament actors and writers could see at their earlier point in history. It could survey the work of God through the centuries and see its deeper meaning and unity. This view allows careful historical interpretation of each biblical document in its contemporary situation. It can give each document its place in history and seek to state what its writer meant to say. But it can also give each writing its place in the total series of Old and New Testament writings, and can see that it has a valid meaning in the total context of God's long-term working which could not have been fully clear to the writers of the earlier works.

The theme of promise and fulfillment must rise above artificial and mechanical forms of thinking. We have noted that the use of Zech. 9:9 and Gen. 12:7 did not accord with sound historical interpretation, and we do not need to continue such methods. Paul uses the fact that Jesus hung upon a *wooden* cross as a reason for saying that Christ took upon himself the curse of sin which belonged to sinful men (Gal. 3:13). It might seem that death upon a metal cross or a stone wall would have provided no atonement. But that would not be fair to the New Testament message. The reference in Gal. 3:13 is but a passing phase of a far deeper understanding of the meaning of the death of Christ. Let us look at the heart of that understanding.

Jesus had voluntarily gone to Jerusalem to further his ministry and make his last appeal to his people. He had given himself for men's good. The disciples who had forsaken him and fled in time of crisis knew that it was not their strength but his steadfastness which had given them ground for hope. They looked back to the Old Testament and found there the picture of a Suffering Servant (Isa. 52:13–53:12), and they knew that Jesus had suffered to serve God's cause and save them. He had fulfilled the deepest insight and promise of the Old Testament. Their faith was not in an artificial interpretation of one passage. It rested on a sound understanding of how much Jesus had deliberately and unselfishly done for them, and also on clear insight into the depths of Old Testament promises.

A true view of fulfillment allows full place to important truths. For one thing, it permits elimination of outworn or inadequate aspects of earlier thought.[14] Not every Old Testament act is a finger pointing directly to Christ. Not every Old Testament law is a prophecy of an event or aspect of his work. As Jesus told the Jews concerning divorce, there are phases of Old Testament teaching that represent what Israel could grasp of God's will at the time (Mark 10:5), and we need not make permanent what was partial and imperfect. Certainly the New Testament writers let considerable areas of the Old Testament fall into the background. They used their center in Christ to find the deep and

[14] On this and the following points see Andrew C. Zenos, *op. cit.*, p. 12.

vital threads of Old Testament revelation; they did not try to perpetuate every detail of their Scripture.

Fulfillment also allows for purification or correction. Jesus did not hesitate to reject Old Testament rules on divorce or the use of oaths (Mark 10:2-12; Matt. 5:33-37). Wherever he could, he appealed to an alternative Old Testament passage in giving a higher and fuller expression of the will of God; he used the Old Testament itself, where he could, to correct itself (Mark 10:6 ff.). But he did not hesitate to say in principle that the Old Testament must not be considered a final law, and Paul clearly declared that the Law was no longer the norm for the Christian (Rom. 6:14). The Old Testament must be read in the light of Christ; it is not an independent law or a final and full statement of the will of God.

The biblical form of fulfillment allows also for a new revelation in the process of fulfillment. The work of Christ and of the Holy Spirit is not confined to slavish fulfillment of what the Old Testament has fully discerned and stated. For that matter, we must not think that the fulfillment of the promises of God was fully completed even in the New Testament period. The final and complete realization of those promises is still to come. Christians with the biblical outlook may have confidence that the fulfillment will come and bring new and unexpected events. An expanding future stretches ahead.

This means that we cannot find in either Testament a chart of current or future events. The theme of promise does not enslave the church to a predetermined and clearly outlined pattern of events.

God had his surprises to give in the New Testament period. The freedom with which Jesus went to the outcasts among the Jews, the guiding of Jewish Christians to preach to the Gentiles, are examples of the way the New Testament generation saw current expectations corrected and expanded by the work of the Spirit of God. We therefore cannot look either in the Old or in the New Testament for a complete outline of future history. The Bible is not that kind of book. God still has his surprises to effect. This is the biblical faith. "What no eye has seen, nor ear heard, nor the heart of man conceived, what God has prepared for those who love him." (I Cor. 2:9.) This is the

91

Christian "openness to the future," the eager expectancy of a faith that cannot yet see what is to come.

The Old Testament is an incomplete book. Jews and Christians must agree on that. Some have thought that the Jews simply stick to the Old Testament, while Christians add the New Testament to it. This view is mistaken. The Jews went on to form an oral tradition, the tradition which Jesus refused to accept as binding, and which the church ignored. They went on to write this tradition down in codified form in the Mishnah, which took definite written form about A.D. 200, and developed further interpretation of their tradition in the Talmud, which builds around the Mishnah a commentary and expansion. Through the centuries orthodox Judaism has built on the Talmud, while later supplementary dovelopments have opened out into freer treatment of the heritage in reformed types of Judaism. Judaism is not the static preservation of the Old Testament. It made the Old Testament the starting point of a long and extensive development in thought and practice.

The Christians too have gone beyond the Old Testament, and like the Jews, have taken the Old Testament with them on that development. But they have gone a quite different route. They have found in Jesus Christ the central and decisive act of God, and in the work of the Spirit in building the church they have seen the ongoing work of God which continues in our own day.

These two parallel developments cannot be equally right and justified. He who takes the one cannot consistently take the other. The crucial question is this: Which line has discerned and developed the true meaning of the Old Testament? Whoever finds in Jesus Christ the center and interpreting clue to the previous and succeeding history is bound to say that the Old Testament is the church's book, that the Christian interpretation of the Old Testament as preparation for and promise of Christ is its true meaning, and that the legal talmudic development of Judaism—sincere as it was—took the wrong fork in the road. The right road led to Christ. To him the Old Testament pointed.

CHAPTER V

Christil and the Kingdom

THE APOSTLES' CREED, WHOSE CORE TOOK FORM ABOUT THE MIDDLE of the second century, moves at once from the mention of the birth of Jesus to his death under Pontius Pilate. Classical Christian thought has often continued this failure to build into its essential confession the ministry and teaching message of Jesus. As we have already noted, traditional Christology, using New Testament titles, has regarded Jesus Christ as prophet, priest, and king. But under the influence of The Acts and especially of the New Testament letters, it has placed the accent on his priestly work in his death and intercession, and on his lordship as the risen, reigning Christ.

The prophetic role has not faded completely from view. Wherever men have denied the humanity and human career of Jesus, the church has roundly condemned this failure to take seriously the human life and historical ministry in Palestine. It has seen that such docetic conclusions would be fatal to its gospel.[1] Yet more than once in the history of Christian doctrine, the ministry and teaching of Jesus have not been given their full and essential role in the confessions of the church.

The Importance of the Gospels

Complete and radical error on this point is fortunately impossible, because the church had the guidance and wisdom to give the Gospels a prominent place in its permanent canon of Scripture. These Gospels will not let either the Christian or the church forget the challenge, promise, and power of the historical ministry of Jesus Christ. Their

[1] On the rejection of Docetism and the importance of the Jesus of history, see D. M. Baillie, God Was in Christ (New York: Charles Scribner's Sons, 1948), pp. 11-20, 30-58.

93

account of what Jesus did and said has an important role in the Christian message and understanding of life.

1. The gospel story of the life of Jesus, while it agrees with the rest of the New Testament that the Christian message is and always must be Christocentric, prevents any idea that Jesus is a rival of God or is independent of his will and work. The Christian message understands God through Jesus Christ; the Christian comes to God through his Son. But the God-centered focus of the teaching and life of Jesus forbids the Christian to think that Christ replaces God or excuses man from clear loyalty to God.

There arises at times in the church a "Jesusolotory" which makes the historical Jesus its sole object of faith and worship. The New Testament paints the picture on a vaster canvas. The eternal God, the Lord of heaven and earth, of past and present and future, of life and death and all that lies beyond, is the only adequate object of faith and worship for the Christian. Jesus worshiped God as his Father; he pointed men to the Father of all mankind; and he worked to bring them into vital fellowship with the great and gracious God, to whom even he looked as Father. The story of Jesus' ministry should help us to preserve the God-centered focus of the Christian message.

2. The ministry of Jesus gives the gospel story its healthy roots in the background and life of Israel. The detailed account of that ministry makes clear the Jewishness of Jesus, his indebtedness to the Old Testament and his forefathers, and the continuity of his work with God's previous work in Israel. To find the gospel rooted in that strange ancient setting creates problems of study and interpretation. But the roots and meaning of the gospel become clear only when we see it in the setting of first-century Judaism. The gospel of Jesus of Nazareth, the Son of David, who lived and taught in Palestine and ministered to human need among his people until he died for those he loved, still rings with reality. The story of Jesus' life helps us to see the relation of Jesus to Israel and his tie with the Old Testament.

3. The figure of the Christ of faith would be vague and indistinct without the vivid accounts of the Gospels. When Paul's letters refer to Jesus, or a Christian preacher speaks of him with faith and reverence, the words are surcharged with more than their normal meaning. They

94

glow with life and power precisely because the Gospels have given the background in the light of which we understand the voice of apostolic faith.

If we could erase from mind and memory all concrete detail that the Gospels have given us, all specific incidents which express the spirit and purpose of Jesus, he could no longer grip the imagination and command the will. He would be at best an elusive shadow whose exact identity and meaning for us we could never know. A fatal vagueness would blight the Christian faith. The gospel would not be able to speak its convincing word from within the human struggle. Its Christ would be just another of those ancient "gods" who lived aloof from human existence, or who died and rose with the cycle of the seasons. Those phantom gods had no vitality. They lost their hold on the mind and will of men.

The great affirmations of Christian faith, its great creedal declarations, its dedication in worship to the Lord Christ, are possible and have meaning only because the teacher and prophet, the healer and friend, steps forth from the pages of the Gospels to confront us and compel our loyalty. To despise the humble life of the prophet of Nazareth would be to lose the exalted Lord of the church.

4. The nature of the Christian life would be obscure if the New Testament lacked the teaching and life of Jesus. It is never enough for Paul or any other preacher to say to men: Repent and believe in Jesus as the Christ, the Son of God, the Lord. In a sense different from that which the question had when Paul first asked it, every Christian continually asks his Lord, "What shall I do?" (Acts 22:10). It is not enough to say: Follow the guidance of the Holy Spirit. Even the leading of the Spirit had definite outline in the Apostolic Church only because a life had been lived, a spirit had emerged in friendship and ministry to others, an understanding of God's will had come to men through a ministry of teaching, and so the Spirit could guide the disciples of Jesus to move out along the line and in the spirit which his life had given. Christian ethics is never a rigid law. Nor is it a vague set of general principles. It faces life in the light of the teachings and life example of Jesus. Only through that concrete preparation can the disciple face and find his way through life's choices and trials.

The church can never outgrow the need of this direct reference back to the ministry and teaching of Jesus; it can never state its doctrine or guide its members in their daily life without giving an essential place to the concrete message of Jesus Christ. To present the New Testament message of Christ the risen Lord, therefore, we must state the essential theme of the teaching of Jesus, and show its deep unity with the apostles' later testimony to Christ and his work.

The Gospel of the Kingdom

For the central theme of Jesus' teaching we must go to the Synoptic Gospels. The writer of the Gospel of John, as he plainly states, chose material from the total gospel tradition to establish the central point he wanted to make: "These are written that you may believe that Jesus is the Christ, the Son of God, and that believing you may have life in his name" (20:31). This Gospel tells who Jesus is; he is the Christ, the Son of God. It tells what he offers men; he offers them eternal life. It tells them what they must do to receive that divine gift; they must believe in Christ the Son. We do not learn from this Gospel what Jesus said on numerous religious, ethical, and social questions, nor does it tell what he did in varied life situations which could guide his followers in meeting such problems. It has a central interest and sticks to its specific chosen theme. The church has always known that on that theme, this Gospel says what Christian faith must say. But this Gospel does not give us the full tradition of Jesus' teaching and ministry. For the range and focus of that teaching, we must turn to the Synoptic Gospels. Only against the background of their more detailed account does the figure of Jesus in the Gospel of John possess its memorable vividness and power.

As soon as we turn to Matthew, Mark, and Luke, it is clear that they agree on the central theme of Jesus' teaching. He came to men with a message of the Kingdom.[2] Matthew almost always—thirty-three times—

[2] Important books on Jesus' teaching concerning the Kingdom include Albert Schweitzer, op. cit.; T. W. Manson, The Teaching of Jesus (Cambridge: Cambridge University Press, 1931); C. H. Dodd, Parables of the Kingdom (New York: Charles Scribner's Sons, 1936); Rudolph Otto, The Kingdom of God and the Son of Man, tr. Floyd V. Filson & Bertram Lee Woolf (Grand Rapids: Zondervan Publishing House, 1938); Frederick C. Grant, The Gospel of the Kingdom (New York: The Macmillan Co., 1940); Cecil John Cadoux,

refers to it as "the kingdom of heaven," although on four occasions (12:28; 19:24; 21:31, 43) this Gospel says "the kingdom of God." All other New Testament writings speak simply of the Kingdom or of the kingdom of God; this latter phrase Mark uses fourteen times; Luke, thirty-two times. These expressions all mean the same thing. The word heaven was often used by Jews as a substitute for the name God, which reverence inclined them to use sparingly. "Heaven" therefore was a reference to God; all of these phrases refer to his kingdom.[3]

Which phrase did Jesus himself use? As a Jew he might have used the expression kingdom of heaven to avoid using the name God. But all the New Testament writers except Matthew say kingdom of God; even Matthew includes four references to the kingdom of God, and other Jewish Christian writers do not shy away from this phrase. So it seems probable that Jesus himself said kingdom of God; this would explain why the phrase is so general in the New Testament writings.

Jesus' use of the phrase implies both a positive and a negative fact. The positive fact is unhesitating faith in the one God, who as the Lord of life is working out his purpose in history.[4] This monotheistic faith in the active, purposeful God, Jesus expresses in this phrase which speaks of the rule of God. The negative fact is the undeniable presence of human sin and moral conflict in the world which God has created. Jesus is realistic; he does not ignore the fact of sin. But he is confident of the power, lordship, and ultimate victory of God. The tension between these two opposed facts finds its solution in the message of the kingdom of God.

In this message the determining fact is God. He is the creator of the world and of man; he is the Lord and King of his world, and he has a purpose for it. He acts in history to achieve his purpose; even the ugly fact of encroaching sin cannot alter his will or defeat it. The Kingdom, then, is his Kingdom; it expresses his character and will and purpose.

The Historic Mission of Jesus (London: Lutterworth Press, 1941); John Bright, The Kingdom of God (New York and Nashville: Abingdon Press, 1953), ch. vii.

[3] See Gustaf Dalman, The Words of Jesus, Eng. tr. from the German (Edinburgh, 1909), pp. 91-96, 217-19; Hermann L. Strack and Paul Billerbeck, Kommentar zum Neuen Testament aus Talmud und Midrasch, vol. I, Das Evangelium nach Matthäus (Munich, 1922), p. 172.

[4] T. W. Manson, op. cit., expresses this by using the words "God as King" in four chapter headings.

In this word Kingdom the basic idea is not that of territory included, although no Christian would doubt that God is the God of the whole earth. Nor is the basic idea that of an administrative organization or program. The central meaning is rather the reign, the rule, the active sovereignty of God.[5] The kingdom of God means essentially the sovereign, active, and effective reign of God. It is not an arbitrary reign. God is just and gracious, and his kindly concern for men makes it possible for Jesus to make the Kingdom central in his teaching, and yet to use the title Father as the most adequate way to describe God's nature. The reign of God is fair; it is gracious and helpful to all who will respond, and so it is a fatherly rule. But it is the reign of the sovereign God, who will not permit wicked men to triumph and will not abandon those who look to him for help in the struggle of life.

Prominent in Jesus' message of the Kingdom is the promise that the effective and full reign of God is coming. (Mark 1:15; 9:1.) This has always been God's world. He made it; he has never lost control of it. But the sin of men and the moral conflict of history has obscured the fact of his lordship, and the existing situation fails to express the kingship of God. The New Testament promise of the Kingdom assures believers that the manifest, full, and effective reign of God is coming. Instead of the moral confusion that has marked the world scene, evil will be defeated, right will be vindicated, the loyal people of God will be given free and secure fellowship with him, and the honor of God will be vindicated.

Characteristics of the Kingdom

1. This message of the Kingdom is essentially religious in character. Social context and personal benefit are secondary. The machinery of government attracts no attention at all. The basic thing is that God rules in his kingdom. The Kingdom is a message about the action and rule of God.

It is therefore non-political in method. To be sure, it will prove fatal in the end to every political power and system which rejects or ignores the will of God. But its method is not political. That is why Jesus put

[5] Biblical thought of God regarded him as a living, active, purposeful Lord. Later ideas of divine existence, being, substance are more Greek than Hebrew. God is the axiom and actor of the Bible.

aside at the start of his ministry all thought of using force to conquer the kingdoms of the world (Matt. 4:8-10; Luke 4:5-8). Instead, he came teaching and preaching. The chief aim of this message of the Kingdom is right relation to God; it therefore demands that men repent for all wrong in which they have shared, and turn henceforth to do the full will of God for their lives (Mark 1:14-15).

Therefore the Kingdom's message is not a nationalistic one. It is not intended to satisfy the selfish interests of the Jews. It can give full place to their privilege as the responsible people of God, but it cannot let them use that privilege for selfish advantage. It calls the nation to obedience to God, who is the ruler of the world, but it also has a concern for those who come from the east and west to sit in the kingdom of Heaven (Matt. 8:11).

Neither is the Kingdom centered in ritual or priestly offerings. Jesus came as the prophet of the Kingdom, and no one thought of him as its priest. He came to lead men to obey God rather than to revise their rituals. The accent of what he said lay on reverent faith and life dedication which lives out the will of God in daily life. The spiritual and moral aspects of religion dominated this message. God wants repentance, faith, and sincere worship, and the test of all this and its indispensable expression is faithful moral obedience shown in daily life with other people (Matt. 5:23-24; 7:16, 20).

2. This message of the Kingdom is inherently social in character. The social aspect is inherent in the God-related life of the Kingdom; it is not a hermit's way of living under God. The word Kingdom cannot be limited to purely personal response to God;[6] it inevitably refers to God's rule over his people. Its background is the Old Testament and Jewish conception of the covenant people of God, who are related to God by being members of his people. No emphasis on the Old Testament thought of the remnant, no stress on individual responsibility, ever eliminated this sense that God exercises his rule over his people. The message of Jesus did not surrender this wholesome social context of faith and life. It vividly emphasized the fact that good living, obedient

[6] Even the rabbinical reference to repeating the Shema as a taking of the yoke of the Kingdom on oneself was not meant to define the Jew's relation to God as individualistic. The Jew repeated the Shema as a member of his people.

living, recognizes and accepts God's rule in the social relations between people. The Kingdom is essentially social.

3. Yet the Kingdom is the home of fully personal life under God. A persistent modern misunderstanding supposes that social and personal are irreconcilable opposites. Quite the contrary is true. Wholesome community life gives respect, honor, and hope to persons; truly personal life is lived in community and unfolds in responsible human relationships.[7]

Certainly Jesus, while he founded his teaching upon the fact of the living God and his rule, and set the individual in social relationships as an essential part of human life, nevertheless put his message before people for their personal decision and claimed their lives for responsible personal obedience (Mark 1:15). That is why he came preaching. He did not try to use compulsion, although his deep earnestness was unmistakable. He would have nothing to do with merely formal religious living. (Matt. 7:21; Luke 6:46.) He appealed for voluntary, responsible decision to accept his message, enter his movement, and take a willing part in his work.

Jesus could establish his movement within the framework of Judaism; it was already common practice for groups to arise, press their interpretation of the ancestral faith, and still remain within the bounds of Israel.[8] Similarly, Jesus had no intention of seceding from Judaism; he considered himself fully loyal to his people's heritage (Matt. 5:17). But he had a new message of the Kingdom to present, and he called men to repent, believe, and shape life in the light of that truth. Because he rejected every usual support of political organization, nationalistic appeal, or formal ritualistic worship, he was the more able to put his message before people so that it demanded intelligent personal decision.

4. This message of the Kingdom was urgently eschatological. Jesus was moved to speak by his conviction that history had arrived at its

[7] See G. Ernest Wright et al., The Biblical Doctrine of Man in Society (London: SCM Press, 1954).

[8] J. W. Lightley, Jewish Sects and Parties in the Time of Jesus (London, 1925). The new evidence of an Essene sect center in the Qumrân region west of the Dead Sea is additional proof of the sectarian divisions of first-century Judaism. The view of George Foot Moore, Judaism in the First Centuries of the Christian Era, 2 vols. (Cambridge: Harvard University Press, 1930), that Pharisaism was normative first century Judaism, does not do justice to this diversity.

climax, that mankind faced its greatest crisis, that God was in the act of bringing his full and effective rule to pass.

To us who live so many centuries later, it is hard to capture the thrilling sense of entering into the period of God's climactic, decisive action. We regard the New Testament story as ancient history. It happened long ago and was only a preparation for the events of our time, in which our pride would like to find something more significant than anything which happened two thousand years ago.

Only by an effort of study and imagination can we even partially capture the electric atmosphere of the teaching of Jesus. He spoke of the unique and epochal action of God, which he discerned in its beginnings and of which he knew himself to be the central agent. John the Baptist had already sounded this note of expectancy (Matt. 3:2). Jesus took it up, suffused it with a sense of the active goodness of God without sacrificing John's stern note of judgment, and carried it to his countrymen to move them to repent and enter into the privilege of this realm of life before it was too late. He had no interest in exploring or describing the details of the future of the heavenly world, as so many apocalyptic writers of his day were incurably trying to do.[9] He wanted men to face the fact of God's coming rule and see the urgent demand it made for repentance, faith, and steady obedience.

Part of the significance of Jesus' miracles lies in their evidence to Jesus that this effective rule of God was beginning. We usually think of these miracles as expressions of Jesus' compassion, and so they are. His human kindness, his care for health of body and mind as well as of soul, find winsome expression in these powerful acts. But Jesus saw more in them. He saw the triumphant power of the Spirit of God at work to banish sickness and death as well as sin and frustration (Matt. 12:28). To those with eyes to see, they were clues that the kingdom of God had begun to be effectively established in their midst.

This prelude pointed to the certain and not too distant coming of the full Kingdom, where God's will would be fully done and his people

---

[9] This is the truth in Maurice Goguel's argument in *The Life of Jesus*, tr. Olive Wyon (New York: The Macmillan Co., 1933), pp. 569-72, that Jesus' thought was eschatological, not apocalyptic. But Jesus, like the apocalyptists, expected the end rather soon. On apocalyptic literature, see H. H. Rowley, *The Relevance of Apocalyptic* (rev. ed.; New York, n.d.). J. W. Bowman, *Prophetic Realism and the Gospel* (Philadelphia: Westminster Press, 1955), denies that Jesus thought in apocalyptic terms.

would find perfect blessedness as God's gift to those who trust him. Evil would be defeated and eliminated, the right would be vindicated, and the justice and goodness of God would be clear.

New, Now, but Still Incomplete

It may help to grasp the meaning of Jesus if we examine three recent interpretations of Jesus' teaching and try to discern their truth and their weakness. The essential issues will become clear as we evaluate the conclusions of three leading scholars, T. W. Manson, Albert Schweitzer, and C. H. Dodd. From each of them we learn much, but none offers a full and balanced interpretation of Jesus' teaching concerning the Kingdom.

1. Jesus spoke of the Kingdom as a new, unique, decisive action of God.

This statement calls in question one aspect of T. W. Manson's otherwise masterly presentation of Jesus' teaching. The basic contention upon which Manson builds his interpretation is that for Jesus the kingdom of God is eternal. "God as King: The Eternal Sovereignty" is the subject of the crucial chapter of his book.[10] He recalls Old Testament suggestions that the kingdom of God is "an everlasting kingdom" (Ps. 145: 13). He knows that no Jew or early Christian could deny that God had always been the Lord of his world, and he understands Jesus to speak of the Kingdom in the same way.

In a real sense, Manson is right. Jesus would never have denied that God had been the Lord of his world since its creation. But it remains a fact that he did not use the word kingdom in connection with such ideas, and Manson cites no saying to show that Jesus so spoke of the Kingdom. When Jesus began his ministry, he announced that the Kingdom was just at hand. He did not say that it had been there all the time, but he regarded it as a new act of God. His mastery of evil spirits in healing of minds and bodies showed that the Kingdom was beginning (Matt. 12:28); this divine kingdom he sees overcoming the kingdom of Satan (Mark 3:22-27). The word kingdom carries for him a vibrant sense of the new action of God in his own time and in his own work. But he never uses it to refer to God's past rule.

[10] Op. cit., ch. vi.

When Jesus spoke of the lordship of God, he was speaking of it as an effective reality. The fact of sin and moral conflict was too plain, and the need of decisive action to establish the effective rule of God was too clear, for him to say that God had been complete King all along. Therefore what he announced was not the past existence, but rather the present coming of the Kingdom—a new, epochal, decisive inbreaking of divine power and action. Only this sense of the newness of the Kingdom does justice to the vivid eschatological note of Jesus' teaching.

2. Jesus spoke of the Kingdom as already beginning.

This statement calls in question the purely future picture of the Kingdom which Albert Schweitzer has brilliantly supported.[11] It is to the credit of Schweitzer that when scholars were content to interpret the teaching of Jesus in gradualistic and evolutionary terms, he jarred the world of scholarship loose from its mistakes and forced them to hear in Jesus' message the note of imminent and decisive divine action.[12] Jesus did not speak as one who expected the world to go steadily on with a slow process of gradual improvement. He rather spoke of radical, imminent divine action to set up God's new order and realize his full purpose (Matt. 10:23; Mark 9:1; 13:30).

In this insistence Schweitzer was undoubtedly right. But his vigorous emphasis on the decisively new order that lay just ahead ignores the equally clear teaching which stated that this new order was already beginning. He had to interpret the parables of growth so that the growth from small beginnings had no meaning (Matt. 13:1-33; Mark 4:1-34; Luke 8:4-8; 13:18-20). He had to interpret the miracle stories so that they did not suggest that the Kingdom was already beginning to come with power (Matt. 12:28). He had to assume, in order to justify his reconstruction of Jesus' ministry, that Mark had reversed the order of events at the decisive stage of the story.[13] He had to give an artificial turn to Jesus' final visit to Jerusalem, and make it appear that Jesus deliberately went there to force his foes to put him to death and thereby

---

[11] Op. cit., especially chs. xv, xix, xx.

[12] Schweitzer was indebted to others for much of what he said. Johannes Weiss, Die Predigt Jesu vom Reiche Gotte (Göttingen, 1900), was his most important predecessor. But it was Schweitzer whose statement of the case has been most influential.

[13] See his book, Des Messianitäts– und Leidensgeheimnis, Tübingen, 1901 (Eng. tr. The Mystery of the Kingdom of God, New York, 1914).

set in motion the wheels of destiny that would bring in the still entirely future kingdom.

His brilliant sketch of events cannot do justice to both aspects of Jesus' kingdom teaching. It catches the sense of breathless expectancy, but it misses the thrill of the already present inbreaking of God's decisive new day. For Jesus, the Kingdom, a new and unique action of God, was beginning to come in his work and movement. A note of partial realization pervaded his message and gave confidence to his expectation of its full impending triumph.

3. Jesus spoke of the Kingdom in its full form as future; the note of forward-looking expectancy was prominent in his teaching.

This statement guards against the one-sided view that Jesus taught a "realized eschatology," an interpretation to which C. H. Dodd has given wide currency. Dodd clearly sees that in the Apostolic Church the original message was that the great complete fulfillment of God's purpose lay in the future. But in Jesus' teaching he finds an accent on already achieved realization. For Jesus the kingdom of God had come. It was present. It is always present when men open their eyes to it. He taught "realized eschatology." [14]

This was a valuable corrective of the "consistent eschatology" school, which contends that for Jesus the Kingdom was entirely future. As Dodd sees it, the sense of present fulfillment was strong both in the teaching of Jesus and in the apostolic message. The Kingdom had begun to come. It was no mere promise for which to wait; the active and powerful working of God was already present. In that sense there was realized eschatology in the words of Jesus and of the apostles.

But this is far from being the whole truth. The fact of conflict between the will of God and the forces of evil remained. Neither Jesus nor any of his followers were in doubt about that. They could not say that the Kingdom had fully come, that God's will was being done on earth as it is in heaven. (Matt. 6:10.) Jesus spoke of the fully realized kingdom as future. He warned his hearers to live by the will of God in order to be ready to enter the Kingdom.

Even at the end of his life Jesus spoke of the still future final drama

[14] See *The Apostolic Preaching*, p. 145; *Parables of the Kingdom*, pp. 108, 113, 198.

(Mark 13; Matt. 24; Luke 21). [15] He used pictorial language, and it is not certain how clearly the church preserved his words on this theme. But this much is clear: he declared that the coming, final action of God through the Son of Man would effect the full purpose of God and establish his permanent reign over all the world. To ignore that future aspect of Jesus' kingdom teaching makes it hard to understand why the apostolic preachers emphasized the future coming so much. It also conflicts with the words of Jesus and assumes that Jesus ignored the moral conflict that still existed in the world.

The Kingdom and Eternal Life

The Fourth Gospel refers to the kingdom of God only in ch. 3:3-5 (cf. 18:33-37). Instead of the Kingdom, eternal life is the recurrent theme. The Synoptic Gospels frequently use the phrase kingdom of God or (in Matthew) kingdom of Heaven, while the phrase eternal life occurs only two or three times in each Gospel. In the Gospel of John the preference is reversed. The kingdom of God is mentioned but twice, while eternal life becomes central.

This eternal life is given at once to the sincere believer. "He who believes in the Son *has* eternal life" (John 3:36; cf. 6:47). Other passages speak of a future full coming of the final order of God's rule (e.g., 5:28-29; 6:39), and those scholars do violence to the Gospel who delete such sayings as a redactor's discordant addition.[16] But the accent in the Gospel of John falls strongly upon the present gift of eternal life to believers. Nowhere in the New Testament is this sense of present privilege more emphatic. It reflects the immense change which the work of Christ, understood in the light of the Resurrection, has made in the human situation for those whose eyes are open.

This change of emphasis was not an essential change in Jesus' message of the Kingdom. To be sure, if Jesus had spoken of the eternal Kingdom, present before he came and continuing in and beyond his ministry, then stress on the fresh privilege of eternal life, given to the believer only now through the earthly career of Jesus, would be a noteworthy difference between the Synoptics and the Gospel of John. And if Jesus

---

[15] For a detailed study of Mark 13, see G. R. Beasley-Murray, *Jesus and the Future* (New York: St. Martin's Press, 1954).

[16] E.g., Rudolf Bultmann, *Das Evangelium des Johannes* (Göttingen, 1941), *in loco*.

had presented the Kingdom as purely future and not yet present in any real sense, the emphasis on present possession of eternal life through faith would be a radical alteration of his teaching. But when we once see that in Jesus' view the Kingdom has already begun to come in his work and movement, the change of atmosphere in the Gospel of John is not radical. The Synoptic Gospels picture the Kingdom as beginning in Jesus' ministry and destined to triumph before too long a time. In the Gospel of John, eternal life is available to true faith now and continues on into the final perfect order of God. In all four Gospels both aspects appear. The Synoptic picture stresses the future note, while the Gospel of John accents the present privilege, but these two aspects appear in both forms of the message of Jesus.

To us today, the term kingdom may seem uncongenial. Our political outlook does not make a kingdom seem the best form of life. So we may tend to prefer the phrase "eternal life." For our present purpose, it is worth noting that the term kingdom protects three aspects of Jesus' mind which the phrase "eternal life" does not specifically state.

For one thing, the term kingdom states clearly that God is our King and Lord, and not merely our elected official. Moreover, the reference to God, whether directly or in Matthew's substitute "Heaven," reminds us that we are not talking merely about our personal state of well-being. In the way of life Jesus presented, God is the central figure and his rule is the basic interest. Furthermore, while eternal life could easily be understood today in purely personal terms and lose its intended sense of community, the word kingdom clearly reminds the Christian that he is one of God's people, and that his life is lived in the mutual relationships of that community. The word kingdom forces us to recognize the social as well as the basically religious aspect of Jesus' message.

Of course, the phrase eternal life, when used by those who know the biblical message, will suggest both the religious and the social aspects of Christian life. We only point out that the expression kingdom of God explicitly includes both of these essential points.

The Kingdom and the Church

The rest of the New Testament lacks the frequent mention of the kingdom of God which we find in the Synoptic Gospels. The phrase does not disappear; it occurs often enough to prove it remained in common use. Reference to it occurs in ten New Testament writings in addition to the Gospels, and these ten documents come from at least four different writers.[17] The kingdom of God was obviously a subject of teaching by all types of Christian leaders and writers.

Yet a change occurs. To put it briefly, attention shifts more to the person of Jesus, to what he has done for man's salvation, and to the church through which this salvation is being offered to the world. We find references in seven writings to the kingdom of Christ.[18] But we can no longer say, as we could say of the teaching of Jesus, that the Kingdom is central in the message of the Apostolic Church. It was present and significant, but it did not have the same place of prominence. Attention focuses on Christ, on salvation through grace received by faith, and on the church.

This shift of emphasis has sometimes been considered the abandonment of Jesus' message. Famous as an expression of this view is the saying of Alfred Loisy: "Jesus announced the kingdom of God, but it was the Church which appeared." [19] The implication, however, that the preaching of the church was radically at variance with the teaching of Jesus is not valid. The shift of emphasis is a fact, but it was essentially a development rather than a surrender of what Jesus had said.

Note two significant facts: the church preserved the kingdom theme by preserving Jesus' teaching; and through its preachers and writers it continued to refer to the Kingdom. These facts show that the church had no intention of abandoning Jesus' message or distorting its basic meaning. We have the right to assume that a theme so prominent in the Gospels and so often mentioned in other New Testament writings steadily held its place in the faith and teaching of the Apostolic Age. We may be sure that preachers and writers did not all say exactly the

[17] Acts 1:3; 8:12; 14:22; 19:8; 28:23, 31; Rom. 14:17; I Cor. 4:20; 6:10; 15:24; 15:50; Gal. 5:21; Eph. 5:5; Col. 4:11; I Thess. 2:12; II Thess. 1:5; Jas. 2:5; and Rev. 11:15; 12:10 refer to (or imply) the phrase kingdom of God.

[18] I Cor. 15:24; Eph. 5:5; Col. 1:13; II Tim. 4:1, 18; Heb. 1:8; II Pet. 1:11; Rev. 11:15 refer to the kingdom of Christ. Cullmann, Christ and Time, p. 151, says that the kingdom of Christ exists now and will last to the end of this age (I Cor. 15:24). Then the kingdom of God will begin. Passages such as Eph. 5:5 and Rev. 11:15, however, argue that it is one Kingdom, which may be called either God's or Christ's.

[19] L'Évangile et l'Église (Paris, 1929), p. 153.

same thing or preserve the words of Jesus with exactly the same details. But the Kingdom remained a vital feature of the Christian faith.

The complaint that the apostolic preaching was not identical with that of Jesus lacks historical perspective. In part this complaint has rested upon indefensible criticism of the Gospels. It has asserted that Jesus did not claim to be the center of his movement or the object of the personal religious loyalty of his followers, and so the Christology of the Apostolic Age is an unwarranted intrusion into an originally non-Christological message.[20] It has asserted that Jesus did not interpret his death as a crucial benefit to his followers, and so all views which find more in his death than a noble example of faithfulness and unselfish devotion to his cause are a later addition.[21] It has been said that Jesus never thought of establishing a brotherhood which would make the church inevitable, but only formed an informal fellowship within the bounds of Judaism, and so the formation of the church was an innovation unrelated to his mind and teaching.[22]

This excision from the Gospels of prominent features which they share in common with other New Testament writings cannot be justified. It deals roughly and skeptically with the Gospels, which were written within a few decades of the life of Jesus and used oral and written tradition from the early years of the church, when numerous eyewitnesses would have protested against radical perversion of the message.[23] It leaves the apostolic preaching and writings without any convincing source or foundation, and unjustly attributes to these preachers and writers an irresponsible disregard or unconcern for facts.

The Gospels picture Jesus as the Christ who died for his cause and his followers and welded his disciples into a fellowship which would withstand opposition and continue his work. Had this picture been the free product of unhistorical imagination, the Gospels would have

---

[20] Typical of this view are W. Wrede, Das Messiasgeheimnis in den Evangelien (Göttingen, 1901); C. C. Torrey, Our Translated Gospels, pp. xv-xlix; R. Bultmann, Theology of the New Testament, tr. Kendrick Grobel (New York, 1951), I, 26-32.

[21] This is the general view of Parsons, op. cit., pp. 23-26.

[22] See note 19. But see R. Newton Flew, Jesus and His Church (London: Epworth Press, 1938); John Wick Bowman, The Intention of Jesus (Philadelphia: Westminster Press, 1943).

[23] See Vincent Taylor, The Formation of the Gospel Tradition (London: Macmillan & Co., 1933); E. F. Scott, The Purpose of the Gospels (New York: Charles Scribner's Sons, 1949).

parroted the later ideas and interests of the church. The very differences in emphasis which we find when we turn from Jesus' kingdom teaching to the message of the Apostolic Church strongly support the essential trustworthiness of the Gospels.[24] They show a tradition of amazing tenacity. They show it coming to us with essential faithfulness, although the church had already been forced to face new issues and to state its message to meet the new situations.

The tradition preserved its essential form. It deserves respect. And the high view of Jesus Christ, the importance of the Cross, and the essential role of the fellowship which Jesus established are integral to that tradition. To delete these aspects of the gospel tradition is unsound criticism; it renders the Gospels themselves unintelligible, and makes it impossible to form any reasonable picture of the origin and growth of the Apostolic Church. The high estimate of the person of Christ, the prominence of the Cross in the way of salvation, and the fellowship of believers in a living community are aspects of apostolic faith which have their basis in the mind and ministry of Jesus himself.

A change in the focus and statement of the Christian message, however, is just what we would expect the church to develop. Momentous events had occurred: the final rejection of Jesus by Jewish leaders, the death of Jesus, his resurrection, and the gift of the Holy Spirit. His followers could not be content to repeat just what he had said. They had to face the fact that he had not won his people by his life and teaching; he had been widely rejected. His ministry and teaching alone had not achieved his purpose. Even his closest disciples had deserted him at the last, and Peter had denied him. They needed something more, divine help that came only through the complete work of Jesus. The Cross and Resurrection were seen to be essential to all future faith and thought.

How could the disciples ignore these epochal events or fail to give them a central place? They lived, worshiped, and witnessed in the light of the Resurrection and in the light of the Cross as the Resurrection had taught them to understand it. Christ had to be the center of their message. Moreover, as the Christian movement spread, included more mem-

---

[24] This point is documented by Burton Scott Easton, *The Gospel Before the Gospels* (New York: Charles Scribner's Sons, 1928).

bers of many communities and races, found the former Jewish setting inadequate, and was rejected by the Jewish leaders and masses, the fellowship of disciples had to become a separate church.

This was not to desert Jesus and his kingdom message. It was to see God establishing his reign through the ministry and death and resurrection of Christ, through the gift of the Spirit, and through the continuing lordship of Christ over his widening church. This continuing work of God had to be told. The presence of Acts in the canon reminds us that the death and resurrection of Christ, and the work of the Spirit through the developing church, were integral parts of the redemptive work of God. They were essential steps in establishing the reign of God. The public ministry and teaching of Jesus were not forgotten, but they were fitted into a total picture that gave the full witness of the church.

This development of the church and its message had to come. We must speak more specifically of the church in a later chapter. For the present we only point out that the message of the Kingdom had a providential importance for the church. There is always a danger that the church will idolize itself. It may lose a sense of its weakness and limitations. It may forget that it is an instrument in the hands of God, and exists to serve the purposes of its Lord, Jesus Christ. The message of the kingdom of God, already partially realized and sure to be fully established in God's good time, can keep the church from being an end in itself. It can also keep Christians aware that when they believe in Christ, they accept the rule of God, the will of God, and the duty of obedience. The kingdom teaching of Jesus dooms the idea that Christians can passively receive and enjoy the blessings God has to give. The church must be the home of active obedience to God; its members must continually show friendly helpfulness to others.

CHAPTER VI

Christ and the Cross

FOR NINETEEN CENTURIES CHRISTIAN FAITH HAS GIVEN
the Cross a prominent place. In symbols and art, in hymns and worship,
in thought and creed the Cross has been characteristic of Christianity.
A tendency to stress the teaching and example of Jesus has marked
recent decades, and this has been a good corrective of earlier tendencies
to minimize Jesus' public ministry. But the Cross has been a focal center
of Christian faith from the first century to our day.

The Cross in New Testament Preaching

This prominence begins and roots in the New Testament itself. Concerning its importance there, two general facts deserve notice.

1. The Cross was evidently a prominent feature of the early Christian
message, and occupies a central place throughout the New Testament
tradition and writings. The sermon summaries in Acts show that it was
a basic feature of the apostolic preaching.[1] The Gospels come to a
decisive point in the passion story, and the fact that a quarter of the
total space of the Gospels tells of the last week of Jesus' life indicates
that the story of Jesus' death always held a prominent place in the gospel
tradition. The apostle Paul confirms this. When he became a Christian,
not more than six years after the death of Jesus, the basic confession and
message delivered to him gave the crucifixion prominent mention (I Cor.
15:3).

Other New Testament writings tell the same story. The Epistle to
the Hebrews gives notable prominence to the death of Jesus. (7-10.) The
Epistle of James is the one exception, unless the murdered "righteous

[1] See ch. ii.

111

man" of 5:6 refers to Jesus: in any case, however, the use of the title Lord (1:1; 2:1) implies the Resurrection, which assumes the Crucifixion. First Peter, written to persecuted Christians, uses the fact of Jesus' death to nerve and steady them in their trials (1:19; 2:21-24; 4:1). First John knows that by his death, Jesus Christ "is the expiation for our sins" (2:2). In Rev. 1:18 the risen Christ himself tells the seer: "I died." The death of Jesus was common Christian teaching.

2. But the other general fact is that the death of Jesus was always interpreted. No Christian ever told the story as a mere news item. It was always explained, and the meaning presented was that which the church had been able to see in the light of the resurrection of Jesus.

Nonbelievers also interpreted the death of Jesus, for it was an event which demanded explanation. But among them a different interpretation prevailed. Saul the persecutor of the church illustrates the difference. Before his conversion he knew that Jesus had been crucified, and he took it to prove that Jesus has been disowned by God and rightly rejected by Jewish leaders. Once converted, he saw in the Cross a quite different meaning; in the light of the Resurrection it had a positive and central place in a message that claimed the faith of men (I Cor. 2:2). But it had that place and meaning only because the Resurrection supplied the interpreting fact that gave the Cross its true place in the Christian message.

Why Was the Cross So Central?

The fact of Jesus' crucifixion and the interpretation of that fact in the light of the Resurrection are beyond dispute. But we need to inquire further why the early church stressed the Cross so much.

1. One suggestion explains this prominence by the influence of pagan cults which celebrated the dying and rising of certain gods in ritual ceremonies. Pagan cults tied to the cycles of nature and concerned with the fertility of field, flock, and family often emphasized such rites. Seasonal changes, especially those in which vegetation dies and then in turn appears to come to life again, stimulated rites which celebrated this death and renewal cycle as a rather magical means of insuring the revival and fruitfulness of nature in a new season of life and harvest. These primitive nature cults were given deeper meaning in the mystery

religions; they came in time to symbolize the promise of future life to those who took part in their ceremonies.[2]

Whether this development had reached an advanced stage by New Testament times is doubtful; direct evidence for its full bloom falls somewhat later. But however that may be, the attempt to explain the New Testament emphasis on the Cross by reference to these pagan rites is misguided. The New Testament doctrine ties back to an historical event, and the Christian interpretation of that event appears so promptly and universally in the church that we can hardly ascribe it to pagan influence. The pagan nature cults reveal a longing for life, and in their later forms a longing for life beyond the grave, but they cannot serve as the explanation of the New Testament emphasis on the Cross.

2. Related to the idea that emphasis on the death of Jesus derives largely from the nature cults and mystery religions is the view that this accent was due, not to the Jewish-Christian circles of the earliest church, but mainly to the Gentile and Hellenistic circles into which the gospel soon made its way.[3] That the Hellenistic Christians stated the fact against their special background, and thus gave it in some respects a new form, is not surprising. But there is no evidence of an early stage in which this interest in the death of Jesus did not exist. The earliest sermons we can find, the earliest gospel tradition we can discover, and the earliest written references, in the letters of Paul, carry the emphasis on the Cross back to the beginnings of the church. Moreover, Jerusalem's leaders, in the later part of the Apostolic Age, did not oppose this message of Paul. He can say that they were in essential agreement with his preaching (I Cor. 15:3; Gal. 2:6).

We do not deny—we rather affirm—that the church grew in its grasp of the meaning of Jesus' death. That is the biblical way of the divine historical action and revelation; the full meaning of the event becomes clear only as time goes on. But there never was a time, even in the earliest days, when the church kept a painful silence about the fact of

[2] On these cults and their strength and weakness see Samuel Angus, *The Mystery Religions and Christianity* (New York: Charles Scribner's Sons, 1925); Harold R. Willoughby, *Pagan Regeneration* (Chicago: University of Chicago Press, 1929).

[3] A survey and critique of views which explain Christian emphasis on redemption by pagan religious ideas of redemption is given by J. Gresham Machen, *The Origin of Paul's Religion* (New York: The Macmillan Co., 1921), chs. vi, vii.

113

the Crucifixion. From the first the disciples included in the Gospel an interpretation of the Cross.

3. Another possible explanation of the prominence of the Cross in the gospel message is that the ridicule and attacks of opponents forced the Christians to say something about Jesus' death. There is truth in this statement. Even if the disciples had wished to forget the Cross, their Jewish opponents would not have let them ignore the harsh fact that Jesus had been rejected and crucified.

The gospel is not a success story of the Horatio Alger or Dale Carnegie sort; it reports an apparently tragic failure by a man whose appeal and life purpose met hostile rejection. Had there been no better reason, the unceasing taunts of outsiders would have forced the church to discuss the death of Jesus and say what they understood it to mean. Christians had to absolve Jesus of any blame or fault that could block loyalty to him. But their references to the Cross had more than apologetic reasons.

4. The only satisfactory explanation of the universal apostolic emphasis on the Cross is that the life and message of Jesus himself had prepared them to think and preach as they did. The view of some scholars that Jesus had nothing to say about his death has radical weaknesses.[4] In the first place, the Gospels all say that he did expect his death and interpreted it (Mark 8:31; 9:31; 10:32-34 and parallels in Matthew and Luke; John 12:33); to deny this is to say that the Gospels are radically in error. In the second place, since no one contradicts the fact that Jesus met opposition during his ministry, to deny that Jesus spoke of his death assumes that Jesus either could not see the gathering storm clouds or could not discern an explanation of his rejection that would fit his message. To assume that he was too naïve to notice the ominous increasing hostility, or that he had no constructive explanation of what was happening, raises such questions about his competence and strength of leadership that only strong reasons could warrant accepting such a view. In the third place, the disciples had an interpretation of the Cross as early as we can trace their message. If they contrived this explanation without any basis in Jesus'

---

[4] This is made clear by the careful study of Vincent Taylor, *Jesus and His Sacrifice* (London: Macmillan & Co., 1937).

words to them, it is hard to account for their steady conviction that Jesus was vastly superior to them in knowledge and penetration.

If Jesus did not foresee or explain his death, we must simply accept the fact. But that view has startling implications. It reduces Jesus to the role of a naïve, unobserving enthusiast or a helpless, cornered idealist; and it implies that the earliest church had no historical sense, since it ascribed to Jesus sayings he never said and to his death meanings that never occurred to him.

We need not accept so radical a discrediting of both Jesus and the disciples, for we possess abundant evidence to the contrary. The varied sources for this evidence, the consistency of their witness, and the inherent probability that Jesus foresaw what was coming and prepared his disciples for it, warrant the conclusion that the gospel tradition on this point is essentially trustworthy. Jesus saw the threat of death; he spoke to his disciples about it. We must examine the evidence in the Gospels more directly.

The Impending Cross

The exact time when Jesus clearly anticipated violent death as the outcome of his ministry is difficult to determine. We can put aside suggestions of later art, in which some object or shadow in the form of a cross gives the boy Jesus a hint of the manner of his death. We need not insist on literal use of the poetic reference to the suffering of Jesus in the infancy narrative (Luke 2:34-35).

The question becomes urgent at the time of the Baptism. Does the voice at the Baptism (Mark 1:11)—with language recalling Ps. 2:7 and Isa. 42:1—indicate that Jesus, when he dedicated himself to the will of his Father, already was aware or then became clearly aware that he must fulfill the role of the Suffering Servant? [5] The fate of the prophets in Israel, and her continual refusal to obey the word of God, could have suggested such a prospect (Acts 7:52). A knowledge of "what was in man" (John 2:25) could have told him, in his days of planning and decision at the Temptation, that urgent preaching which left the decision to the hearers could arouse opposition and end his

[5] See John Wick Bowman, *The Intention of Jesus* (Philadelphia: Westminster Press, 1943), pp. 35-40.

career. But we should not press scriptural allusions not directly quoted, especially since the allusions cited do not refer to death. Nor should we build on the *a priori* contention that Jesus must have known how difficult his work would be.

Even so clear a passage as Mark 3:6, which tells of a definite plot against Jesus' life, must be used with care. The form critics have taught us that most units of the gospel tradition were handed down without clear and explicit information as to just when and where the events and sayings took place. Mark 3:6 is the climax of a series of controversies.[6] In them opponents attack Jesus for his disregard of Jewish law and customs, and he gives a telling reply which the church has used and preserved in the Gospels. We must not insist that these events all happened in close sequence; their chief connection is topical. Quite likely they were collected in this series to serve the teaching needs of the church. The decision reached in Mark 3:6, therefore, cannot be clearly dated.

Two things, however, are quite clear. One is that Jesus throughout his ministry encountered opposition. Great crowds thronged about him on occasion, but when the full extent of his demands became clear, many turned back, and even when the crowds were enthusiastic, the background of official opposition persisted. Jesus had challenged the validity of the oral traditions which to Pharisees formed part of the revealed Law of God (Mark 7:9-13); he had challenged the authority of established leaders and spoken for God without official support or authorization (Matt. 5:20). He had rebuked men who profited by the sufferings of their fellows (Mark 12:40), and had asked those satisfied with respectable, lukewarm religious observance to give complete obedience to God (Matt. 7:21; Luke 6:46). These acts made enemies. Jesus faced opposition, and as his ministry continued, it mounted instead of decreasing.

It also became clear to Jesus before the end of his Galilean ministry that this opposition could cost him his life. The martyrdom of John the Baptist was a warning. The continued and even intensified opposition of the religious leaders was a warning clue to danger ahead.

---

[6] See Martin Albertz, *Die synoptischen Streitgespräche* (Berlin, 1921), for a study of Mark 2:1–3:6.

Jesus could easily have avoided the danger by withdrawing from his ministry or by fleeing from the Palestinian scene. But he had the deep and driving conviction that God had called him to preach the message of the dawning kingdom to the people of Israel. It was his duty to preach "whether they hear or refuse to hear." (Ezek. 2:5.) His entire teaching and ministry had a determined and, in a sense, aggressive aspect. His parables, as Charles W. F. Smith has pointed out,[7] are not neutral discussions of truth; they are weapons in a campaign to force Israel to face its responsibility before God. To put it another way, Jesus presented himself and his message to Israel with the demand that they render a decision on his claim. If they refused him, he could see that, humanly speaking, catastrophe awaited him.

This crisis became even more inevitable when Jesus set his face to go to Jerusalem (Luke 9:51). Commissioned to preach to Israel and to require a verdict, he could not do his work by remaining in the north country of Galilee. The final decision could be reached only in "the holy city" itself. It was the center of Jewish life; the temple and the religious leaders of the people were found there; from there decisions went out to Jews all over the world. Not until he had preached in Jerusalem, and brought his claim to decision there, could his work be considered done. But this took him into the place of maximum danger, and involved him in the series of events which he foresaw would lead, as far as human eye could see, to his death. Jesus must have gone there fully aware of the immense danger which this step involved.

Jesus Foretells His Death

These facts throw light on the series of Synoptic passages in which Jesus predicts his coming death. The disciples had recognized in Jesus the fulfillment of their ancestral hope of a great Messianic leader. But he had to teach them that his course would not be one of easy triumph; he faced rejection and violent death. This forecast occurs three times in each of the Synoptic Gospels. The effect is particularly strong in Mark (8:31; 9:31; 10:32-34). Its importance in the eyes of Mark is clear from this rhythmic repetition, which begins immediately after the climactic Messianic confession by Peter near Caesarea Philippi.

[7] In *The Jesus of the Parables* (Philadelphia: Westminster Press, 1948).

The very structure of what follows the three predictions makes that importance still clearer. Each passage gives first the explicit prediction by Jesus. Each then gives some response or action by the disciples which shows that they do not understand or accept what Jesus has just told them (Mark 8:32; 9:32-34; 10:35-41).[8] Jesus then repeats the prediction, applying it to the disciples to show them that they must meet life in the same sacrificial spirit. (Mark 8:33–9:1; 9:35-37; 10:42-45.)

This thrice-repeated threefold pattern shows how important this prediction is in the structure of Mark, as well as in Matthew and Luke. The pattern may have been given its regular literary rhythm by Mark; in stating details of the predictions, he may reflect knowledge of the precise manner of this fulfillment. But after considering the life situation of Jesus, we need not doubt the essential trustworthiness of the picture. Jesus spoke to the disciples of his coming rejection, interpreted it to them, and showed them that they must accept the same lot and live in the same spirit of dedication with which he was facing his death.

To catch the significance of these passages, it is important to note that Jesus does more than predict his death. The fact of impending death, so threatening as to be for all practical purposes certain, is clearly stated. But Jesus does not end with that. In each case he goes on to speak of vindication and triumph. He looks beyond the death to the resurrection. His death will not be mere doom or irrevocable defeat, but an inevitable step in achieving God's purpose. His death will prove the doorway to a new stage in which new victory for God is certain. Deep faith and strong confidence are expressed in these predictions; they end in the prediction of resurrection and victory; the promise of redemptive benefit from the death is implicit in all of them and is explicit in Mark 10:45.

Jesus' strong anticipation of death appears also in the parable of the wicked vinedressers (Mark 12:1-12). These tenants in their master's vineyard have rejected many messengers of their master and have refused to give him his due. They finally reject and kill his son. But the will of the master prevails; judgment falls on the rebellious tenants, but the master's ownership and will stand vindicated.

This parable often arouses suspicion, in part because it is allegorical

[8] Cf. Robert Henry Lightfoot, *History and Interpretation in the Gospels* (New York: n.d. Bampton Lectures for 1934), pp. 117-20.

in form; it describes the history of Israel as a continual rejection of God's prophets, with its climax in the rejection of his Son. The story, however, is clear in narrative; its meaning grows out of the story without forcing; and the presence of allegorical features in parables is not without parallel. Another objection is that this parable anticipates the death of Jesus and so must have been created after his death. This wrongly assumes that Jesus did not or could not foresee where his course was taking him.

The story really does not reflect the accent of later Christian thought, for it does not conclude—as a parable created in the Apostolic Age would end—with the vindication of the Son in the Resurrection. It is after all a preresurrection parable. It indicates that Jesus anticipated his death and by this story confronted his opponents with the fact that in rejecting him, they were opposing the will of God and rejecting God's unique messenger.[9]

The Last Supper

An even clearer prediction of death and interpretation of its positive meaning for Christian faith and thought is the Last Supper.[10] The Gospel of John does not tell that Jesus symbolized his death by breaking and distributing the bread and by taking and passing the cup, but its earlier discourse, about Jesus as "the bread of life" (6:35), shows conclusively that the author knew that story. The somewhat vague references in Acts (e.g., 2:42) to the "breaking of bread" reflect that story indirectly. But for the actual report of this symbolic, interpretive action we must turn to the Synoptic Gospels and to Paul's account (Matt. 26:26-29; Mark 14:22-25; Luke 22:17-20; I Cor. 11:23-26).

These four accounts raise many questions. Matthew is closely allied to its main source, Mark; but Luke presents peculiar problems. His

[9] Werner Georg Kümmel gives a vigorous argument that this parable originated in the Apostolic Age: *Das Gleichnis von den bösen Weingärtnern* (Mark 12:1-9), in *Aux Sources de la Tradition Chrétienne* (essays in honor of Maurice Goguel), Neuchatel, 1950, pp. 120-31. For a compact summary of the opposite view, see Vincent Taylor, *The Gospel According to St. Mark* (London: Macmillan & Co., 1952), pp. 472-77.

[10] Two excellent recent studies are A. J. B. Higgins, *The Lord's Supper in the New Testament* (London: SCM Press, 1952), and Joachim Jeremias, *The Eucharistic Words of Jesus*, tr. Arnold Ehrhardt (New York: The Macmillan Co., 1955).

longer text is much like Paul's account, but his shorter text gives a form unlike either Mark or Paul. According to the longer text, Jesus passes two cups, one before and one after the bread. But if we accept the shorter text, which much good ancient evidence supports, the cup is passed first and then the bread. But it is not only the number of cups and the order that raise questions; the actual words with which Jesus comments on the bread and cup vary in the four accounts.

For our purpose we need not decide which text of Luke is authentic or precisely what Jesus said concerning the bread and the cup. Certain facts are common to all four accounts, and they are vital for our present discussion. In every account Jesus refers to his coming death in symbolic act and interprets it in words. He indicates that it will not be a defeat nor will it end his movement; it will rather benefit his followers and thus continue and advance the cause for which he has lived. He speaks of his death with hope; he assures his disciples that it offers them help and ground for hope. He has been giving them leadership and help without which they could not have found the truth or the power to live for God. In his death he will give his life willingly to provide them the help which they as failing followers need in order to go ahead.

Thus Jesus foresaw and foretold his death. He assured his disciples that his death would not end his work and defeat his cause, but would rather further the work he had undertaken and benefit those who had cast their lot with him. His disciples did not find it easy to accept this view. The crucifixion of their Master shattered their outlook, and scattered them until the Resurrection brought them together with new understanding and purpose. Clearly they found it hard to give rejection and death a place in the plan of God for his Christ. They clung too hard to the easy success psychology expressed in much current Messianic hope to be able to see how God really fulfills his purposes.

The modern church should not find it hard to understand the disciples. We are as obsessed with success psychology as they were. We feel that one so good and helpful and worthy as Jesus should have commanded universal admiration and obedience. We too find it difficult to give the Cross a vital and natural place in God's way of carrying out his purpose. It seems to us a strange and unexpected event.

The Cross in the Old Testament

This means that we, like the disciples of Jesus, have not read the Old Testament with proper discernment. It is no easy success story. The people of Israel come from wandering nomadic forefathers. They find their national unity and basis of common life in the experience of escape from slavery in Egypt. This leads to further wandering and to the slow and painful conquest of the Promised Land. But Israel never unites in full and steadfast loyalty to the Lord, and never responds steadily and gratefully to God's chosen leaders. Moreover, this people which has suffered slavery continues to know opposition; their history recounts continual oppression and subjection by foreign powers. They rarely enjoyed complete freedom.

God's leaders in Israel had an even harder time than the common people. The faithful spokesmen for God almost always met resistance, and at times they suffered actual persecution. In Heb. 11 we find a summary of the hardships of God's people during that period. It uses later legends as well as Old Testament evidence, but makes clear the central point. Both the loyal core of Israel and the faithful prophets of God knew from personal experience something of what the Cross means to discerning Christian believers.

The truth that God's work goes forward and his will gets done through costly sacrifice is as clear in the Old Testament as it is on Calvary. The event on Calvary is the central and decisive embodiment of God's way of saving men through unselfish and costly dedication which furthers God's will in the face of all opposition. But Calvary is the consistent climax of the spirit of dedication which the Old Testament continually illustrates. Jesus carried forward the way of sacrificial living repeatedly presented in the Old Testament story.

This Old Testament spirit of costly service to God's cause found supreme portrayal in the Suffering Servant figure of Second Isaiah.[11] The insight that suffering is not senseless, or even deserved in all cases, but may be accepted in the service of God and prove a benefit to those for whom it is accepted, comes to clearest expression in the great Servant

[11] See the works listed in n. 13 of ch. vii; also O. Eissfeldt, "The Prophetic Literature," in ch. v of The Old Testament and Modern Study, ed. H. H. Rowley (New York: Oxford University Press, 1951).

poem in Isaiah 52:13–53:12. The message of this passage is no isolated feature of the total Old Testament outlook. It is the most vital expression of a principle implicit in the entire story, the principle called later the principle of the Cross.

Some recent scholars have questioned whether Jesus, and even the earliest New Testament preachers, connected his impending death with the Suffering Servant passage in Isaiah.[12] The assumption behind this question has been in part that furthering God's will through suffering was a strange idea, which would not have occurred to Jesus. We have been trying to show that when read with discernment, the Old Testament—and the Suffering Servant passages in particular—offered the clear clue to what God was doing and the way he was doing it. A deep-seated unity connects the experiences of the loyal in Israel, the experiences of her faithful prophets, and the experiences of Jesus. It should not surprise us that to interpret what he saw happening to him, Jesus seized upon the Suffering Servant passages, where this recurrent note of the Old Testament story finds climactic expression. He lived in the atmosphere of Scripture and he penetrated into its deepest meanings. He turned to it when he faced the fact of hardening rejection; he found in the Suffering Servant idea the preliminary portrayal of what he in his death was to embody in supreme clarity—the principle of the Cross, the working out of God's redemptive purpose through suffering willingly accepted to serve God and God's people. Precisely in the Cross we find one of the deep bonds between Jesus and the Old Testament, between the Old Testament and the New.

Thus far we have noted the prominence of the Cross in early Christian preaching. We have seen that this message was not a later addition to the original message, or a mere apologetic necessity, but arose in the mind of Jesus himself as he faced increasing evidence of general rejection by the Jewish leaders and people. He saw what was coming, and interpreted it in a positive way to his followers. This spirit of dedicated, costly living, undeterred even by the advance of impending death, was not a new note in biblical preaching, but rather continually occurs in the

[12] E.g., Rudolf Bultmann, *Theology of the New Testament*, tr. Kendrick Grobel, vol. I (New York: Charles Scribner's Sons, 1951), p. 31. But see Wm. Manson, *Jesus the Messiah* (London: Hodder & Stoughton, 1943).

life of the loyal in Israel, and especially in the life of God's prophets. We still need to discuss in detail what the early church thought of the meaning of the Cross and what unity there was between Jesus' ministry and his death.

Early Interpretation of the Cross

The first witnesses to the resurrection of Jesus had to interpret the death of their Master.[13] We recognize, of course, that Paul was the first great Christian theologian. But he certainly was not the first to begin serious thinking about the meaning which the death of Jesus has in the Christian story. Deep inner questionings, and the necessities of preaching and replying to opponents, led the first disciples to face this question. Not that they found a full answer at once. As is usual when God reveals his purpose in history, the event only gradually unfolded its full meaning. Not even yet has the church reached static completeness in its theology of the Cross. The earliest Christians had a much more rudimentary theology than Paul and later Christian thinkers, though the essential teaching found adequate expression in the Apostolic Age.

Too often we think that this theology of the Cross was worked out quite apart from the actual lives of the people who gave it form. But it was not done in that way. It was rather linked with their life experience. They had failed to understand Jesus during his lifetime. They did not grasp and were unwilling to accept what he said about his impending death. They were not steady in the face of danger; they fled when danger to Jesus endangered their own lives. Then the Resurrection rallied them; they reassembled; and moved by the Spirit of God, they began their Christian witness to what God had done in Christ and was now doing by his Spirit.

In this witness, as we have said, they had to speak of the death of Jesus. They had to find meaning in it. But they had to do this first of all for themselves. They had not deserved the privilege of being with Jesus, nor had they been worthy of it. They had not stood by him in his hour of final danger (Mark 14:32-50); even the inner trio of disciples fled to save their own lives. They did not deserve to lead his cause and

---

[13] See Vincent Taylor, *The Atonement in New Testament Teaching* (1st ed.; London: Epworth Press, 1950), part 1.

witness to him. But Jesus during his ministry had given them all they would hear of teaching and counsel; he had stood steady for God's work even when they all failed; he had now given them restored confidence and new opportunity.

They could not escape the fact that what Christ had done, he had done first of all for them. It had been for their benefit; they had not deserved it. They could only accept it, witness gratefully to it, and say that God in Christ had done for them what they could not do for themselves. Out of their failure had come a realization of the forgiving goodness of God and his Christ. Out of it had come a realization that the death of Christ was, as he had promised, a way in which he in his faithfulness had given them gracious benefit. When Paul reports that the earliest Christians taught that "Christ died for us" (Rom. 5:8), we are likely to think that this was just doctrinal theory. That would be a radical mistake. This theology grew out of the personal experience of those who were nearest to Jesus. They had known best his teaching; they had known his faithfulness and his promise that his suffering would benefit them; and they had learned by humiliating experience that this was God's way of helping men.

Only a doctrine of grace and of the saving benefit of the death of Christ could do justice to what had actually happened to those who stood closest to Jesus in his last hours and in the thrilling days of his resurrection appearances to his followers. Nothing in the following survey of New Testament views is mere theory; it is explanation of experienced benefit, and the attempt of grateful men to say what this mysterious event meant in God's plan and for their faith.

We possess no adequate information by which to reconstruct in clear detail the earliest stages of Christian thought about Jesus' death. It is certain that his disciples accepted that death as a fact. They gave no basis for the later attempts of a few embarrassed Christians to deny that Jesus really died. They accepted the fact. Christian thinking had to start from that.

They were certain, however, that it was not the final fact. They were witnesses to the resurrection of Jesus, and this fact dominated their thinking. Seen in its light, the death of Jesus could not warrant rejecting him or taking his death as defeat. The Resurrection meant that the death

124

could not be merely an irrelevant or negative fact. It fitted somehow in God's plan.

One defensive fact was always clear. The execution of Jesus was a crime against human law and order (Acts 2:23). Jesus had done nothing to deserve such torture and death (Luke 23:22; Acts 3:14; II Cor. 5:21; I Pet. 2:22; I John 3:5). His life had been wholesome and helpful; "he went about doing good" (Acts 10:38).

The church early asserted the sinlessness of Jesus. In positive content this affirms Jesus' full loyalty to God, his fitness to lead God's cause, and his full devotion to people's needs. The negative form of the statement probably reflects the need Christian preachers faced to show that Jesus did not deserve condemnation either by Jewish leaders or the Roman governor. No fault of his justified his execution. Those who condemned him did wrong by standards of human justice, and sinned against God in rejecting his chosen Christ.

Foretold in Scripture

In finding the positive meaning of Jesus' death, the church made instant and continual use of the Scriptures they had inherited. God's work in history has unity. His climactic work in Christ carries forward what he has done in Israel and what he has promised in Israel's Scriptures.

Suppose we ask where the New Testament writings have their origin. We may give more than one answer. We may say: in the teaching and work of Jesus; or, in the telling of the story about Jesus in the light of the Resurrection. But while these statements are true, another answer is part of the truth: in the process of understanding God's work in Christ in the light of the Scriptures. For the disciples it was axiomatic that their Scripture, our Old Testament, was the background of the present working of God in Jesus and the church.[14] If the Crucifixion was neither the final fact nor a damaging fact, but rather one to be understood in the light of the Resurrection, it must be consistent with what the Scripture teaches, and the study of Scripture to get its light on the events of Jesus' career becomes an urgent necessity. "Christ died for our sins in accordance with the scriptures." (I Cor. 15:3.) The assertion

[14] Cf. C. H. Dodd, *According to the Scriptures* (New York: Charles Scribner's Sons, 1953).

that the death of Jesus was foreshadowed and foretold in Scripture formed part of the earliest interpretation of the Cross (Luke 24:45; Acts 13:29).

Early and Continued Interpretation

What has a place in God's plan and has been foreshadowed and foretold in Scripture must have meaning for Christian faith and living. The church at once explored that meaning. Peter interpreted the death of Jesus at Pentecost. (Acts 2:23.) The early church told Paul, within a few years of Jesus' death, that the death was "for our sins" (I Cor. 15:3). Other Christians generally accepted Paul's emphasis on the benefits of the death of Jesus.

Thus the interpretations we find in New Testament writers reach back into the period before the actual writing of these documents began.[15] An unbroken line runs from the earliest Jewish-Christian Church into later Gentile-Christian faith and thought. The fact which we have established, that this interpretation had its roots in teaching that Jesus gave his disciples, explains this consistent line, and leaves no reason to suspect that the earliest disciples differed essentially from Paul and other New Testament writers of later decades. We can be confident that a deep unity of faith underlay the healthy variety with which Christians understood and expressed the meaning of the Cross. They agreed that this death was grounded in God's plan, served to carry it forward, and gave rich benefits to the followers of Jesus.

The death of Jesus serves occasionally as an example to his followers; they should have the mind or spirit in them which they had seen in Christ Jesus (Phil. 2:5-8; I Pet. 2:21). The appeal to the example of Jesus does not occur often. It was present in the teaching of Jesus (Mark 8:34), found expression in Philippians and in First Peter, and undoubtedly nerved many a Christian witness in times of danger or condemnation. But the gospel emphasis was not on the death of Jesus as an example of courage, perseverance, and fidelity to God. Instead of these concerns, in which Jesus could be imitated, the church centered more on the unique aspects of that death which his followers could not repeat

[15] See the hints in Maurice Goguel, *The Birth of Christianity*, tr. H. C. Snape (New York: The Macmillan Co., 1954), pp. 98-103.

or parallel. Christ had done something for them which they could never have done for themselves. They could only recognize and accept it with gratitude.

The death of Jesus was to Christians a way to triumph. It led to his resurrection and exaltation; as the Fourth Gospel says, on the Cross Jesus was lifted up and glorified (John 3:14; 12:32; 13:31-32). It was the pathway to glory, divine honor, and regal activity. It had deep meaning; it was decisive in God's working for men; but it was seen to be so only when viewed as a part of the total divine work which included the resurrection and lordship of Christ.

"Christ Died for Our Sins"

The church did not find the central meaning of the Cross, however, either in its illustration of the spirit of life that all disciples should show or in the fact that it was the prelude to later glory and authority. The dominant concern of the New Testament is that the death of Jesus brings help and benefit to sinful men.

Back of this concern is the clear recognition that the central human problem is sin. Without this recognition the New Testament makes no sense at all. Sin is the background of the entire gospel story. The gospel is a message of deliverance from sin by the action of God in Christ. And the Cross has a central place in this message of redemption.

In the face of that sin and its ruinous consequences, the Cross expresses God's active, gracious love for erring men. The Cross is often interpreted as an expression of the wrath of God. It does show that God takes sin seriously; he cannot tolerate it or compromise with it. He can deal with it only by condemning it and acting to remove it. He alone can solve that problem, and he acts in Christ to meet it in a way that will redeem men. Love, holy love, prompts his action. The Cross speaks first of all of the love of God. "God shows his love for us in that while we were yet sinners Christ died for us." (Rom. 5:8.) "God so loved the world that he gave his only Son." (John 3:16.)

To interpret God as a stubborn, angry God, reluctant to do anything for men and needing to be pacified by Christ, is blasphemy; it misses the central New Testament note. God acted out of holy and gracious love to help men, and the Cross is the supreme expression of that love.

127

The Cross is equally the expression of the love of Christ (II Cor. 5:14-15; Gal. 2:20). Kindly concern for people and especially for his followers marked his ministry; it expressed itself with climactic intensity in his voluntary acceptance of death to fulfil God's will and benefit his followers. His death showed the completeness of his dedication to God and love for man. It willingly accepted the uttermost sacrifice to give the help which kindness, friendship, and teaching combined had thus far failed to give. It was at one with the love of God in its purpose of redeeming men. He knew what he was doing. He was acting out of steadfast good will to accomplish what even his life and ministry had thus far failed to achieve.

Keenly aware of the outreaching love of God and the unselfish love of Christ, the church inevitably saw that the suffering of Christ was vicarious; it was "for our sins," "for you," "for us," "for me" (I Cor. 15:3; I Pet. 2:21; Rom. 5:8; Gal. 2:20). No wonder the church remembered what Jesus had said of the suffering of the Son of Man as a ransom for many (Mark 10:45). As a captive is redeemed by the payment of a ransom price, so they in their failure and sin had been delivered and given new life by Jesus' death on their behalf.

Paul can even speak of the death of Christ as a substitutionary sacrifice (Gal. 3:13; II Cor. 5:21). This offends some and puzzles many.[16] The idea is widespread today that we all must answer for ourselves; no one else can take the penalty for what we do.

It is curious how difficult people make this idea of Paul. As a matter of fact, it is a constant feature of human life that parents, friends, and sometimes even strangers act in moments of danger or over long times of strain to relieve endangered or helpless people from whatever danger besets them. People are reached by unselfish love, and recaptured for physical life or moral renewal, precisely by unselfish dedication of others, who pay a cost and suffer a penalty or burden which they had no need to assume apart from human love or kindness. The feature of vicarious helpfulness and even of substitutionary suffering to rescue and deliver others is not the moral outrage some take it to be. God has built it into the very heart of the gospel, and wherever his Spirit and will prevails,

[16] C. A. A. Scott, *Christianity According to St. Paul* (New York: The Macmillan Co., 1927), sees the presence of sacrificial ideas, but I think he would not use the word "substitutionary."

it finds continual expression. To the Christian it finds supreme expression in Jesus' unselfish, sacrificial acceptance of death to further God's cause and help his people.

We dare not claim to understand all that was in Paul's mind when he spoke of the vicarious and substitutionary sacrifice of Christ.[17] Nor can we fathom the full meaning in God's purpose of the single perfect sacrifice of which the author of the Epistle to the Hebrews speaks (10:12-14).[18] But these men spoke of more than a cold idea. Their lives had been touched and their relation to God radically changed by what Christ had done. Christ did not deserve condemnation, while they did, and yet Christ had been condemned and they had gone free—released not only from the guilt but also from the power of sin.

These early Christians were not so concerned to explain how this had happened as to witness to the fact that it had happened to them and to many others they knew. Christ died for them; it was a great truth, in view of their spiritual failure, that he had died instead of them. They did not seek to escape condemnation for their sins; they could not worship a God who did not condemn them; they accepted that condemnation. They had been deeply in the wrong and unable to do anything about it; but they had found when they confessed their guilt that Christ had given them the deliverance they had not deserved. This was the miracle of grace which Christ's death had brought. It had been costly; it had been vicarious; it had been effective.

"The Message of Reconciliation"

Sin for these early Christians was not merely a private, personal matter. It was of course a personal responsibility, and they were grateful that Christ's work had reconciled each one of them to God. He had done more than care for the guilt of their sin. Of course, he had done that, but he had also broken the grip of sin on their lives, and had brought them back into living fellowship with God.[19] This reconciliation, the work of the crucified and risen Christ, is the theme of perhaps the profoundest passage about Christ's death in the entire New Testament.

[17] See Elias Andrews, The Meaning of Christ for Paul (New York and Nashville: Abingdon Press, 1949), ch. iii.

[18] See C. Spicq, L'Épitre aux Hebreux, vol. I (Paris, 1952), ch. x.

[19] See Vincent Taylor, Forgiveness and Reconciliation (London: Macmillan & Co., 1941).

"All this is from God, who through Christ reconciled us to himself and gave us the ministry of reconciliation" (II Cor. 5:18; cf. Col. 1:20).

Taken alone, this verse could be understood in a highly individualistic way, as though the death of Christ had as its intention the deliverance of numerous hermits from their personal sins. But while the New Testament never cancels individual responsibility, and never loses the sense of personal privilege which the gospel gives, it also keeps clearly in sight two other facts.

The Defeat of Evil Powers

For one thing, the New Testament knows that there is a network of evil powers and forces in life which oppose the Christian and the cause of Christ. It was not merely individuals that brought Christ to his death. Hostile groups and sinister forces combined against him. What Christ did was to defeat all the combined evil the world contained.[20] Paul and other early Christians thought of this hostile array in personal terms. Christ defeated "the principalities and powers" and destroyed their domination of mankind (Col. 2:15). We often think that we improve on Paul by substituting for evil spirits our abstract ideas of evil principles. It may well be that Paul laid hold of deep truth when he sensed that sinister social and even cosmic forces of evil were arrayed against Christ and mankind. He interpreted the victory of Christ not only as a help to individuals in their moral need, but also as a victory over all hostile powers in the universe. From Jesus (Luke 10:18) throughout the Apostolic Church to the end of the New Testament, there is this sense that the victory of Christ has cosmic dimensions.

But there is also another understanding of the social range of the Cross. The new life and order to which Christ's death gives access is a life in community, a Kingdom and not a hermit's cell. The benefit of the death of Christ is deliverance from personal guilt and sin—yes; but it is also deliverance from bondage to evil persons and powers, and is gracious acceptance into the fellowship of those who are free to do God's will.

[20] See Gustaf Aulén, *Christus Victor*, tr. A. G. Hebert (London: The Sheldon Press, 1931); Oscar Cullmann, *Christ and Time*, tr. Floyd V. Filson (Philadelphia: Westminster Press, 1950), part III, ch. iii.

The Cross Consistent With the Ministry

The Resurrection throws light on all this meaning of the Cross, but the Resurrection does not crowd out the fact of the Cross or its vital role in expressing the very nature of God, of Christ, and of Christian living. This will become clear as we see how the entire career of Jesus of Nazareth blends with the Cross into one consistent picture. We have shown that the Cross is consistent with the Old Testament. We have pointed out how the early church found its meaning as they realized what Christ had done for them and learned that they should embody the same spirit. The career of Jesus draws all this together and unites life, ministry, and death in a picture of unique consistency.

Here is a historical figure, subject to all the essential limitations of human life. Against the Docetic tendency to free Jesus from such limitations, against pious attempts to stress the divine side of his nature so that the human becomes insignificant, the church held fast to the plain fact that he had lived a full human life, at a certain point in history, in a certain small and politically unimportant country. He was a member of a subject people, and was himself without distinctive status among that people. Regardless of his place of birth, he came to his ministry from the "backwoods" in Galilee (John 1:45-46).

He came from a good and respected family, but they were of the wholesome common folk of his day. He was born as a helpless babe, and even the doctrine of the Virgin Birth, which the church saw was necessary to state and protect the divine nature of Christ and the divine initiative in salvation, does not obscure the humble dependence of the small and growing child. He had no outstanding education, although he obviously had been taught to read the Scriptures of his people and had been trained in Israel's way of worship and life. To his home-town contemporaries he did not seem a genius or distinguished person; they could hardly believe their ears when they heard him teach with confident authority in their synagogue (Mark 6:2 ff.; Luke 4:22). Even his brothers did not accept his claims during his lifetime (John 7:5), and at one point his family appear to have desired to withdraw him from the public eye, for fear his burning zeal for God's cause might bring the family into disgrace (Mark 3:21, 31-35).

He went to hear John the Baptist and submitted to baptism, so that later it was a problem to the church to explain how one who had been subordinate to the Baptist could be their Lord—the Christ and Son of God. In his temptation he turned from the externally impressive, expected program of the messianic leader of God's people. Because he was seeking the willing response of each person, he took the slow way of teaching, making friends, and building understanding and loyalty without depending on outward authority and power.

Jesus' ministry had the air of humility about it. He was content to work mainly in the cities and villages of Galilee instead of in the great "holy city" Jerusalem. He did not seek or possess official standing among the religious leaders of his people. He was happy to deal mainly with the common people. He had no steady income, no office equipped for religious administration, no trained staff, no highly trained intellectual leaders on whom to rely for the development of doctrinal or promotional literature. The tenor of his teaching was not self-assertive; he used such words as repent, believe, obey, serve, sacrifice, suffer, love. He met opposition, persecution, rejection, and finally death.

All the way his was a life without outward claim to distinction and without the use of external pressure and compulsion. He lived in the spirit in which he died, with his interest centered not on self-promotion or personal privilege, but on the deepest needs of others, and his desire was to help every one of his people whom he could reach, regardless of the cost to himself. The spirit that took him to the Cross was the spirit that had expressed itself throughout his ministry, and it was a spirit consistent with the entire situation of his personal life and public work.

This is a clue to the nature of the Gospel. The humble one is exalted. Sacrificial love actually saves people. Unselfish suffering has redemptive power. God is at work in all this. He conquers through ungrudging self-giving, without surrender of his holiness or righteous purpose. God is like that. He loves his people and at great cost acts on his own initiative to save them. The Cross is not a passing feature of history, but the clear expression of the nature and spirit of God. He is the seeking Father. He is "a righteous God and a Savior." (Isa. 45:21.)

Christ expresses in human life and historical act the very nature of God. The Cross is God's way to save. And to everyone who has seen this fact, it shows how man is to act. The Cross is man's way to live.

CHAPTER VII

Christ and the Father

IT IS CHARACTERISTIC OF THE CHRISTIAN GOSPEL THAT IT centers in one historical figure. Many other religious messages give the same basic place to God. But the gospel's message about God does not take the form of general theological argument. Its essential form is not a system of moral demands. This message is not put in the form of a general ideal. It requires theology to understand and state its meaning; it embodies a radical demand for obedience; it enshrines the highest ideal. But it does all this by telling of a central historical person. His career drives the believer to develop a theology. His message and personal claim lay upon the believer a radical and comprehensive moral demand. His person and work control the ideal which the believer forms for his worship, thought, and life.

The heart of the gospel is this specific witness to a person. Jesus Christ is central in the gospel; the Christian message about God and man, about faith and life, finds living expression in him.

Since this is so, we must ask who Jesus is and what relation he holds to God the Father. This question has been close to the center of attention in all that we have said thus far. It could not be otherwise, for at every stage Jesus is central for faith and dominant in Christian thought. Yet to do justice to his decisive role, we now must ask: Just who was he? Who did the apostolic witness say that he was and is?

Christ's Work the Basis of Christology

It was with good reason that we deferred until now the discussion of this question. We tried to follow the order which the New Testament story itself suggests. The early Christians did not begin by stating the

133

full view which Christians should hold concerning Jesus Christ. They first met a vital person who claimed their attention and then won their loyalty. As they lived with him, and as they later saw the developing results of his life and work, the sense of his greatness grew upon them. They repeated the biblical pattern, in which a great event finds full understanding and appreciation only with the passing of time.

Thus all that Jesus Christ meant to faith and all that believers must say of him came more clearly to light with the passing of the years. The essentials of the high view of his person emerged with amazing rapidity, but its full and formal statement took time.

All of this Christology grew out of a vivid sense of the unique meaning of his work. What he had said and done, what he had meant to his hearers and followers, led them to fuller statement of what he was. This is why we first described Jesus as the herald and bringer of the Kingdom, and as the effective redeemer of men, before attempting to sum up what the New Testament says of his personal greatness. It was his unique and decisive work which led to the high Christology of the Apostolic Church. That Christology seems unreal wherever the sense of his redemptive work fades or is feeble.[1] But to those who have grasped the greatness of what he has done, is doing, and will do for his people, that Christology proves convincing. This sense of the immeasurable benefit of the work of Christ prompts the New Testament writers to speak as they do about the personal identity of Christ and his unique relation to God.

Their procedure is not surprising. It is similar to what we find in the biblical witness to God. The Bible has no interest in general propositions about the nature and characteristics of God. It is God as known in what he has done and is doing who is the subject of the biblical witness.[2] Because he has done great things for his people, because he is the living God who acts in history and is the sovereign Lord of men, the Bible must make great affirmations about him and his importance for human life and thought. Just so, the work of Christ leads to high statements about his nature and relation to God.

[1] Cf. the notable statement by Melanchthon: "This is to know Christ, to know his benefits."

[2] This point of view is presented in a World Council of Churches symposium edited by Alan Richardson and W. Schweitzer, *Biblical Authority for Today* (Philadelphia: Westminster Press, 1952). See especially the essays in part 3.

A Human Life—With a Difference

Jesus was a man. He was a first-century Jew who was born in a Jewish home, brought up in a Galilean village, taught the Jewish heritage, trained in the specific trade of carpenter, roused to his specific role in history through the preaching of John the Baptist, and subject throughout his life to the essential limitations of human life. He did not know everything (Mark 13:32); he knew what it was to get tired (John 4:6); he knew the sting of unfair treatment and desertion by former friends; he suffered pain and experienced physical death.

Even in the Apostolic Age there began the tendency, which has never completely disappeared, to rescue Jesus from the apparently degrading participation in the common lot of mankind.[3] The Docetists soon claimed that he only *seemed* to be truly human. With healthy insight the church stoutly rejected this temptation to substitute mere appearance for the hard reality of actual human experience. To say that he never knew physical trials and limitations or the moral struggle of life might seem to honor Jesus and protect his greatness, but the church knew that to say this was to surrender the very basis of the gospel story. This story testified that God had acted in history, in this central person, for the salvation of men. "The Word became flesh" (John 1:14); Jesus was a real man; God did his work through a life which shared the human lot.

Yet this, as believers always knew, was human life with a difference. They expressed this sense of difference in at least three ways.

1. Not in the original apostolic witness, as far as we can tell, but before many years, they testified that the beginning of his life on earth was due to the miraculous act of God (Matt. 1:18-25; Luke 1:26-38). Whether the doctrine of the Virgin Birth is taken as literal fact, and Jesus had no human father, or whether it expresses in poetic form the deep theological fact that the coming of this unique life into history was the direct result of the purposeful act of God, it is clear that the church had to say that God was back of this birth.[4] This life did not just happen.

[3] A wholesome emphasis on the Jesus of history, and a vigorous attack on Docetic tendencies in modern theology, appears in D. M. Baillie, *God Was in Christ* (New York: Charles Scribner's Sons, 1948).

[4] The best argument for the literal fact as the necessary protection of the theological truth is by J. Gresham Machen, *The Virgin Birth of Christ* (New York: Harper & Bros., 1932). On the other side see Elwood Worcester, *Studies in the Birth of the Lord* (New

Its origin was due to divine love, which was here at work to carry out God's saving purpose for his people. The church could not accept the idea that Jesus was only a human being who turned out unusually well, so that God tardily awoke to the fact that here was someone he could use for his work; it had to find the origin of this life in God's act. Jesus can never be fully explained by reference to his human ancestry. God came into human life here in a unique way to work out his central purpose of redemption.

2. Another conviction that Christian faith found both true and essential to faith was that Jesus was not guilty of personal sin. As we have already suggested in chapter 6, this conviction probably came to its earliest clear expression in answer to charges and slanders which opponents brought against Jesus. The church insisted that he had always acted justly. Though Jewish leaders condemned him as a dangerous man and Pilate executed him as a rebel and criminal, he was innocent of any wrong. He was "the Holy and Righteous One"; "he committed no sin"; Paul can call Jesus "him who knew no sin" (Acts 3:14; I Pet. 2:22; II Cor. 5:21). But he was more than negatively guiltless; he was positively obedient to God's will and loyal to God's purpose; and the gospel therefore included the conviction that "he went about doing good" (Acts 10:38). This was not what humanity was like in others, but it was what humanity should be. He was in actual life what all men ought to be, free from fault and loyal to the will of God.

3. The life of Jesus was distinguished from other human lives by a third point of difference. The church came to see in Jesus a new start for humanity, a new leader who gives to all of his people a share in a renewed human race. This conviction did not often come to explicit expression. At first there existed only a general agreement that things had been radically changed by the coming of Jesus, so that his followers could live in a new life situation. The apostle Paul, however, gave a more specific formulation when he referred to Jesus as "the last Adam" (I Cor. 15:45; cf. I Cor. 15:22; Rom. 5:12-19).[5] In contrast to Adam, whose sin had deadly results for his descendants, Jesus gives men mem-

---

York: Charles Scribner's Sons, 1932). Vincent Taylor states both sides in *Historical Evidence for the Virgin Birth* (New York and London: Oxford University Press, 1920).

[5] See Elias Andrews, *op. cit.*, pp. 93-96.

bership in a new form of human life—both now and at the final resurrection.

In these assertions that Jesus represents human life with a difference, we see an example of a frequent tendency in New Testament thinking about Jesus. The New Testament disciples and writers recognize and defend his real humanity. They know he shares many qualities with other men and leaders. But they are never satisfied to describe him as being like other men. Deep conviction born of faith makes them emphasize the differences between Jesus and others who may share a quality or title. His oneness with mankind is a fact. But it is not the only fact. And they cannot rest until they have at least partly understood and stated the difference they sense. He was a man but his birth required more than a human explanation, his life was free from the moral flaws which mar other men, and he began a new stage in the life of humanity which puts him, like Adam, at the head of a new race of men.

As we turn now to study the titles which Christians used to express the work and nature of Jesus, we see again how they sensed the uniqueness of Jesus. They knew that he shared many titles with other divinely sent leaders, but they could only describe him satisfactorily by reaching out for titles which recognize his unique role and nature.[6]

Prophet and Teacher

Jesus was a prophet and teacher. In this he was like many Old Testament spokesmen for God. He followed the prophet John the Baptist, and like John, he gathered disciples and taught men. He was much like the rabbis of his day. The rabbi had his followers, who learned their message and their place in Jewish leadership by accompanying their leader, hearing him, watching what he did, and discussing problems with him. It is not surprising that Jesus, according to Matthew, Mark, and John, was called Rabbi and was considered by many a rabbi with a group of disciples who were learning his interpretation of the Law (e.g., Matt. 26:25; Mark 9:5; John 3:2).[7]

[6] For a brief study of over fifty of the titles of Jesus, see Vincent Taylor, *The Names of Jesus* (New York: St. Martin's Press, 1953). On the six titles Reginald H. Fuller considers most important, see his *The Mission and Achievement of Jesus* (Chicago: Alec R. Allenson, Inc., 1954), ch. iv.

[7] The R.S.V. uses "Master" for the translation of most of the gospel uses of "rabbi."

The Gospels contain several titles which among Jews all point to the same general view of Jesus. Preacher, teacher, Rabbi, Master, prophet—they all carry the idea of a God-given message, a teaching ministry, and a group of followers who live with their master and learn his message by personal relation rather than merely in a classroom. Because he taught with a fresh note of direct authority, and never with a mere desire to hand on inherited ideas, and because he always spoke with the burning consciousness that God was speaking through him an urgent word which not only challenged the mind but also demanded the decision of men, the one of these titles which most fully represents the relation of Jesus to his hearers is that of prophet.[8] The people who heard him knew that in him lived again the rugged independence and power of the noted prophets of former times (Mark 8:27-28). This man was speaking for God and claiming men's lives for God.

To be a prophet was to be one of a high and select group of Israel's leaders. It was to be God's spokesmen among his people and to bring God's word and claim to his people. But high as the role was, it came to its climax in a still more unique role. There had been in the Old Testament and in Judaism the expectation that God would send a special prophet, a climactic spokesman for God's purpose. This expectation appears in Deut. 18:15: "The Lord your God will raise up for you a prophet like me from among you, from your brethren." Another form of this special expectation was the idea that Elijah would return at the end to perform the final prophetic work before God's final action in history (Mal. 4:5).

In popular thought the possibility was considered that Jesus might be the expected Elijah or the prophet like Moses (Mark 6:15; 8:28; John 1:21). But while Jesus and the early church were ready to grant these roles to John the Baptist (Mark 9:13),[9] they did not apply them to Jesus himself. That would have been to give to Jesus a preparatory role, inferior to the role of the Messiah himself, and both Jesus' own conviction of his own role and the universal belief of the early church reserved to Jesus the highest role Israel could assign—the role of God's chosen Messiah. Popular expectation, as we have noted, held Jesus to be a

[8] See H. A. Guy, New Testament Prophecy (London: Epworth Press, 1947), ch. iii.
[9] John the Baptist rejects such identification in John 1:21.

prophet; indeed, he spoke of himself as one (Luke 4:24). Yet his own thought and that of his followers could not stop at that. They could not rest content even with giving him the role of the great final prophet whose work prepared for the coming of the messianic age. His role was not preliminary but decisive, for he was the Christ.

The role of prophet, however, carries authority in a way which recalls a more favored title used in the church. The prophet was not a mere teacher and announcer of God's word to men. His work was effective in carrying forward God's will.[10] He could speak with authority and command loyalty. This aspect of Jesus' work his followers fully recognized, but, as we shall see, they preferred to indicate it by calling him their Lord. After the Resurrection the title prophet seemed inadequate to express his dominant role, and the title Lord continued and surpassed the note of authority which the title prophet expressed.

The Messiah

Jesus was "an Israelite indeed" (John 1:47), loyal to his people and deeply concerned for their good; and he was specifically the expected Messianic leader, the Christ of Israel. This we have noted in considering his relation to Israel and the Old Testament. He so understood his role, and while his disciples during his ministry could not understand the place of suffering in that work,[11] they came to grasp this connection, and they never doubted his messiahship once the Resurrection had interpreted his death as a part of God's plan and a factor in achieving God's work.

Yet messiahship was a role which in its generally accepted form he could not fulfill. It commonly included too strong a nationalistic and military atmosphere. And he clearly rejected the nationalistic and military features which the Messianic hope expressed in the Son-of-David idea.

The dream that a great Son of David would liberate Israel and give

[10] See H. Wheeler Robinson, *Inspiration and Revelation in the Old Testament* (New York: Oxford University Press, 1946), part IV, especially pp. 170 ff.

[11] Since W. Wrede explained all such passages as a dogmatic intrusion into the gospel tradition (*Das Messiasgeheimnis in den Evangelien*, Göttingen, 1901), many have considered them unauthentic. But see A. E. J. Rawlinson, *St. Mark* (2nd ed.; London, 1927), pp. 258-62; and T. W. Manson, "Realized Eschatology and the Messianic Secret," in *Studies in the Gospels: Essays in Memory of R. H. Lightfoot*, ed. D. E. Nineham (Oxford: Basil Blackwell & Mott, 1955), pp. 209-22.

them a leadership both political and spiritual inspired many of Jesus' contemporaries (II Sam. 7:12, 16; Isa. 11:1; Jer. 23:5).[12] Both Jesus and the church accepted this view in a spiritual sense. Yet he was wary of permitting people to call him the Son of David, because it would encourage people to think of him in political and military terms, and because by plausible misinterpretation it could be taken by the Romans as a call to revolt against Roman rule.

His sense of the unsatisfactory nature of the Son-of-David title was so great that toward the end of his life he took the initiative in declaring that the Messiah would not be the Son of David in the way that people expected him to be (Mark 12:35-37). This unexpected declaration may be interpreted in two ways. It may completely reject any connection of the Messiah with Davidic descent and the Son-of-David expectation. Probably Jesus did not intend to go so far. But at the very least, it declares that the Messiah is not bound to conform to the political and military pattern of David's reign—a pattern which many Jews expected the Messiah to repeat. In either case, it is clear that for Jesus the title Son of David gave at least in part a false idea of the messianic role of God's Christ.

The Suffering Servant

Moreover, even the role of Messiah required restatement. It was a title elastic in meaning, but in general usage its meaning was practically identical with the Son-of-David title. Jesus' basic rejection of political and military methods inherent in the latter title forced him also to break with most current ideas about the Messiah.

Even the anticipation that the Messiah would have prestige and easy triumph could not express Jesus' conviction. The spirit of his entire ministry was one of humble and unselfish service to others at cost to himself; the principle of the Cross was, as we have said, inherent in his entire ministry. And as hostility to his message and leadership continued to confront him, he increasingly saw that the way of God's anointed leader could not be one of unbroken prestige and easy triumph. The

[12] See Ch. Guignebert, *The Jewish World in the Time of Jesus*, tr. S. H. Hooke (New York, 1939), Bk. II, ch. iv, especially pp. 138 ff., and J. Klausner, *The Messianic Idea in Israel*, tr. W. F. Stinespring (New York: The Macmillan Co., 1955).

Messianic idea took form in the light of the Suffering Servant figure who climaxes Old Testament prophecy (Isa. 52:13–53:12).[13]

The practical effect of this was to eclipse the popular Messianic expectation and idea. While Jesus could hold that he was fulfilling the genuine spiritual center of that expectation, he could never let his followers rest content with current views; the criticism of those views was the notable thing about his attitude to Messianic expectations. The interpretation of messiahship in terms of voluntarily accepted suffering became his dominant note.[14] The Messianic fulfillment had historic significance in carrying forward the hope of Israel, but it was a fulfillment which transformed the inherited expectation. He purified and refined it in the light of the deepest levels of Scripture.

This helps to explain the fact that the word Christ or Messiah soon dropped out of use as a title of Jesus. The church preserved it, for it expressed the tie of Jesus with the Old Testament, with Israel, and with Messianic expectation. But it was preserved by being made a proper name, and when thus used, the way was clear for other titles to declare his role in more clear-cut and adequate terms. Every New Testament writer if questioned would have asserted instantly that Jesus was the expected Messiah or Christ of the Jews. But the total work and meaning of Jesus were too great to express in that term, and it therefore could not be the center of New Testament testimony about the person of Christ.

The Son of Man

The title Son of Man was another title whose former meaning was utilized and yet transcended. It was the favorite self-designation of Jesus, occurring thirty-one times in Matthew, fourteen in Mark, twenty-five in Luke and thirteen in John. This might have been expected to guarantee its permanent place in the usage of his followers. But like the title Christ, it was both honored and soon dropped from current church use. Except for one use by Stephen in Acts 7:56, it never occurs in the New Testament outside of the Gospels, where it is always a direct or quoted word

[13] On the interpretation of the Suffering Servant passages see Christopher R. North, *The Suffering Servant in Deutero-Isaiah* (New York: Oxford University Press, 1948); H. H. Rowley, *The Servant of the Lord and Other Essays on the Old Testament* (London: Lutterworth Press, 1952), pp. 3-88.

[14] So William Manson, *Jesus the Messiah*.

of Jesus himself. With a sense of historical accuracy, the church preserved it in his sayings. By preference it used other titles to express his
greatness.

This title Son of Man was deeply rooted in the Jewish background.
In fact, the New Testament gives no title to Jesus for which some
Jewish background cannot be found. "Son of man" was used in Ps. 8:4
to refer to man. It frequently occurs in Ezekiel as God's address to the
prophet, frail, human, but yet God's spokesman (e.g., 2:1). In Dan.
7:13 occurs a passage of great importance. Here the seer sees in vision
"one like a son of man"; that is, one in human form. He represents "the
people of the saints of the Most High." (Dan. 7:27.) The idea is
collective. Later, in such writings as the Book of Enoch, "Son of Man"
became used of a specific individual and he was closely linked with the
presence, power, and action of God.[15]

This individual reference recurs in the words of Jesus, who uses "Son
of Man" to refer in a veiled way to himself. But something of the collective reference of Daniel may remain in his meaning.[16] We today tend
to draw a sharp distinction between an individual and a collective reference, but the Hebrew sense of solidarity did not do that. Both a personal
and a collective reference might be present, with now one and now the
other predominating. This appears to be the case in the references to
the Servant in Deutero-Isaiah. It likewise may very well have been true
in Jesus' references to the Son of Man, although as far as the evidence
in the Gospels goes, the individual, personal reference to himself certainly predominated. But however we settle this question, the Old
Testament and Jewish background of the Son-of-Man title is beyond
question. It was not familiar or widely intelligible to Gentiles.

For Jesus the title blended features from more than one Jewish source.[17]
It had that sense of humble life and frail human existence which the
Old Testament conception included. Because Jesus saw increasingly
that his humble and frail human life was moving toward actual suffering

[15] See Rudolph Otto, *The Kingdom of God and the Son of Man*, tr. Floyd V. Filson
and Bertram Lee Woolf (Grand Rapids: Zondervan Pub. Co., 1938), pp. 176 ff.

[16] T. W. Manson has argued for this view in *The Teaching of Jesus*, pp. 211-36.
Cf. also Theo Preiss, *Life in Christ*, tr. Harold Knight (Chicago: Alec R. Allenson,
1954), ch. III, "The Mystery of the Son of Man."

[17] See Andrew C. Zenos, *The Plastic Age of the Gospel* (New York: The Macmillan
Co., 1927), pp. 66-68.

and death, he referred to his coming death in terms of what would happen to the Son of Man. The victory of God's people as depicted in Daniel, however, and the heavenly honor and role which the Book of Enoch reflects, were also taken up in Jesus' references to the coming triumph and victory of the Son of Man. Yet the victory did not eclipse the fact of rejection and impending death. The Christ must suffer, as Jesus came to see; the Son of Man must suffer.

The central Old Testament figure for Jesus' life and thought was not the expected Christ or the Son of Man but the Suffering Servant. All other titles get their meaning from that central figure. Just as Jesus used the title Christ with an adapted meaning, so he poured his own meaning into his favorite self-designation Son of Man, and it was the meaning derived from the Suffering Servant coupled with the triumph which God had promised his Servant. He was the Son of Man in the form of the Servant.

It is easy to see why the church did not continue to use the Son of Man title in its preaching and thinking. The title was not discarded; it retained its rightful place in the sayings of Jesus. But it was a term with no clearly fixed meaning even for Jews; Jesus had to define it in terms of what he undertook to do, and in terms of the Servant figure of the Scripture. It was not clear or adequate even to his Jewish believers. To Gentiles it was a strange and uncongenial term. The New Testament writers therefore use other titles to express in a fuller and clearer way what Jesus means to them.

Savior, Mediator, High Priest

An important group of titles conveys the early Christian conviction that through Christ, God has provided for his followers redemption from sin and death. These titles are not descriptions of his nature or person so much as statements of what he has done and still does for those who put their faith in him.

Since Christians had received through him release from sin, guilt, and fear of death, he was their Savior (e.g., Luke 2:11; Acts 5:31; 13:23; Eph. 5:23; Phil. 3:20; II Tim. 1:10; Tit. 1:4; 2:13; 3:6; II Pet. 1:1).[18] This title is not used often to refer to Jesus, and it is not frequent in the

[18] See the word study by Burton Scott Easton, *The Pastoral Epistles* (New York: Charles Scribner's Sons, 1947), pp. 229-32.

earliest writings, but the gratitude it expresses for spiritual help received is an attitude which constantly appears from the earliest days of the church.

Since Christians as sinners had felt their separation from the holy God and had found in Christ the way to reconciliation and reunion with the Father, he was their Mediator (I Tim. 2:5; Heb. 8:6; 9:15; 12:24).[19] This term too occurs but rarely, although it likewise expresses the general Christian sense that through Christ the barriers that blocked fellowship with God had been removed and believers could now worship and serve God with confidence and joy. Christ had brought the grace of God to men, and had brought men to God, as no other had done or could do. Therefore, he was not merely one mediator among others equally capable of giving such help; to all who believed in him, he proved the sole and unique Mediator.

To the writer of Hebrews, who thought in terms of the priestly ritual and ministry of the Old Testament, Christ was the true High Priest.[20] He had done effectively what the Levitical priesthood could only typify and promise; he had put an end to all human priesthoods, for he had offered the one effective sacrifice for sin and now continually makes intercession for his people. He ministers in the heavenly tabernacle. Upon his entrance there he first offers his sacrifice for men's sins. That sacrifice need never be repeated. There he remains to offer priestly intercession for his people in all their need (Heb. 4:14; 7:25; 9:1–10:14).

All such titles seek to express how adequately Christ has provided salvation from the guilt and grip of sin. They express the conviction that he has done more than human ministry could ever have accomplished. Only God could deal thus with sin. The greatness of his work points to a personal greatness that transcends human nature. Implicit in such titles is a high Christology.

"Jesus Christ Is Lord"

Most frequently used of all New Testament titles for Jesus is the title Kyrios, "Lord." The title Christ soon became a proper name, and

---

[19] The noted study by Emil Brunner, The Mediator, tr. Olive Wyon (New York: The Macmillan Co., 1934), is a general theological study rather than an exegetical study. It sees the importance of this biblical term for understanding the gospel.

[20] See C. Spicq, op. cit., Vol. I, especially pp. 291-300.

so does not really occupy the central theological role that its continual use might at first suggest. Lord was the universal and central title which the church used to suggest the decisive role and importance of Jesus Christ. It occurs in every New Testament writing except the three Johannine epistles; obviously the entire church joined in the use of this high title.

It was a word which had had wide use. By original meaning "Lord" was an adjective, which described someone as "having power or authority." It was used of men who had authoritative position; it was especially used of kings. It was also widely used of gods; as Paul said, in the pagan world there were "many gods and many lords" (I Cor. 8:5). Its common use for deities of the time occurs in ancient writings, inscriptions, and papyri.[21] But the Greek Old Testament also used it to refer to God himself. It translated not only the Hebrew word for Lord but also the word Yahweh. Thus the word had a wide usage, ranging all the way from a polite term of social address to the title of the one true God of Israel. It did not necessarily express divinity, but it could do so, and often did.

The New Testament use of Lord for Jesus appears to go back to Jesus himself. In a famous passage, which we may accept as authentic, for it would never have occurred to the church to invent it, Jesus says that the Messiah is not the Son of David. He is David's Lord (Mark 12:37). The early sermons of Acts, which embody very early Christian tradition, use the title of Jesus (Acts 2:36). The Aramaic exclamation and prayer of I Cor. 16:22, Maranatha, "Our Lord, Come!" (cf. Rev. 22:20), confirms the other evidence that the title was no late intrusion into Christian vocabulary, but was known and used in the early Aramaic-speaking days of the church.[22]

Once the Christians were convinced that Jesus was risen and exalted to the right hand of God, where he had a position of honor and authority on behalf of the Father, the naturalness of designating him by the title Lord is manifest. He was acting for God the Father and with the

---

[21] Adolf Deissmann, *Light From the Ancient East*, tr. Lionel R. M. Strachan (New York: Doubleday, Doran & Co., 1927), pp. 349-57.

[22] For the opposite view see Wilhelm Bousset, *Kyrios Christos* (3rd ed.; Göttingen, 1926), pp. 77-101. A. E. J. Rawlinson answers him in *The New Testament Doctrine of the Christ* (New York: Longmans, Green & Co., 1926), pp. 231-37.

Father's power and authority. This high position of present honor and authority enables us to understand a remarkable practice of the early Greek-speaking church, in which they applied to Jesus their risen Lord Old Testament sayings which referred to Yahweh (whose Hebrew name had been translated "Lord" in the Greek Old Testament). Even during Jesus' earthly ministry the title could have meaning for disciples as they thought of his miraculous power and authoritative teaching. But its New Testament use for that period is sparing, and the evidence indicates that only for the period after his resurrection and exaltation did the title seem fully suited to be his common and central title. He was then effectively and unquestionably the anointed Lord, who had acted for God in his earthly career and was now acting for the Father to continue and complete the divine purpose.

"Judge of the Living and the Dead"

Coupled with this title Lord was the title Judge. It was common early Christian expectation that all men, including the Christians, must face divine judgment at the last day. The basic Christian message announced that the risen Lord would act for the Father at that judgment. He would have and exercise the authority to pronounce the final divine judgment on all mankind. The pictorial portrayal of the judgment in Matt. 25:31-46, a section which many Christians have taken as a non-Christological passage, teaching only human kindness, indicates that Jesus himself thought of his work as extending to that final judgment. Moreover, his sayings about denying before the Father those who have denied him also indicate that his word will be decisive at the end (Mark 8:38; Luke 12:8-9). So it is not surprising that the early church picked up this note of Jesus' teaching and spoke of him as the active authoritative agent of the Father's final judgment (Acts 10:42; II Cor. 5:10).

Neither the title Lord nor the designation as Judge is in itself a statement as to the nature of Jesus. But the task which these titles assign him is no human task. The universal use of the title Lord and the wide reference to him as Judge show that in the worship and thought of the earliest Christians, Jesus already occupied a place which demanded a high doctrine of his person. He was exercising the power and authority

146

of God himself. His unique role and work called for a Christology adequate to express what he had done, was doing, and was expected to do.

Christ and the Father

Thus the urge and drive of Christian worship and thought rapidly pushed the Christians to link Christ explicitly with the Father. As far back as we can trace the mind of the early Christians, this conclusion is already pressing itself upon Christian consciousness. In their worship they were unhesitatingly ascribing to Christ what they could only expect from God. And worship was the forerunner of explicit Christology.

We can see in the earliest letters of Paul the material of which later Christological formulations were made. In these earliest New Testament documents Paul prays that the readers may receive the divine gifts of grace jointly from "God the Father and our Lord Jesus Christ" (Gal. 1:3). These are divine gifts; they come jointly from the Father and Christ. The doctrine of the deity of Christ, while not explicitly formulated, is already implicit in the worship and confession of these earliest New Testament writings. The early church never passed through a preliminary stage in which their thought centered in a merely human Jesus. As far back as we can trace early Christian worship and thought, they centered about a divine Lord. Questions remained; clear and explicit definition was still to come; but the essential position is present from the first.

The Son of God

No attempt occurs to identify the Lord Christ with the Father. Not even John 10:30 means that. The sense of the real human life of Jesus of Nazareth was too vivid to permit identification with the Father. But the link uniting the Father and the Lord of the church was close and unique. It was widely expressed by calling Jesus the Son of God, or simply the Son. While this title was widely used to refer to angels (Gen. 6:2), to Israel (Ex. 4:22), and even to men or outstanding human agents of God (II Sam. 7:14), the Christians used it from the first to designate Jesus and assert that he had a unique and intimate bond with the Father himself. It occurs so frequently and so naturally in the letters of Paul that it plainly was no new title, but one long

147

accepted and nowhere challenged (e.g., Gal. 2:20). It therefore is not surprising that it is common usage in the later New Testament writings, especially since it expressed the closest relation to God and suited well the risen and exalted Christ.

It may be suggested that this title was congenial to Hellenistic Christians, but would not have found use among the early Jewish Christians of Palestine. Evidence points to the contrary conclusion. The Gospels indicate that the title had been a part of the gospel tradition all along, and that it had been used during the ministry of Jesus, and even by Jesus himself. Jewish and Aramaic setting is suggested by the peculiar idiom of Mark 5:7, "What to me and to you, Jesus, Son of the Most High God?" (that is, "What have we in common?" or "What have we to do with each other?"). Both the Marcan and the Q tradition report that Jesus spoke of himself as the Son (Mark 13:32; Matt. 11:27; Luke 10:22); the continual usage of the Gospel of John has substantial Synoptic parallels.

This title could express mainly the messianic role of Jesus, and undoubtedly in some uses this is at least part of its essential meaning (e.g., Matt. 3:17; 4:3; 16:16).[23] However, it almost inevitably implies also a unique and close relation to God the Father, and as the early church thought about it, they became convinced that Jesus was the Son of God in a sense that transcended special function and included unique nature and relation to God. The later Nicene definition of this unique nature, that the Son is of the same essence as the Father, was not yet clearly in mind, but that definition has broad base in the strong New Testament affirmation of the divine nature of Jesus as the Son of God.

The Logos

Closely allied with the title Son of God was the title Logos or Word. Both titles indicate a vital link with the nature of God. Both suggest clearly the divine nature of Jesus, the Son or incarnate Logos. Both, however, preserve the sense that the reference to God is not exhausted by speaking of the Son or Logos; in a real sense the Father can and must be distinguished from this Son or Logos.

[23] Gustaf Dalman, *The Words of Jesus*, Eng. tr. from the German (Edinburgh, 1909), studies the title on pp. 268-89.

The title Logos had a long and varied history before it came to be applied to Jesus. It is interesting to read the controversy as to whether its real roots are Jewish or Hellenistic. Scholars of Semitic competence assert the kinship of the title in the Gospel of John with the Semitic background.[24] They can cite the idea of the Word in quite ancient Mesopotamian sources. They can point to the role of the creative word of God in the Old Testament and apocryphal writings. They can show that this concept is personified (Pss. 107:20; 147:15; Isa. 55:11), a fact which may serve as some preparation for the personal use of the Logos in the Gospel of John. They can show how the word of God is powerful in the prophets. They can also refer to the wisdom teaching of the Old Testament and later writings (Prov. 8:22-31; Wis. of Sol. 7:22-8:1), where wisdom is assigned the same roles of presence (or agency) at creation, activity in God's providential guidance of his world, and illumination of man—features found in the Johannine Logos idea. They may include a reference to the Aramaic word *Memra* or Word, used in rabbinical writings to represent the outgoing speech and action of God.

Yet scholars versed in Hellenistic philosophy and religion in Hellenistic sources find striking parallels to the Johannine prologue. It is not simply that Heraclitus, the Greek philosopher, and the Stoic school spoke of the immanent Logos. Philo, the Hellenistic Jew of Alexandria, seeking to show the unity of the Mosaic Law and the Greek philosophy, uses this philosophy to interpret the Law in terms of the Logos, the active, outgoing Word of God, whom Philo can even call a "second god" to indicate the divine nature and dignity of the Logos.[25]

The truth is that the Logos idea has both Semitic and Hellenistic roots, and that is precisely why the writer of the Gospel of John could use it effectively to introduce his work. It expressed, as did the title Son of God, the idea of an agent of God, divine in nature, present in men, and active in history to carry forward the divine purpose. The Christian

[24] E.g., William Foxwell Albright, *From the Stone Age to Christianity* (Baltimore: Johns Hopkins Press, 1940), p. 285.
[25] On Philo and the Logos teaching of the Gospel of John, see C. H. Dodd, *The Interpretation of the Fourth Gospel* (London: Cambridge University Press, 1953), pp. 54-73, 263-85. Dodd also discusses other Hellenistic parallels and the Semitic background. See also C. K. Barrett, *The Gospel According to St. John* (London, 1955), pp. 127-30.

use of Logos to explain how a specific person of history could be both decisive for redemption and divine in nature has no full parallel in earlier use of the term. Only the Christians testified that "the Logos became flesh" (John 1:14)[26] and by his death as the Lamb of God "takes away the sin of the world" (John 1:29). But there had been wide preparation for this Christian use, and its meaning was close to that which Son of God came to carry in the Apostolic Age.

The deep kinship between the titles Son of God and Logos quickly appears when we compare key passages in the New Testament. Comparison of I Cor. 8:6 with Col. 1:13 ff. shows that the position in both passages is the same, although the former is too brief to be entirely clear. The three clear key passages are John 1:1-18; Col. 1:13-23; and Heb. 1:1-4. In the first of these passages the gospel writer uses the title Logos; Paul and the writer of Hebrews use the more familiar title Son. Yet they agree in all essentials. They speak of one who is divine in nature and acts for the Father in creating the world, upholding it, and effecting redemption for God's people.

Thus Logos in the Gospel of John and Son in Colossians and Hebrews have essentially the same content. But Logos was too technical and philosophical a word to gain general currency. Son or Son of God was the title which the church preferred from the first, in part because it had roots in Judaism, in Jesus' own usage, and in gentile areas. The title grew in the content it carried; the stress on the divine function of the Son was not lost, but the assertion of the divine nature of the Son grew clearer as time went on.

"Our Great God and Savior"

This tendency and interest of the church came to its climax in the use of the word God to state the nature and role of Jesus Christ. Thus the church made explicit the affirmation of divine nature which it implied in the titles Lord and Son of God. The New Testament does not often use the designation God for Christ, and it is not possible to determine how many passages contain it. Some cases are ambiguous; the reference may be to God the Father rather than to God the Son. It is possible, but not probable, that Jesus Christ is called God in Rom. 9:5;

[26] Cf. Augustine, *Confessions*, bk. VII, ch. ix.

more likely the expression is an ejaculation of praise to God. Tit. 2:13 is another passage which is uncertain, but here the reference to Jesus Christ as both God and Savior is more probable. The same problem that the Titus passage presents is shown in II Pet. 1:1, and with the same probability that "our (great) God and Savior Jesus Christ" is the correct translation. Phil. 2:6, in saying that Christ Jesus had existed in the form of God, comes close to open use of the word God to define the identity of Jesus Christ. The Gospel of John clearly and unmistakably uses "God" in referring to the Logos in 1:1 and to the risen Jesus in 20:28.

The worship of the Apostolic Church had been preparing for just such an affirmation. And worship, rather than intellectual curiosity, is theology's cradle and basic stimulus. From the beginning of the Apostolic Church, Jesus had been hailed by believers as both Christ and Lord. As Lord he had effectively exercised the rule of God over his people. He had been regarded as being, with the Father, the joint source of the divine blessings which the Christians received. Prayer to him was not unknown (Acts 7:59). Obviously Jesus was no mere man to these Christians. He was so linked with God the Father that they had to recognize his high rank and unique nature as "our great God and Savior." The use of the designation God to define that high nature was the logical crystallization of the attitude which worship and thought had presaged throughout the course of the Apostolic Age.

Yet the rarity of the use of God as a designation for Christ had its good reasons in the consciousness of the Christian believers. They could never forget the human life of Jesus of Nazareth. They could not let his life disappear in the infinite reaches of deity. They insisted on his true human life, his dramatic human struggle and victory, his historic ministry and his convincing obedience to his Father's will. In a very real sense Jesus was subject to the Father, and it is not surprising to find Paul giving clear expression to that subordinate role in I Cor. 15:27-28. The church had to come to clear confession of the deity they implied when they reverently recognized Jesus Christ as exalted Lord, and when in worship they addressed the Father through him. But they refused to lose sight of the human life which was the focal point of history and the instrument of the decisive divine action of history. And when they used the word God of Jesus Christ, they did not mean to identify him with the Father. The human life of Jesus meant that the term God could not wholly state the nature and significance of Jesus. But the reverse was also true. The transcendent greatness of Christ the risen and exalted Lord meant that from the first the church could not express his greatness in terms of purely human greatness. God was present and active in Christ. Risen and exalted, he was exercising the functions of God; he was again "in the form of God" (Phil. 2:6). In this respect, the church could not rest until it dared to call him God.

Summary

It will be well to summarize the results of the study we have made in this chapter.

1. First of all, we see, though our list is by no means complete, the amazing variety of titles which the New Testament uses of Jesus. This variety results from a driving urge to describe adequately and accurately what Jesus Christ has done for his followers. Because his work has been so unique, effective, and fruitful, believers continually seek out titles which will more adequately describe the One who has done such unparalleled good and has played so central a role in God's work.

2. In the second place, we see a sifting process under way. The search for adequate terms leads the church to drop some terms as inadequate or not clear; "Servant" is an example. The church gives other titles a lesser place because they cannot serve adequately the widening needs of worship and mission work. "Messiah" or "Christ" drops from central use as a title for this reason. And the Church enlarges the content of terms which previously had not carried so rich a meaning. The title "Logos" is an example. This milling process, in which the church experiments and rejects some terms because they are not sufficiently clear or comprehensive or expandable, is an impressive testimony to the immense significance which Jesus had for faith, worship, and thought. The search goes on until the highest terms are seized, used, and even expanded in content, because nothing less can express what the worshiping, thinking church wants to say.

3. In the third place, the church increasingly concentrates its atten-

tion on those titles which express unique position and unique relation to God. Minor titles occur in great number; Jesus is called prophet, teacher, apostle, shepherd, and many other things which could also be applied to other divinely sent leaders. But the center of attention moves to the unique role and unique titles which can rightly be used only of Jesus himself. They are titles which relate him uniquely and essentially with the Father, or which can also be used of the Father. Jesus, like the Father, can be described as Savior, Lord, and even God. Only titles which express his uniqueness in history, his effective redemptive work, and his divine nature finally satisfy the consciousness of the New Testament church. The terms may expand with the passing of time, and the essence conception of Greek philosophy may in time give new shading to the Christian thinking of earlier generations; but the solid basis of later doctrinal statements is present in New Testament worship and in its use of high and unique titles to express the identity and significance of Jesus. His life is recognized as standing in unique and permanent relationship with the Father.

4. The fourth important fact is that this development has roots in the consciousness of Jesus himself. Scholarly attention most often centers on the question whether Jesus thought of himself as the Messiah the Jews expected. We have seen good reason to conclude that he did so think of his role. But an even more central question is whether he thought of his role as that of Lord and Judge and Son of God. Not merely in the early church preaching and letters, not merely in the Gospel of John, but also in the Synoptic Gospels we find a clear answer. He expected to fulfill the role of authoritative Lord of God's people. He warned his hearers that they would have to reckon with him at the last judgment, and he was conscious of holding a unique relation to God.

Criticism has often tried to date late and so discount the key passages which point to this conclusion. It is a desperate measure. It would require us not only to discredit all the basic attitudes of the first generation of disciples, but also to reject the common witness of all the Gospels and their identifiable sources. The one way in which we can intelligibly explain the origin of the New Testament writings and make logical the rise of the Christian church is to accept the common basic testimony of the entire New Testament: Jesus knew that he had the unique and decisive role of all God's work in history; he knew that he stood in a unique relation to the Father in his personal life and nature; and so he gave to the church the basis for identifying him as Christ, Suffering Servant, Savior, Lord, Son of God, and even in a real sense God. This makes sense of these writings. No other view leaves of them anything but discredited wreckage of deluded opinions.

Historical study, no matter how rigid it may claim to be, gives no reason to reject this consistently high New Testament view of Jesus Christ. Such historical study will find here a consistent, naturally developing, and wholesomely varied witness to the unique and divine nature of Jesus. Only faith can accept and really understand that witness. But only lack of clarity or openness can lead a student to deny that it is the essentially united witness of the New Testament.

5. The key passages about the Logos and the Son of God point us to still a fifth fact about the New Testament view of the person of Christ. A tendency emerges to expand the role of Christ from the brief historical career of Jesus of Nazareth to the full sweep of the world's history. Just as the God of Israel is the God of creation and the God to whom all must finally answer, so Jesus Christ is not merely the Suffering Servant who redeems men by his work at a definite period of time, but also the agent of God in creation and in judgment as well as in redemption.

There are three things to note about this amazing affirmation.

a) It was early; it occurs in I Cor. 8:6 and in Col. 1:13-23, and so was present and apparently unchallenged in the circles Paul knew in the middle fifties of the first century.

b) It was an expression of the church's sense of the immense greatness and significance of Christ. His work and relation to God were no passing phases of the divine plan; he was so deeply related to God that he must be related to the divine activity throughout the course of history. All through history he is God's agent in the divine work: in creation, in upholding and carrying forward the life of men, in redemption, in lordship over God's people, in defeating evil, and in judging all God's creatures.

c) Yet this development of faith and thought was held within bounds. Christian faith and thought felt driven to go this far to express the full greatness of the person of Christ. But the sense of the radically new work which he had done in his earthly career, death, and resurrection remained vivid and constant; the church never let the wider work of the Son or Logos obscure that human life and work. It is part of the greatness of New Testament faith and thought that it never let itself be dazzled into neglecting the heart of its message, that God came into human life in Jesus Christ and through that human life did the highest divine work and achieved the highest divine purpose.

That historical action must be kept central. Therefore the church never gave the central place to the wider view of the Son of God as active in the total cosmic work of the Father. The maximum revelation, the greatest divine work, the one effective redemption came through Jesus of Nazareth.

When theology loses this fact from view and gives the accent to general lofty propositions, it loses the New Testament emphasis and denatures the Gospel. The highest view of the person of Christ keeps the work of God in Jesus of Nazareth at the center of attention and thought. It is the task of biblical and all Christian theology to grasp and state in fullest context, but with unblurred historical perspective, that central divine work of all time. Indeed, it was the concern for what God did in Jesus of Nazareth that led to the high Christology of the New Testament. The return to the New Testament understanding of what God did in Jesus of Nazareth will always confirm the church in that high Christology.

CHAPTER VIII

Christ and the Spirit

TO UNDERSTAND THE ROLE OF THE SPIRIT OF GOD IN THE life and thought of the Apostolic Age we must think in post-resurrection terms. Nowhere is it clearer that to understand the New Testament message, we have to allow full force to the effect which the resurrection of Jesus had on the worship and thinking of his disciples. It is both necessary and profitable to look back to the earlier stages and see what the role of the Spirit was in those earlier times. But once Christians knew that Jesus had been raised from the dead, their thought of God's working proceeded in the light of that basic fact, and they even gained new light on earlier events from what God had done in Christ and was doing through the Spirit. It was as a sequel to the Resurrection that they received the Holy Spirit, and they thought of the Spirit in the light of that event.

With this perspective in mind, we may turn to three brief background studies before we consider directly the gift of the Spirit to the church and the Spirit's work in the church. We need to study: 1. the place of the Spirit in the Old Testament, 2. the work of the Spirit in the life and career of Jesus, and 3. the importance of the exaltation (or ascension) of Jesus for New Testament thinking about the Holy Spirit.

The Spirit in the Old Testament

In the Old Testament the Spirit of God is essentially the power or presence of God at work in this world. He works here through his Spirit.[1] This implies that he greatly transcends this world which we

[1] See the article by George Johnston on "Spirit, Holy Spirit," in A Theological Word Book of the Bible, ed. Alan Richardson (London: SCM Press, 1950); also Norman H. Snaith, The Distinctive Ideas of the Old Testament (Philadelphia: Westminster Press, 1946), ch. vii.

know. In his infinite greatness he cannot be confined within the limits of man's observation and action. Yet God, great as he is, is no absent or unconcerned deity. God, or the Spirit of God, creates the world and human life, and maintains that life by his power.[2] Indeed, inherent in the very idea of the divine Spirit is the sense of activity and power. The Spirit is no passive presence. Where the Spirit is, divine action takes place, and men receive gifts for special work. The Spirit "comes upon" men at critical times or when there is special need, and causes striking effects and notable achievements.

One specific effect of the coming of the Spirit upon a man is the gift of wisdom which makes him able to perform his special work or mission. Bezalel receives wisdom and skill for his work on the tabernacle (Exod. 35:30-35). The Spirit moves the judges to lead in war and to govern (Judg. 3:10). The Branch, the descendant of David, will have the Spirit of wisdom given him for his messianic work (Isa. 11:2). Later, especially in the Apocrypha, the Spirit gives wisdom to men and this makes them friends of God (Wis. of Sol. 7:27; 9:17). Here appears a more settled indwelling of wisdom than early references to the gift of wisdom for specific tasks and crises.

This gift of wisdom and guidance lay back of the utterances of the prophets and the writing of the scriptural books.[3] It was essential to the very nature of the prophetic mission that the prophet spoke as prompted by God. This direction may simply be traced to God, but at times it is assigned to the working of the Spirit of God (Mic. 3:8; Isa. 61:1). No real difference exists between these two ways of speaking, except that the reference to the Spirit's working more clearly preserves the sense of the transcendent greatness of God.

The role of the Spirit in writing the books which came to constitute Scripture was not emphasized so early. The New Testament shows, however, that by the days of Jesus and the Apostles this idea was clearly present. David spoke as "inspired by the Holy Spirit." (Mark 12:36.) A more general statement is that "men moved by the Holy Spirit spoke

[2] I think Rudolf Bultmann's existentialist approach to the New Testament message fails to do justice to God's transcendent greatness, and Bultmann finds no real role for the gift of the Spirit to men.
[3] Cf. E. F. Scott, The Spirit in the New Testament (New York: Doubleday, Doran & Co., 1923), pp. 27 ff.

from God." (II Pet. 1:21.) Whether we understand the Greek of II Tim. 3:16 to say that "All Scripture is inspired by God and profitable" (R.S.V.), or that "Every Scripture inspired by God is also profitable," the fact of divine inspiration is recognized in either case. The Holy Spirit is not mentioned here, but this passage parallels the others which specifically refer to the inspiring activity of the Spirit.

One aspect of the Old Testament message about the Spirit has special relevance for the New Testament. This is the promise of the eschatological gift of the Spirit. Just as the Spirit prompted the prophet to speak for God (Isa. 61:1), just as the Spirit had guided in the past (Isa. 63:11-14), so God's people needed the same Spirit for their life. There was an unfulfilled need: "Where is he who put in the midst of them his holy Spirit?" (Isa. 63:11). The divided people of God will revive to a new unity: "I will put my Spirit within you, and you shall live, and I will place you in your own land" (Ezek. 37:14). We hear as a climax the comprehensive promise:

I will pour out my spirit on all flesh; your sons and your daughters shall prophesy, your old men shall dream dreams, and your young men shall see visions. Even upon the menservants and maidservants in those days, I will pour out my spirit (Joel 2:28-29).

The Old Testament thus concludes with a sensed need of a further and greater gift of the Spirit, and with the promise that the Spirit will be given to all men. When John the Baptist promises this gift (Mark 1:8), he is renewing the voice of Old Testament prophecy.

The Spirit of Christ and the Prophets

Even in the references to Old Testament prophecy and inspiration we begin to note the curiously close relation between Christ and the Spirit which recurs in several parts of the New Testament. The usual biblical statement is that God or the Spirit of God inspired the prophets and the writers of the Old Testament, but in I Pet. 1:11 we read that "the Spirit of Christ within them" was "predicting the sufferings of Christ." This reminds us that Christian thought, before it could rest content, found itself forced to give cosmic scope to the work of Christ. It ascribed to Christ the Son an active agency in creating and upholding as well as in redeeming the world; and it looked forward to the completion of his work at the end of the age. Similarly here, in this one passage, the thought moves back to the words of the Old Testament prophets, and the writer is certain that the divine Spirit which moved the prophets to speak in ways now seen to point to Christ was in a real sense the Spirit of Christ himself.[4]

Yet the dominant note of the Christian message accented the newness and centrality of what God had given men in the historical career of Jesus Christ. This historical sense was too vivid to let the church give Christ a role as prominent in Old Testament times as he exercised in the first century. The decisive nature of that fresh invasion of human life and history in the first century had to be protected. And it could not be protected if Christ and the Spirit were identified. So even in speaking of the Christian period First Peter does not identify them; it is not the Christ but the Holy Spirit who inspires the preachers of the Apostolic Church (1:2, 12). We might have expected the writer to say that just as the Spirit of Christ inspired the Old Testament prophets, so he inspires the apostolic preachers. But his shift to the inspiration of the Holy Spirit is characteristic of the New Testament; it makes tremendous affirmations concerning the work of Jesus Christ, and cannot exclude him from any area of the work of God throughout history, yet it keeps the major emphasis solidly and persistently on the historical career of Jesus Christ and its results in the church.

The Christian will read the Old Testament story with the knowledge that the Son of God was involved in the whole story, but he will remember that this earlier role was veiled and preparatory. It is only in Jesus of Nazareth that the Son comes to full historical manfestation; it is there that Christian interest and emphasis must center.

The Spirit in Jesus

Preparatory to the gift of the Spirit to the church was the work of the Spirit in the coming and ministry of Jesus.[5] At first sight this might

---

[4] Cf. Edward Gordon Selwyn, *The First Epistle of St. Peter* (London, 1947), pp. 133-39, 259-68.

[5] See Henry Barclay Swete, *The Holy Spirit in the New Testament* (London: Macmillan & Co., 1910), pp. 11-62; Hans Windisch, "Jesus und der Geist nach synoptischer Ueberlieferung," in *Studies in Early Christianity*, ed. Shirley Jackson Case (New York, 1928), pp. 209-36; C. K. Barrett, *The Holy Spirit and the Gospel Tradition* (London, 1947).

seem the central coming and work of the Spirit, and we have no intention of minimizing the importance for New Testament faith of this work of the Spirit in Jesus' historical career. The Spirit was active in bringing Jesus onto the historical scene. Yet we must remember two things: The Gospels rarely refer to the work of the Spirit during the ministry of Jesus; and for the Christians of the Apostolic Age the gift of the Spirit which they had received was so linked with the resurrection and exaltation of Jesus that what preceded was not the same to them. It was the time when, from the point of view of the gift which the church had received, "as yet the Spirit had not been given" (John 7:39). The church's thinking about the Holy Spirit is basically post-resurrection thinking; what happened earlier was important but preparatory to the gift as the church knew it.

The Spirit was active in the coming of Jesus to the stage of history. According to Luke, this preparation began with the conception of John the Baptist (Luke 1:15) and continued through his career.[6] The activity of the Spirit guided Elizabeth and Zechariah to express the significance of the birth of John and Jesus (1:41, 67). The Spirit was to fill and direct John the Baptist (1:15). The Holy Spirit had guided Simeon and led him to expect God's help through his Christ, and it led him into the temple when the child Jesus and his parents were there (2:25-27). Both Luke 1:35 and Matt. 1:18 say that the conception of Jesus by Mary was the work of the Holy Spirit. This new life had no ordinary human origin; only the specific miraculous working of God by his Spirit can explain it. This series of references to the Spirit interprets the meaning of the career which is about to begin, and asserts that God is here present and working with unique redeeming purpose. The "favor of (with) God," twice mentioned (Luke 2:40, 52), suggests that this divine presence and working was a constant fact in the developing life of the boy and young man Jesus.

All four of the Gospels refer specifically to the Spirit in connection with the baptism of Jesus.[7] The Spirit descended upon him at the time he was baptized (Matt. 3:16; Mark 1:10; Luke 3:22; John 1:32). This pictorial description tells us that at this occasion the divine presence

---

[6] Swete, op. cit., pp. 12-37; Barrett, op. cit., ch. ii.

[7] Swete, op. cit., pp. 38-49; Barrett, op. cit., ch. iii; W. F. Flemington, *The New Testament Doctrine of Baptism* (London, 1948), ch. iii.

and working advanced to a new stage. If we thought of the presence of the Spirit in static terms, we could ask why and how this gift came at this late date in the life of Jesus. If the Spirit had been present at every stage, how could it be given at baptism? This is a fair question. Once faced, it will lead us to see that the references to the Spirit in the infancy narratives are preparatory. They are poetic passages of deep theological truth; they say that God was uniquely present and active in the birth of John the Baptist and especially Jesus, but they are not the central affirmation about the role of the Spirit in the career of Jesus.

For all the gospel writers it is the coming of the Spirit on Jesus at his baptism which is the decisive explanation of his ministry and work. The reason for this is not hard to find. Biblical thought about God connects his presence not with inner moods and passive contentment, but with purpose and action, mission and power. In both the Old and New Testaments the Spirit's presence means that God is present and active with power. The Spirit came on Jesus to move him to take up his ministry, to give him power to fulfill it, to lead him to act to carry out his mission at this crucial central point of history. Just as in the Old Testament the Spirit seized men and led them to prompt and notable action, so in the case of Jesus the Spirit came upon Jesus to lead him to act and carry out his God-intended task.

The resulting sense of compulsion explains the urgency with which he faced the issues of his coming work (Mark 1:12); the temptation had to come at once; he had been given a new role, a central task, and impelling power with which to fulfill God's purpose. He had to ask how to use the power of the Spirit in his messianic work; he was driven by the Spirit to face current expectations, chart his course, and set out upon it.[8]

It is with this sense of urgency with which he was seized at the baptism that he enters upon the ministry. We often hear of the patience and meekness of Jesus. There is truth in this, but something else must be said. His family even suspected a lack of mental balance in the great zeal and drive with which he set about his work; they tried to take him home to let him calm down and become more "normal." But he brusquely rejected their attempts and continued on his way, driven by

[8] Swete, op. cit., pp. 50-55; Barrett, op-cit., ch. iv.

a sense of urgency, for the Spirit was directing him and the sense of the lateness of the time gave him added haste (Mark 3:21, 31-35).

It is not certain that the Nazareth sermon of Jesus, as reported in Luke 4:16-30, occurred so near the beginning of the ministry as Luke's order of events implies. Perhaps Luke puts it so early because it sums up the spirit and purpose of the whole ministry,[9] while Mark indicates better the actual time of occurrence by putting it somewhat later in the ministry (Mark 6:2). In either case, it is clear that Jesus was conscious, as the church later knew, that the Spirit in him gave his ministry urgency, power, and direction.

Specific references to the working of the Spirit in Jesus are not numerous in the story of his ministry, but vivid touches show the general view which these narratives reflect. He knows that it is by the power of the Spirit that he casts out demons, giving health of body and poise of mind and spirit to sick and deranged men.[10] He is certain that no one can successfully deny this. He burns with indignation when opponents try to discredit him by saying that he can expel demons from troubled lives only because the archdemon, Satan himself, controls him and can dictate to the lesser demons in other people (Mark 3:22-30).

To Jesus this is blasphemy. He knows that it is the Spirit of God who is active in him; yet his enemies can look at the beneficent work which the Spirit is doing through him and call it the work of the devil. Jesus does not stop to defend himself; he denounces this blasphemous attempt to say that the power within him is the devil, when he knows it is the Holy Spirit of God. He can see no hope for people so perverted in outlook. He has no vindictive desire to see them come to ruin. But since they can look at the good works which he does by the Spirit's power and call them the work of Satan, they have so reversed spiritual facts and so lost spiritual sight and understanding that he sees no hope for them. For our present purpose this incident is revealing; it shows how clearly conscious Jesus is that he acts by the power and guidance of the Spirit.

Yet the church, as we have indicated, did not think that this work of the Spirit in Jesus climaxed the Spirit's working or expressed the full

[9] Burnett Hillman Streeter, The Four Gospels (4th ed.; London: Macmillan & Co., 1930), p. 220: "It seemed to him to sum up the history of the Christian message."
[10] Barrett, op. cit., ch. v.

162

meaning of the Spirit's mission. The importance of the historical Jesus was too great for that; he was no common human agent of God's purpose; he was the Christ, the Redeemer, the Son of God. The gospel centered in him; from his work great results were to flow. And there was an event to follow his ministry which determined the apostolic experience and thought of the Spirit.

Christ and the Gift of the Spirit

The Holy Spirit is the gift of the risen Christ to the church. This is the central New Testament message concerning the Spirit. It later raised theological problems which the church discussed once it had reached a clear statement of the deity of Christ. They concerned the relation of the Spirit to Christ. Did the Father alone send the Spirit? Or was Christ the Son also involved in giving the Spirit to the church? [11] The ultimate answer of orthodox Christianity was that the Spirit proceeded from both the Father and the Son. With this theological statement of the Trinity and the relations between Father, Son, and Spirit we are not concerned. We are thinking of the New Testament. There we find the data which led the church to its later theological formulation.

In one way or another the New Testament expresses the conviction that Christ was active in the giving of the Spirit. All four Gospels indicate at the outset, in the words of John the Baptist, that the coming Messiah will bestow the Holy Spirit on those who follow him (Matt. 3:11; Mark 1:8; Luke 3:16; John 1:33). The Gospels tell this so confidently because they know that this promise has been fulfilled. The Gospel of John points forward to the time after Jesus has been glorified, through death and resurrection and ascension to the Father, as the time when the Spirit will be given (7:39). And it goes on to tell how, on the evening of the day of Jesus' resurrection, he fulfilled this promise for the ten disciples who were with him (20:22). This is the beginning and pledge of the wider and fuller gift of the Spirit to the entire later church.

[11] The Western Church answered this question in the affirmative in the *filioque* controversy. Cf. H. Wheeler Robinson, *The Christian Experience of the Holy Spirit* (London, 1928), pp. 250, 258.

The Book of Acts dates the actual gift of the Spirit several weeks later than the Fourth Gospel does. On the day of Pentecost, fifty days after the Passover on which Jesus died, the Spirit came on the waiting and worshipful church (Acts 2:4). And it was Christ who "poured out this" gift (2:33). This seems the better dating of the event. The Gospel of John, moved as often by a dramatic sense, tells of the gift of the Spirit by the risen Christ on the resurrection day to make it clear that this gift is directly due to what Jesus Christ has already done for men, and that the giving is his own definite act.

Other books of the New Testament have no reason to tell just how and when the Spirit was first given to the church, but they show the close link between Christ and the Spirit in the thinking of the church. Paul says that "God has sent the Spirit of his Son" (Gal. 4:6); the Spirit is here tied to Christ as in I Pet. 1:10-12. In two notable passages (Rom. 8:9-11; II Cor. 3:17-18) the Holy Spirit is so interrelated with the risen Christ that they cannot be clearly distinguished, even though, as II Cor. 13:14 illustrates, they are not completely identified. These passages clearly show that Christ was involved in the gift of the Spirit to the church.

The Book of Revelation has a curious reference to the fact that the Lamb has "seven eyes, which are the seven spirits of God sent out into all the earth" (5:6). This implies that the Lamb, the crucified but now risen Christ, sends out the Spirit; the unusual mention of seven spirits appears to mark the fullness and wide range of the gift and work of the Spirit.[12]

Thus the references in the Four Gospels and in Acts, together with supporting hints in Paul's letters, in First Peter, and in the Book of Revelation, reflect the early Christian witness that Christ was actively involved in the gift and work of the Spirit.

A Gift of the Exalted Christ

It is the risen Christ who so acts. Nowhere do these writings hint that Jesus during his ministry bestowed the Spirit on his followers. That gift was a post-resurrection gift. Here as always, New Testament

[12] Isbon T. Beckwith, *The Apocalypse of John* (New York: The Macmillan Co., 1919), pp. 424-27, thinks the reference rests on Zech. 4:2-10, where "the same symbols represent the Spirit of God active in the world."

faith and thinking moves in the post-resurrection framework. Our Protestant churches too often have thought of Easter as the end of the church year and of Jesus' resurrection as the end of the gospel story. The period of the church then becomes a time of inaction for Christ, who has no role or task in the present period. The New Testament never suggests this idea. For its writers, Jesus' resurrection is the open door through which he entered upon the further work which in God's plan he was still to accomplish.

Therefore the ascension or exaltation of Christ is so prominent in New Testament thought. That it is important, a statistical summary makes clear. The literal ascension story, to be sure, occurs only in a poorly attested closing sentence of Luke (24:51) and in the opening chapter of Acts (1:9). However, eleven different New Testament writings, by at least seven different writers, indicate that Jesus has been given or now occupies a place at the right hand of the Father (Matt. 22:44; 26:64; Mark 12:36; 14:62; Luke 20:42; 22:69; Acts 2:33-34; 5:31; 7:55; Rom. 8:34; Eph. 1:20; Col. 3:1; Heb. 1:3; 8:1; 10:12; I Pet. 3:22. I Cor. 15:25 and Rev. 3:21 mean the same thing, but do not mention "the right hand").[18] Obviously this was a constant feature of New Testament thought from earliest times.

These passages express truth in a figurative form. The New Testament writers were not so devoid of imagination that they always spoke in coldly literal terms. To say that Jesus Christ ascends, or that he sits down at the right hand of God, is to say that he withdraws from his former visible presence with his people, that he receives honor and recognition from the Father for what he has done during his earthly career, that he now takes up an active role in carrying out the further work of the Father, and that as the agent of God's further rule and action he is the Lord of his church.

This thought may be uncongenial to many modern Christians, but it is an essential part of the basic message of the Apostolic Church. Jesus did not become inactive or lose touch with his people; he was now active with increased power and with continuing concern for those who followed him. To understand the New Testament faith and thought

[18] Cf. Oscar Cullmann, *Christ and Time*, tr. Floyd V. Filson (Philadelphia: Westminster Press, 1950), p. 151.

concerning the Spirit, the church, the Christian life, and the future hope, we must take with full seriousness the exaltation of Christ to the right hand of God and his continuing activity as Lord.

It is of course true that in addition to saying that the risen and exalted Christ sends the Spirit, the New Testament can and does say that God does so (Gal. 4:6). Concerning this and many other divine gifts and actions the New Testament can say either that God the Father does them, or that Christ does them, or that God does them through Christ. Part of the evidence for the high and unique role of Christ in New Testament faith and thought is precisely this recurrent intertwining of the work of the Father and the Son in actions and gifts which can only be expected and received from the divine source. So the fact that according to some statements the Father sends the Spirit does not discredit or conflict with other early Christian testimonies that Christ sends the Spirit to his church.

Thus Christ continues and carries forward his work through the gift and activity of the Spirit. The New Testament view of the Spirit is Christ centered. Risen and exalted, Jesus Christ through the gift and work of the Spirit continues to be the active head of his people and the active agent of the Father until he completes the divine purpose for the world.

The Work of the Holy Spirit

When we ask what the Holy Spirit does, we must correct at once a widespread modern view. For many modern Christians the Spirit's chief or only work is to give an emotional lift, an inward joy. This certainly was part of the New Testament experience of the Spirit. It is noteworthy how often joy is mentioned when the context deals with the work or presence of the Spirit. The gift of the Spirit of God did not leave the disciples unmoved. Not that the experience was identical with the gift and working of the Spirit. But where the Spirit really came into a life, the result was abounding joy.

The speaking with tongues, of which we hear in Acts 2:4 and I Cor. 12–14,[14] was a curious and primitive expression of Christian ex-

[14] See E. F. Scott, op. cit., pp. 93-108; P. G. S. Hopwood, *The Religious Experience of the Primitive Church* (Edinburgh: T. & T. Clark, 1936), ch. vii.

perience. It seems to have come from an uprush of emotional joy and a powerful urge to express it, and the result was unintelligible or unconnected ejaculations. Such a primitive expression was open to ridicule, but pride sometimes led those who spoke with tongues to belittle clear thinking and ethical earnestness.

This emotional speaking, however, was a real expression of the Spirit; it was an excited outpouring of the sense of joy which gripped the believers when they sensed that their Lord had given them the very presence and power of God in their lives. We must not deny the genuineness of such primitive experience. But we need not envy those who so reacted, and we must not let such expressions lead us to neglect quiet worship, clear thought, fellowship in worship, and wholesome daily obedience to the will of God. We need to look further for the full and higher working of the Holy Spirit in the New Testament Church. The thrill and joy of the Spirit's presence were real, but they were by no means the most important effect of the Spirit's presence.

Witness to Christ

One constant work of the Spirit was to witness to Christ; he assured the church that God worked in Christ, and interpreted to the church the meaning of Christ's career. Only the Gospel of John specifically states this role of the Spirit (14:26; 15:26).[15] But in fact the church knew from the beginning that the gift of the Spirit was given to enable it to witness to Christ (Acts 1:8). The Gospel of John only states explicitly what is implied throughout the New Testament.

The Holy Spirit, the gift of God through the risen and exalted Christ, carries on the work of Christ, recalls the historical career of Christ and its meaning, and interprets to the church what Christ's work means for its present life. The Spirit was not a vague presence; he received character and identity through the connection with Jesus Christ risen and exalted, and this fact prevented the church from falling victim to all sorts of vagrant and conflicting impulses. The Spirit inevitably leads the church to say, "Jesus is Lord" (I Cor. 12:3). In thus recalling that career of Jesus and the lordship of the risen Christ, the Spirit leads the

[15] Cf. W. F. Howard, *Christianity According to St. John* (Philadelphia: Westminster Press, 1946), pp. 71-80.

church to remember, use, write down, and so preserve in our Gospels the story of Jesus. The Spirit is prominently active as witness to Christ.

Guide to Truth

The Spirit actively reveals truth and gives guidance to the mind of the church. We have noted how the church accepted the fact that the Spirit, even before the Pentecost gift, had given the Old Testament prophets the word of the Lord and had guided the writers of Scripture to give God's word in written form. The same light and guidance are given now to the Apostolic Church. Prophets are named in the Book of Acts; Agabus is one example (11:28; 21:10); Barnabas and Saul are among the prophets and teachers in the church at Antioch (13:1). Paul indicates that in the church at Corinth, prophets regularly took part in services of worship, and that he himself had and exercised this gift (I Cor. 12:10, 28; 14:19). The Spirit gave prophetic guidance to the church in crises and also in more regular services of worship.[16]

It is important to note the role of the human mind in the guidance of the Spirit. References to speaking with tongues might suggest that when the Spirit comes into a life, the mind must abdicate. There is little to support this view. It is noteworthy how clearly Jesus thinks and how he appeals to his hearers to think and answer his questions. The preaching of the church tells a story and interprets it. It uses the mind; it challenges the mind as well as the imagination and the will. Worship, too, involves at least some recognition of the truth of the message; faith includes mental action. When the Corinthian church tended to stress emotion and minimize intelligent use of the mind in worship and fellowship, Paul protested. He recognized this incoherent emotionalism as a legitimate expression of spiritual life, but he definitely minimized it, and he insisted that it was better for the church to speak intelligibly; this was the higher gift of the Spirit, the clear intelligent expression of Christian truth and guidance (I Cor. 14:18-19).

Effective in Conflict with Evil

Another work of the Spirit was effective conflict with evil. This appears in the ministry of Jesus.[17] Only one stronger than Satan can defeat

[16] H. A. Guy, op. cit., ch. iv.
[17] Barrett, op. cit., pp. 53-68.

and expel him, and the fact that Jesus expels demons from the lives of troubled people shows that the Spirit is working in him. He therefore is indignant at the charge that he acts by the power of Beelzebub—that is, Satan. As we have said, he knew that the very Spirit of God was the power at work in his life to perform these mighty acts, which repelled the encroaching hold of Satan on human lives (Mark 3:22-30). The work of the Spirit in such healings is a sure clue to those with discerning eyes that the Kingdom is dawning in what Jesus is doing (Matt. 12:28; but cf. Luke 11:20).

Not only in the life of Jesus, but also in the lives of his disciples, the Spirit will give help in time of persecution (Mark 13:9-11). When taken before hostile magistrates, the Spirit will guide the believer in answering his accusers, and will make his answer a witness to Christ. This promise of Jesus, which gives his followers assurance, is fulfilled in the Book of Acts. There the church lives under the guidance and power of the Spirit, and the leaders are fearless and ready to witness when arrested and brought before Jewish and Roman authorities (Acts 4:8, 29-31; cf. 18:9-10). Similarly, the seer John, when in the Spirit on the Lord's Day on the island of Patmos (Rev. 1:10), was given courage in the time of persecution and received a message of reassurance and hope to give the rest of the church. When hard times came and danger threatened, the Spirit sustained the church and gave it courage and voice. The Spirit was active in the conflict which Christ and his followers waged with opposing forces.

This is likewise the testimony of the Gospel of John. In the farewell discourses, in which the role of the Spirit or Counselor is repeatedly mentioned, one aspect of his work will be to "convince the world of sin and of righteousness and of judgment" (John 16:8). The New Testament sees the historical scene as a battleground between good and evil, between God and Satan; Jesus was centrally active in the conflict against evil; the Spirit will carry forward that conflict and support the people of God as they share and perhaps suffer in the struggle.

God's Gift to All Christians

The life of the church is life in the Spirit. This is not simply the life of man's spirit as opposed to his life on the physical plane; the

New Testament did not think in such purely human terms. Life in the Spirit is Spirit-given, Spirit-inspired, Spirit-led life. Some wrongly read the Book of Acts as essentially an account of human heroism and activity. Luke presents it, however, as the action of the Holy Spirit in Christ's church.[18]

One noteworthy aspect of this Spirit-centered life of the church is the gift of the Spirit to all Christians. This universal gift was not known in earlier days, and it was a bright eschatological promise of Joel 2:28-32 that in the last days God would give the Spirit to all his people. The church lived in grateful consciousness that God had now fulfilled this promise. All who believed received the gift of the Spirit (Acts 2:38; Rom 8:9). The church had this rare democracy in which all its members shared the divine gift of the Spirit.

Unity and Fellowship with Varied Gifts

In this common gift the church found its unity. There might be and there were many diverse gifts, but the one Spirit gave them all (I Cor. 12:4-11).[19] Each Christian was able to serve and help the church through the working of the Spirit in his life. Indeed, the Spirit's ministry was so rich and varied that all needed gifts were present, and all worked together to make the one church fully equipped for mutual help and effective world witness. When Paul speaks of the unity of the church in Eph. 4:1-6, he mentions the work of the Spirit even before he mentions "one Lord" and "one God and Father of us all." Christians have "the unity of the Spirit in the bond of peace." That is why "there is one body and one Spirit"; the one Spirit builds the church in unity and sustains it in its oneness. This is not a human achievement; it is the divine work of the Spirit of God.

The resulting fellowship in the church is not a product of human skill in adaptation and organization. It is basically the "fellowship of the Holy Spirit" (II Cor. 13:14), whether this means human fellowship created and sustained by the Spirit or, as is more likely, fellowship which all together have with the Holy Spirit. The unity of which we

[18] Cf. Richard Belward Rackham, *The Acts of the Apostles* (11th ed.; London, 1930), pp. lxx-lxxvi.
[19] Swete, *op. cit.*, pp. 184 ff.

have spoken is created as believers share "participation" or "fellowship" in the Spirit (Phil. 2:1). Christian lives are bound together in common worship, in Christian sympathy and understanding, in mutually helpful concern. This happens because all are moulded by the Spirit's work in the church.

Power to Witness and Work for Christ

The Spirit gives to these Christians the power to do the work of the church. This task is basically to witness to Christ and to God's grace, expressed and offered in him. This witness is not an independent human testimony. It is because the church has received the Holy Spirit that it is prompted and able to give effective witness. This is the promise of Acts 1:8; the Book of Acts and other New Testament reflections of the life of the Apostolic Church testify that the promise was fulfilled. The church had power, but it was not the church's own power; it was divine power; the Holy Spirit working in the church enabled it to witness to Christ and to carry forward Christ's work.[20]

That power found expression in many ways. It appeared in the endurance with which the church faced hardship and persecution. It prompted courageous public preaching and bold defense under varied and difficult situations.

It explains the miracles of the church. The "signs and wonders and mighty works" which Paul had done in his ministry (II Cor. 12:12), he twice ascribes to the powerful working of the Holy Spirit (Gal. 3:5; Rom. 15:19). Our modern study of the New Testament miracle stories might well begin with these three passages. They are firsthand testimony of one who knew that remarkable events had occurred during his ministry. They could rightly be called mighty works or miracles. But he knew he had not done them by his human power. That the Spirit of God had worked through him was the only explanation with which Christian faith could rest content. The Book of Acts fully confirms this point of view of Paul. Great acts were done, but it was "the name of Jesus Christ" (3:6) or the power of the Spirit (4:29-31) which brought them about.

[20] E. F. Scott, op. cit., pp. 108-19.

The Guide of Christian Worship

Even in Christian worship it was the work of the Spirit which ex-plained the helpful participation of each member in the service they shared. Luke describes how the early disciples spoke with tongues under the prompting of the Spirit (Acts 2:4; 10:46; 19:6). Whether this was actually, as he seems to say, speaking in foreign languages, or was rather—as we are inclined to conclude—highly emotional and joyous expression of faith and loyalty, it is in either case the outward expression of the presence of the Spirit of God.[21]

Similarly, Paul tells how the church at Corinth, when it came together to worship, was thrown into confusion because so many members wished to take part at once. Some prophesied, others spoke with tongues (here it plainly is joyous unintelligible speech), others had a hymn to sing, a scripture passage to quote, or an interpretation of the gospel to give (I Cor. 14). These for Paul are all true acts of worship, if a sense of love and a spirit of good order guides the speaker. But they are all gifts of the Spirit.

True worship, Paul implies, is never the unaided action of man, even the devout man. It is rather the attitude and expression which the Holy Spirit prompts and guides. This was no passing or minor idea of Paul. He ascribes to the Spirit even the earnest cry of prayer in which the believer says "Abba! Father!" (Gal. 4:6). It is only through the Spirit that man understands God's gifts and goodness and properly expresses his gratitude in worship. It is only through the Spirit that the Christian who has learned these things in worship can express them truly so that others receive spiritual help.

This is not merely the view of Paul. John the writer of Revelation was in the Spirit when he saw and heard his vision and was directed to write it to the seven churches. Man receives and speaks the revelation through the Spirit's working. The Spirit is the key person in true Christian worship.

[21] For a brief sketch of such phenomena see Swete, op. cit., pp. 379-82; Alexander B. Macdonald, Christian Worship in the Primitive Church (Edinburgh: T. & T. Clark, 1934), pp. 42-43.

The Guide in the Choice and Work of Leaders

This leadership of the Spirit controls all aspects of human leadership in the church. The Spirit guides in the choice of leaders; the Spirit gives them competence and power for their work. It is in harmony with this that Jesus prayed all night before choosing the Twelve. The Book of Acts often notes that leaders are chosen and plans made under the guidance of the Spirit. Such men were to be "full of the Spirit" (6:3). The selection of Barnabas and Saul was directed by the Holy Spirit, who sent them out to preach (13:2, 4).

It was in response to the guidance of the Spirit that the church made crucial decisions. An example is the agreement that Gentiles did not need to keep the Mosaic Law to be saved, but must only accommodate their table practices somewhat to enable all Christians to eat together without offending the feelings of Jews (Acts 15:28).[22] The Spirit led the prophet Agabus to predict famine in Judea and thus led the church to send famine relief (11:28); he guided the apostles in the choice of further fields of mission work (16:6). It was the Holy Spirit who made the elders "guardians" ("bishops") of the church at Ephesus (20:28).

These expressions of the Spirit occurred in groups where worship and search for the will of God were preparing the Christians to receive divine guidance. They came through one or more participating members of the groups. The human mind and voice had their part to play.

We may shrink from such a picture and see immense possibilities for self-deception and mistake in such circumstances. The early church knew the pitfalls of such Spirit-led life in the churches. A man could pretend to a piety he did not have (Acts 5:3). Unfit men could try to do miracles in the name of Jesus (Acts 19:13). Prophets could lead in worship and yet fail to express the true will of God; other prophets needed to discern whether the utterance was a genuine word of the Spirit to the worshiping church (I Cor. 14:29).

In the face of such risks the wise decision of the church was that which Paul phrases thus: "Do not quench the Spirit, do not despise prophesying, but test everything; hold fast what is good" (I Thess. 5:19-21). The guidance of the Spirit is indispensable in the Christian

---

[22] On the Jerusalem conference see Maurice Goguel, *The Birth of Christianity*, tr. H. C. Snape (New York: The Macmillan Co., 1954), pp. 295-303.

Church.[23] Even the risks which this brings must be readily accepted. The use of intelligent judgment is not excluded but rather required. The church has a duty to single out and reject utterances, proposals, and choices which are not the will of the Spirit. But it would be fatal to Christian faith, worship, living, and leadership if the church were to renounce the leadership of the Spirit in the choice of its leaders and in their work.

The church cannot live by the independent human thought and decisions of even its best members. The grace and work of God initiates, supports, and guides all Christian faith, worship, action, and leadership. The Spirit makes that divine work effective in the church. To seek and follow the leading of the Spirit is absolute necessity for every Christian and for all genuine church leadership.

The Giver of Authority to Church Leaders

In the New Testament the leaders of the church speak with authority. Their role is not merely advisory. Peter speaks for the Holy Spirit in denouncing the deception which Ananias and Sapphira attempted; he announces their death as divine judgment for their fault in tempting and lying to the Holy Spirit of the Lord (Acts 5:3, 9). Luke notes that Paul was full of the Holy Spirit when he rebuked and pronounced judgment on Elymas for trying to keep the proconsul at Paphos from accepting the gospel (Acts 13:9).

Paul assumes the same authority to lead in disciplinary action when immorality mars the life of the church at Corinth; "the power of our Lord Jesus" leads to action, and Paul pronounces judgment "in the name of the Lord Jesus" (I Cor. 5:3-5). He does not refer to the guidance of the Spirit in this case, but the situation is essentially the same. He can say that the living Christ, the head of the church and Paul's Lord, directs his life; or, he can say that the Holy Spirit works in the leaders and members of the church.

The Fourth Gospel states most emphatically the authority which the gift of the Spirit gives to the actions of church leaders. When the risen Christ bestows the Holy Spirit on the disciples present with him on the evening of the Resurrection Day, he declares that their actions

---

[23] Cf. J. Robert Nelson, *The Realm of Redemption* (Greenwich, 1951), ch. ii.

will now be fully authoritative and will have the full support of God: "If you forgive the sins of any, they are forgiven; if you retain the sins of any, they are retained" (John 20:23).[24]

The use of this passage to support absolute power for an ecclesiastical hierarchy, or to support apostolic succession, is ill-conceived. It is not certain that in the picture of this Gospel only members of the Twelve were present. It is practically certain that this is a dramatic anticipation of the historical giving of the Spirit at Pentecost, when all of the disciples present were given the Spirit; so even if the Gospel of John were trying to channel the gift and power of the Spirit through a narrowly limited few, this view could not be regarded as historical.

But a more weighty objection prevents using this verse to grant to a hierarchy the monopolistic right to assure people of forgiveness or warn them of continuing guilt. It would turn into mechanics what happens when the Spirit moves Christ's spokesmen. Suppose a leader is not prompted by the Spirit and does not show the fruit of the Spirit in his life. How can he speak with accuracy and authority the absolution or condemnation of God? Wherever God's chosen leaders act under the guidance of the Spirit and in accord with his purposes, their assurance of divine pardon and their warning of continued guilt has divine sanction. It is the presence of the Spirit and the obedient response to the Spirit that gives to Christian leadership its authority and power. No Christian should ever want it otherwise.

The Spirit in the Individual Christian

We think of essentially the same work of the Spirit, but with another focus, when we consider the work of the Spirit in the Christian believer. This is a part of the work which the Spirit does in the church, but it is important to state the effects which the gifts and actions of the Spirit produce in the individual Christian's life.

The Cause of Conversion

The initial conversion and renewal of the Christian are the work of the Holy Spirit. At first, to judge from the earliest records, this fact was not clearly recognized. The act of faith was prominent. Although Chris-

[24] On the meaning of this passage see Howard, op. cit., pp. 141-42.

tians valued highly the gift of the Spirit at the start of the Christian life, they did not say that conversion itself was the Spirit's work.

But as Eph. 2:8 says, even faith "is not your own doing; it is the gift of God." Every step of salvation is achieved and effected by God. It did not satisfy Christian faith and conscience to ascribe the beginning of the Christian life to human action, and let the Spirit take over only at a later stage of Christian experience. To be sure, a man must make his decision; he must believe and be baptized; but he needs a radical renewal which can only be God's work. "Unless one is born of water and the Spirit, he cannot enter the kingdom of God." (John 3:5.) "He saved us, not because of deeds done by us in righteousness, but in virtue of his own mercy, by the washing of regeneration and renewal in the Holy Spirit, which he poured out upon us richly through Jesus Christ our Savior." (Tit. 3:5-6.)

The New Testament can ascribe this life-renewing conversion to God in a general way, or can consider it the result of the work of Jesus Christ and his lordship over his people, but it can also say that the Spirit of God brings about this change. The Spirit brings men into the Christian faith and life.

"To Be With You Forever"

This coming of the Spirit to effect renewal at the outset of the Christian life is not a temporary visit. The Christian's life is henceforth Spirit-possessed. He does not control or own the Spirit; the Spirit controls and dominates his life. It is a continuing gift, which he has not deserved. He can only accept it as God's free gift of the divine presence and power.

In the farewell discourses of Jesus in the Gospel of John, discourses in which the gift and work of the Spirit are prominent, it is emphasized that the Spirit will be steadily with the disciples; they can count on his helpful presence (John 14:16). Though the Spirit is not subject to the will of believers, the New Testament speaks of him as "the Holy Spirit who dwells within us" (II Tim. 1:14). One is not a Christian unless "the Spirit of God really dwells in you" (Rom. 8:9). The Christian life is a God-related, God-guided, God-empowered life; the Spirit

176

gives meaning, understanding, direction, and power to every phase of Christian living.

The Voice of Christian Confession and Worship

The Spirit prompts believers to grateful, courageous confession of Christ. He continuously carries forward the divine work which Jesus Christ began; he guides the life of the disciples so that they honor Christ in confession and behavior. True confession of Christ as Lord is a Spirit-inspired utterance (I Cor. 12:3). Even when standing before hostile rulers and judges, the Spirit will lead the believer to acknowledge Christ as Lord and speak in witness to him (Luke 12:11-12; Acts 4:29-31).

The Spirit is equally active in Christian worship.[25] Whenever the believer cries " 'Abba! Father!' it is the Spirit himself bearing witness with our spirit that we are children of God" (Rom. 8:15-16). All of the expressions of worship which Paul names in I Cor. 12-14 are Spirit-prompted. The true Christian in every service of worship prays, speaks, sings, and takes his part by the working of the Spirit. Thus both personal and private worship on the one hand, and public common worship on the other, are real and effective and beneficial because the Spirit of God is present and active in them.

The Power of Daily Life Obedience

The Spirit gives the believer power and guidance to be fruitful in living. This life is not merely a verbal witness to Christ, though the power the Spirit gives the Christians aims primarily to enable them to give a strong and persuasive witness. Nor is it merely a life of worship, though the spiritual gifts bestowed on each Christian enables all to share helpfully in common worship and to worship sincerely in private. It is also a fruitful moral life, in which the believer understands the will of God and follows that divine will in daily obedience.

This tying of the gift of the Spirit to daily moral life is one of the distinctive features of New Testament faith and thought. Numerous ancient religions knew ecstasy and enthusiasm in worship services. They claimed to experience the indwelling of God in such times of religious

[25] A. B. Macdonald, op. cit., ch. v.

exaltation. Almost all of these faiths expected their adherents to conform in life to the will of the god which they worshiped. But pagan
cults never equaled the moral seriousness which emerges in the prophetic
demand of the Old Testament and finds deepened echo in the New
Testament. Here faith and daily living are tied together in one united
witness to God; the whole life is to be an act of obedience to God.

It was Paul, the great preacher of grace and faith, who took a leading
role in this insistence on moral fruitfulness in Christian living.[26] Like
other cults, the church sometimes tended to esteem most highly the
spectacular features of worship. When the Spirit seized a worshiper and
made him speak with tongues or otherwise show intense enthusiasm,
this seemed to some the highest level of Christian experience.

It is to the everlasting credit of Paul that he fought this morally
shallow view. He did it by insisting on two related points. One was
that the highest worship and living includes the clear use of the mind.
He himself could speak with tongues. But in public worship he preferred to speak five intelligible words which would help others rather
than to speak ten thousand unintelligible words (I Cor. 14:18-19).
True faith, genuine and high worship, good Christian living, requires
the use of the informed and active mind. This discredits the merely
emotional and spectacular.

Paul also protected the true nature of Christian living by finding the
chief fruit of the Spirit in the morally wholesome and socially helpful
expressions of faith. For the sanity, wholeness, and moral fiber of the
Christian life, no words of the Bible excel those which Paul wrote to
the Galatians: "The fruit of the Spirit is love, joy, peace, patience, kindness, goodness, faithfulness, gentleness, self-control" (5:22-23). Where
the Spirit comes into a life, it fosters an inward spirit of good will,
sympathy, gentle kindness, and quiet trust, and it produces in the
actions of the believer outgoing helpfulness and intelligently expressed
concern for the good of others.

The result is that faith cannot be an idle, ineffective thing. For Paul
it was "faith working through love." (Gal. 5:6.) The Spirit makes of

---

[26] E. F. Scott, op. cit., pp. 139 ff. On this and other aspects of Paul's thought see
R. Birch Hoyle, The Holy Spirit in St. Paul (New York: Harper & Bros., 1928).

the Christian life a good and fruitful life, dedicated to the welfare of others and devoted to the service of Christ's church.

Summary

It may help to summarize the chief points of New Testament faith concerning Christ and the Spirit.

1. The Spirit is the same divine Spirit which was active in Old Testament times and in the Old Testament writers. But because the work of Christ was so central for all future faith and life, God's act in Christ forms the background for all the New Testament words about the Spirit. The Spirit carries forward that work of Christ.

2. The Spirit is thus a witness to Christ; his main work in the world is to lead the church to give its witness to Christ.

3. The Spirit is the gift of the risen, exalted Christ to his church, and is so closely related to the living Christ that at times the New Testament writers do not keep them clearly separate.

4. The Spirit is given to the church. This includes the gift of the Spirit to each individual Christian, but the Christian receives the Spirit as a member of the church, and the guidance of each individual life is such as to make that person a loyal, worshiping and working member of the church. The one Spirit binds Christians together into a unity, yet meets the varied needs of each Christian and gives to different individuals varying gifts to use for the common good.

5. The Spirit reveals God's truth to the worshiping, witnessing, thinking church. He first of all interprets the meaning of God's redeeming and revealing work in Jesus Christ. He keeps that always in view. But he also leads on to new truth not yet expressed in the teaching of Jesus (John 16:13). The truth he reveals will always be consistent with what Christ taught and revealed in his life; it will be a growing and fuller revelation and application of the truth essentially given in the work and words of Christ.

6. The Spirit is given to all Christians, as a steady presence and indwelling. It is not the special privilege of the few to receive the Spirit. All Christians have that privilege, and with the gift goes the responsibility to witness and to live for Christ.

7. Those who lead receive the Spirit for their work, and they do

that work in the strength that gift provides. When they yield their lives to the guidance and working of the Spirit, their leadership and decisions—even in judgment—will be the work of God and will stand.

8. The great mark of the Spirit-filled life is not emotional thrill but power. The Spirit gives power to witness, power to live, power to do remarkable actions.

9. The Spirit builds in the Christian a morally wholesome life of loyal obedience to God's will. The real fruit of the Spirit will therefore be a rich cluster of morally wholesome and socially helpful attitudes and actions. Religion and morality are here one united whole. Neither exists without the other. The good life is impossible without the presence, power, and guidance of the Spirit. True faith and worship cannot exist without inevitably working out into attitudes and acts which build good character and embody social helpfulness.

10. The Spirit is not under the control of the Christian. The reverse is true. The true Christian lives under the guidance and control of the Spirit of God, and is happy that this is so.

11. The Holy Spirit is not a general atmosphere or abstract principle, but is personal in nature. Anthropomorphic language about God has limitations, but it is truer to the New Testament to say "he" than it would be to say "it" when referring to the Spirit of God.

12. The Holy Spirit is not the collective spirit of mankind, nor is he some angelic being; he is definitely divine. He is God present, active, and powerful in the life of his church and in the lives of his people. The New Testament never states fully the relation of the Spirit to God the Father. It certainly implies that the Spirit's presence and work in the church and the Christian do not exhaust the greatness, scope, and action of God. Nevertheless, the Spirit cannot be considered less than truly divine in nature and working. Where the Spirit is, God is present and at work.

CHAPTER IX

Christ and the Church

DURING THE LAST HALF CENTURY PROTESTANT THOUGHT CON-
cerning the church has undergone continual change.[1] For decades it
emphasized individualism. Some even viewed the relation to Christ as
essentially a personal matter; the relation to the church was a matter
of convenience or was at least of secondary importance. Personal conversion, personal devotional life, personal integrity—these were essential. One could be a good Christian without belonging to the church.
So thought many sincere people.

Why was this so? In part it reflected the American freedom and
"rugged individualism" which our national history had fostered. In part
it rested upon the sound observation that personal decision and personal
responsibility are essential in truly Christian living. But our question is:
How far did this extreme individualism have a basis in the gospel?
For it claimed to have solid biblical basis.

This view claimed a biblical basis in the rise of "individualism" in the
prophets. It regarded Jeremiah and Ezekiel as prominent pioneers in
this trend.[2] The early stages of Israelite history had a strong group bond,
but these key prophets, it was argued, threw responsibility back upon the
individual.

Jesus, it was asserted, carried this tendency to its proper conclusion.
Throwing off the racial and national ties of religion, he preached a

[1] A helpful survey of recent Protestant study of this subject, with continual attention
to the New Testament data, is that of J. Robert Nelson, *The Realm of Redemption*
(Greenwich, 1951). See also George Johnston, *The Doctrine of the Church in the
New Testament* (London: Cambridge University Press, 1943); Stig Hanson, *The Unity
of the Church in the New Testament* (Uppsala, 1946).

[2] See Harry Emerson Fosdick, *A Guide to Understanding the Bible* (New York:
Harper & Bros., 1938), pp. 61 ff.

purely spiritual and moral message directed to each individual. Both he and the apostles after him appealed to the individual, worked for personal conversion and personal dedication, and thought of life with God in essentially individualistic terms. The church developed as a helpful aid, but the heart of the Christian life lay in the individual's relation to God and integrity before God. The New Testament movement centered in personal witness, personal evangelism, and a missionary outreach which converted individuals, who then broke loose from their social setting and followed Christ as Lord.

The Limits of Individualism

This argument captures a vital note of the New Testament message. John the Baptist, Jesus, and the apostles denied that racial and national ties are an adequate basis for religious fellowship (Matt. 3:9; 8:11-12; Acts 10:34-35). Numerous biblical passages emphasize personal responsibility, which is inherent in all healthy social and religious life. Men like Joshua and Paul stood firm, no matter what others did (Josh. 24:15; Gal. 2:11). The leaders of Israel had long seen that not all of Israel was loyal to their God, and that the hope of the people rested on a remnant. The prophets pressed home to each Israelite the importance of standing firm and living loyally for God. When people tried to excuse their moral failure or their social plight by blaming it all on their ancestors, it was right to tell them that, "The soul that sins shall die" (Ezek. 18:4). Each person and each generation has its inescapable responsibility.

When Jesus called Israel to repent and prepare for the imminent Kingdom, he appealed to individuals to take their stand. The apostles continued this appeal in Israel, and when the Christian movement enlarged its appeal and challenged people in gentile lands and circles to join this minority movement, the necessity of personal decision was crystal clear. At every stage of the biblical story, personal responsibility is recognized, and at times of crisis and transition it receives special emphasis.

But this does not change the fact that Israel was a people, that the movement of Jesus arose within Israel, and that the Christian movement was from the first a fellowship of believers. The New Testament reflects the constant assumption that to become a follower of Jesus Christ means to enter the fellowship of Christ's people. We need to see clearly the biblical idea of the people of God.

The Covenant People of God

The covenant is a common, basic, and highly significant fact throughout the Bible.[3] Israel lived in the consciousness that she was bound to God through a definite covenant (Exod. 24:8). In a wider sense all mankind was thus bound to God, as the covenant made with Noah indicated (Gen. 9:9). But Israel had a closer tie in her special covenant relation with God. Preparatory to this was the covenant of God with Abraham and through Abraham with his descendants (Gen. 15:18). The main covenant, however, was that made at Sinai-Horeb, where, through Moses, Israel acknowledged God as their God and bound themselves to do God's revealed will, in answer to God's election of Israel and his rich gifts and promises to his chosen people. This covenant Israel broke time after time, but out of this tragic history grew a deeper understanding of the faithfulness of God, who refuses to give up his people and continues to work to realize in and through them his holy will (Hos. 11:8).

This covenant was not an agreement between equals. It was an agreement in which God graciously gave to his chosen and dependent people favors which they had no right to claim. God's superior and commanding position and his rich grace are implicit in this biblical idea of covenant. For the Old Testament is not in essence a book of law. At the heart of it is the revelation of the outreaching goodness of God, and at the basis of his relation with Israel is the gracious gift of the covenant relation.

God granted repeated renewals of the covenant to errant Israel, but the inadequacy of the Mosaic type of covenant became clear in the end. This insight finds clearest expression in the great forward look of Jer. 31:31-34. The prophet foresees that the old covenant will be replaced by a new one. God will write his law or will upon the hearts of his people,

[3] On God as the Covenant-God, see Snaith, op. cit., ch. v; Walter Eichrodt, Theologie des Alten Testaments, 3 vols. (Leipzig, 1933-1939).

and they will yield him a loyal obedience that springs from an inward understanding and acceptance of his will. The covenant idea persists, but a better covenant will meet the needs of men.

The covenant relation carries over into the New Testament.[4] Both John the Baptist and Jesus rebuke Israel, but they do not break with Israel. Their ministries call Israel to repent and take her rightful place in the coming kingdom of God. Jesus lives with deep loyalty to his people—to their Scriptures, their heritage, and their worship in both synagogue and temple. Even mounting official opposition did not drive him into gentile lands; he remained one of God's covenant people, and he regarded his work as a stage in God's dealing with them. When he came to the end of his life, faced the fact of impending death, and undertook to teach his disciples their future relation to him, he gave them broken bread and wine as symbols that his death would establish the new covenant, which would continue the old covenant relation but would realize the new relation with God which Jer. 31:31 ff. had anticipated (Matt. 26:28; Mark 14:24; Luke 22:20; I Cor. 11:25).

The disciples clearly understood that Jesus retained the ancestral covenant bond with Israel. Proof of this is their reluctance to leave Jerusalem and their faithfulness in carrying their message into temple and synagogues (Acts 2:46; 6:9). Paul too knows of the church's close tie with Israel (Gal. 3:17). Even in his gentile mission he never surrenders it; he looks forward to the time when all Israel will be saved (Rom. 11:26-27). But he too speaks of the new covenant which the death of Jesus has established (II Cor. 3:6). The writer of Hebrews likewise stresses that new, better, eternal covenant (7:22; 8:6, 8; 9:15; 12:24; 13:20).

This combination is characteristic of the New Testament. The church is continuous with the Old Israel and inherits its covenant with God. Yet its life and relation to God has a new center in Jesus Christ. Both aspects are basically religious and inherently social; they put the tie with God first, but they realize this tie in the setting of God's people. A new stage has come, but the covenant bond has not been broken;

---

[4] See, for example, Frederick C. Grant, *An Introduction to New Testament Thought* (New York and Nashville: Abingdon Press, 1950), pp. 247-48, 315-16.

it has only been given a new center in Christ and a new effectiveness through what he has done for men. His followers are still the people of the covenant.

The Church and Israel

The church thus preserves the tie with Israel. This bond does not rest on custom, expediency, or human wisdom, but on the purpose and work of God. What he has done in Christ is the crown and climax of his work for Israel. The church therefore cannot break that tie with Israel or disown the heritage received from Israel. They feel a deep unity between their own common life and worship and the faith, life, and worship of Israel before Christ. They unhesitatingly take over the Scriptures of Israel as their Scriptures. The Jews are the nucleus and constitute permanently an important group within the new covenant people.[5]

But a sifting was taking place within Israel. The Christians were conscious of being *the true Israel*. They did not secede. On the contrary, they knew that they were full members of God's people. In the first days of the church all its members were Jews or had become Jewish proselytes (Acts 6:5) before coming into the church; they had a sense that they belonged to Israel and were the true Israel. To be a true Jew was to believe in Christ, who had been sent to fulfill the promises of God to his people and to carry out God's purposes. So the disciples remained in Judaism. They worked by their Christian witness to win other Jews to share their faith, which continued and completed the inherited faith of their fathers.

In time the sense of being the true Israel gave way to the sense of being *the new Israel*. They centered life in Christ; they could not conform to the views of non-Christian Jews. The sense of God's great new work in Christ and of Christ's great new gifts held their life centered in Christ. So one of two things had to happen: either the other Jews had to accept this Christian witness, so that Judaism became God's willing instrument to carry forward his purpose made known in Christ,

[5] Cf. G. A. Danell, "The Idea of God's People in the Bible," *The Root of the Vine* (London: A. & C. Black, 1953), pp. 23-36.

or the disciples who centered their life in Christ would be forced out of traditional Judaism and required to organize their life in a separate form.

The continued refusal of Jewish leaders and of most Jews to accept the gospel witness to Christ forced the disciples to accept the latter alternative. Against their will they were driven out of Judaism. But they did not surrender their heritage from Israel. The faith, history, Scriptures, and promises of Israel had pointed forward to Christ; therefore the Christians were the true successors and rightful heirs of those earlier generations. They were the new Israel, the covenant people of God, related to him through that renewed covenant relationship. They were indeed personally responsible, but they were not individualists. The greatest gifts in life, the greatest privileges they possessed, the rich promises which assured them of a bright future, were theirs as members of the people of God.

Since God initiates the covenant, the church as the covenant people is not a voluntary human association or a human invention but a divine creation. The church is continuous with Israel, yet what God has done in Christ is so decisive and effective that the new stage of God's dealings centers faith, worship, life, and thought in Christ.[6] It ties the benefits of the covenant to the relation of faith in Christ. By the very nature of God's covenant, the church is where men find God's righteous will and outreaching grace. It is the Christian's home, where he receives God's gifts, acknowledges his obligation to fulfill God's will, and finds his fellowship and place of usefulness precisely as a member of God's covenant people.

The New Testament, like the Old, knows no purely individualistic way of life with God. It does indeed demand a personal decision and responsible living, but all that God gives and all that man should do are set in the framework of that covenant relation. Christ, the risen and exalted Christ, is the rallying center and head of the people of God.

[6] Tracing a common pattern in the successive stages of God's people, W. J. Phythian-Adams calls this relation "homology" in The Way of At-one-ment (London: SCM Press, 1945).

Did Jesus Found the Church?

The long-standing Christian view makes Jesus Christ central as the founder and head of the church. This view, however, has met more than one challenge in recent decades.

1. The determinative role of Christ fades into a minor place when the church is regarded as already fully present in the Old Testament period.[7] This view exaggerates the continuity with Israel. To be sure, the Bible thinks in terms of a continuous covenant people of God. But the decisive divine action in Christ and the incomparable new privilege which this people of God receives through Christ's work give this people's life a new basis and form.

2. Another view which weakens the tie between Jesus Christ and the church is the purely apocalyptic interpretation of his teaching. This view holds that for him the Kingdom was entirely future. He therefore was only announcing and preparing for the great era soon to come. Besides, he did not look for a church at all. As Loisy said, "Jesus announced the Kingdom, but it was the church which appeared."[8] The implication is that since Jesus preached what did not come to pass, his kingdom teaching is discredited, and he can hardly become the Head and Lord of a church which he did not foresee.

We have seen good reason, however, to conclude that Jesus saw the beginning of the Kingdom in his own person and ministry.[9] He was gathering the nucleus of the Kingdom. The movement he was heading was the earthly preliminary form of the final Kingdom. He was actually heading the movement which God would expand to become the triumphant divine order of the future. Thus a deep continuity linked the fellowship, which he headed in the days of his ministry, with the church that followed and the final Kingdom to which he looked forward.

3. Still a third view which denies a decisive role to Jesus in the

[7] When Calvin, e.g., says that "from the foundation of the world, there has never been a period in which God had not his church in it" (Institutes, Book IV, ch. i, paragraph 17), he does not intend to obscure the unique work of Christ, but he is open to misunderstanding.

[8] L'Évangile et l'Église (Paris, 1929), p. 153. Cf. also Werner Georg Kümmel, Verheissung und Erfüllung (2nd ed.; Zürich, 1953).

[9] See chapter v.

church dates its real founding in the Apostolic Age. Jesus was but a prophet, a great teacher, a good man. He did not think, nor did his followers think during his lifetime, that he personally had a permanently central role in his movement.[10] The creative forces and the creative minds and spirits from which the church arose must be dated later. He was but the historical incident around which—by some strange chance—other factors clustered to give the church its start, without really owing their origin or power to him.

For the moment it is enough to say that this statement would have shocked the Apostolic Church and aroused it to indignant protest. If this strange chance happened, the Christians never suspected it. To them Jesus Christ was the center of history, the rightful object of their faith and loyalty. We must believe them, for the alternate view is historically absurd. It makes no sense to say that they were complete dupes, and then say that they had the acumen, intellectual force, and moral sturdiness to originate the gospel and the church.

4. Finally, the almost complete absence of the word church in the Gospels appears to some a decisive argument. It occurs only in Matt. 16:18; 18:17. This is thought sufficient to show that Jesus himself had no idea or intention of founding or heading the church. The answer to this objection reminds us that Jesus did not secede from Judaism. He was and remained one of the covenant people of God; his work was continuous with God's earlier work for that people and was its crown and fulfillment. That people would have deep roots in the past but would now go on in the new form under his leadership. The essence of the church was present in his thinking and purpose. God's people would live henceforth on the basis of what God had done in him; he would be the central figure of the future as well as the fulfillment of God's past promises.[11]

We do not mean, nor does the New Testament say, that Jesus described the church just as it developed in later generations. He said almost nothing about the exact form and government of the church. His interest centered in people and in the relation they would have to

---

[10] Cf. MacKinley Helm, *After Pentecost* (New York: Harper & Bros., 1936), p. 55.
[11] Similarly R. Newton Flew, *Jesus and His Church* (London: Epworth Press, 1938).

God and other people if they accepted his leadership and gifts. He was sure that God's kingdom was coming, and he gathered a group to witness to its coming and prepare others for it. He appealed to Israel to become the instrument of God's will; even in his death he was challenging Israel to accept his appeal and follow his lead. He did not speak of the later development except in broad outlines. It was only later, when Israel officially and generally had rejected his claim, that the exact outward form of the separate church emerged.

But the evidence is that Jesus lived as one of the covenant people of God. He preached the dawning rule of God. He called men to share his fellowship in that dawning Kingdom, to witness to it, and to prepare for its full coming. As the Messiah of the Jews he assumed the central role in that people of God, so that henceforth to belong to that people was to live under his leadership. He called for a loyalty to him and his cause which transcended all other loyalties. So the way his disciples must take when the Jews or any other group rejected their witness was clear; they had to take their separate way; they had to continue to witness to Christ and serve his cause. He thus created a group that would stand against all opposing groups and acknowledge him as its center and leader. The Last Supper was a promise that his group would continue by the benefit of his work and in spite of the world's opposition. His death, resurrection, and exaltation to lordship sealed and confirmed that work.

Thus there emerges, as a direct result of the ministry, death, resurrection, and continuing leadership of Jesus Christ, a definite group which owes its existence, its faith, its fellowship, its witness and kind of life to him. The historical study of the New Testament has seen numerous attempts to explain the rise of the church without giving the essential credit to the intention and work of Christ.[12] None of them is historically credible; the only explanation which really explains what happened is the New Testament explanation that Jesus Christ by his total work brought the Christian church into being.

[12] Two instructive critical surveys of such trends are: Olof Linton, *Das Problem der Urkirche in der neueren Forschung* (Uppsala, 1932); F. M. Braun, *Neues Licht auf der Kirche* (Köln, 1946).

Christ's Relation to His Church

How does the New Testament sum up the relation of Christ to his church?

1. Jesus Christ is "the church's one foundation." In an equally true and even prior sense the church is, as Paul called it, "the church of God" (I Cor. 15:9). But he established it through Christ, and because the role of Christ the Son is so central and decisive, the historical fact is that Christ founded it. As we have noted, the apostles unanimously held that the church was no creation of man; it resulted from the work of Christ their Lord. They were not the foundation. They owed all that they were to what Christ had already done and continued to do for them (Eph. 4:7, 11). He was the church's one foundation.

One figure which Paul uses to express the important role of Christ describes him as the chief cornerstone (Eph. 2:20).[13] Even this, however, is not an adequate figure, for the cornerstone was only one stone, even though it was the large keystone of the building. This figure does not express the full uniqueness of Christ as founder of the church.[14]

Another figure used by Paul more clearly expresses his meaning. He simply says that Christ is the foundation, and no other foundation can be laid (I Cor. 3:11). This is the central Christian witness. God founded the church on the person and work of Jesus Christ. All the divine work of the past has its place; all the accompanying factors in the emergence of the church contribute in their way; but the decisive action, the actual foundation, the supreme role, belongs to Christ and to Christ alone. This is the New Testament view.

2. Jesus is the church's redeemer. This is the testimony of several New Testament writers. "For the Son of man also came not to be served but to serve, and to give his life as a ransom for many." (Mark 10:45.) "I lay down my life for the sheep." (John 10:15.) So the church is "the church of the Lord which he obtained with his own

---

[13] In opposition to Edgar J. Goodspeed, The Meaning of Ephesians (Chicago: University of Chicago Press, 1933), and C. Leslie Mitton, The Epistle to the Ephesians (Oxford, 1951), I accept Ephesians as a general letter of Paul. For this view see Ernst Percy, Die Probleme der Kolosser- und Epheserbriefe (Lund, 1946).

[14] The statement that the twelve apostles form the twelve foundations of the New Jerusalem (Rev. 21:14), does not intend to dispute the basic role of Christ.

190

blood" (Acts 20:28); "Christ redeemed us from the curse of the law" (Gal. 3:13); "in him we have redemption through his blood" (Eph. 1:7). This is the general New Testament view. And it is early; Paul was told at conversion, and even earlier may have known the claim, that "Christ died for our sins" (I Cor. 15:3).

Some scholars have considered this view a later addition to the original teaching of Jesus and the earliest Christian preaching.[15] They have said that all the Prodigal Son had to do was to rise and go to his father (Luke 15:20); there was no barrier, no need of redemption, no hint of any mediator; he just acted by his own power and initiative, and nothing more was needed. They have said that at the Last Judgment, according to Jesus' picture, only men's attitudes toward their fellows will count (Matt. 25:31-46). They have said that the themes of ransom, redemption, and the mediation of Christ (e.g., Mark 10:45) are later additions to the tradition.

One thing is certain. The earliest New Testament writings know the redemption theme and accept it. It permeates the earliest letters, those of Paul, who knows of no challenge to it in the church.[16] To remove from the gospel tradition all trace of the central role of Christ for Christian faith and all mention of the benefit his death gives his followers would be a major operation. It would require us to say that at the very start of the Apostolic Age, in the matter of a few months at the most, these views gained unquestioned acceptance into a tradition that previously had known nothing of them. This is a violent and implausible historical reconstruction.

It is pitiable special pleading to demand that the full range of Jesus' thinking must be clearly expressed in every parable and saying. The parable of the Prodigal Son expresses vividly the free grace and forgiveness of God, but it does not attempt to explain everything involved in salvation. The picture of the last judgment makes the point that man's treatment of his fellows is an essential part of his relation to God; it also makes the Christologically important point that the Son of Man will act for the Father in passing the final judg-

[15] E.g., Ernest William Parsons, *The Religion of the New Testament* (New York: Harper & Bros., 1939), p. 29.
[16] Elias Andrews, *op. cit.*, ch. iii.

ment, and men's treatment of their fellows is part of right relations with the Son of Man.

In his teaching Jesus made it clear that men sin and need forgiveness. He spoke for God and offered forgiveness to those who would repent. He worked to help men find the way to God and good living. He gathered disciples and became to them a source of strength and guidance. Yet they failed him. They were slow and dull, and at the end deserted him. He went to the Cross in steadfast dedication to his work, but they failed in loyalty to him.

They knew that their privilege in the church, after Christ had risen and sent the Spirit, was not their own achievement. They could only rest back on his unselfish work and the benefits it brought to them. Experience and grateful conviction led them to say that the church was founded on Christ's sacrifice and work. They had faith, fellowship with one another, and new life, but they had it because God had acted to save them; through Christ he had redeemed them from their fault and weakness.

At the very first the doctrine of redemption was not fully and explicitly formulated in the minds of the church and its preachers. But the basic fact, that the church owed its life to the vicarious work of Christ, was present from the beginning. Even during Jesus' ministry, his closest disciples sensed it. The post-resurrection church knew it. Christ was the church's redeemer; only so had it come into being.[17]

3. Jesus Christ is the church's teacher. The orthodox emphasis on the Cross and Resurrection sometimes minimizes his teaching. This is a radical error. For one thing, it makes the figure of Jesus vague. What he is, what he does for men, becomes clear and definite only when it is clear what he stands for; and to learn this we must go continually to the Synoptic Gospels and study his acts and teaching. As Form Criticism has recalled, the church preserved and used the teaching and stories of Jesus in its worship, controversy, and instruction. The tradition was continually in use to give the church needed

---

[17] I know that the appeal to early Christian experience has limitations. But the eager search for background influences must not lead us to forget what happened to the first disciples and what their experience taught them.

light on the Christian way of life.[18] Through this tradition Jesus became the permanent teacher of the church.

Of course Jesus had not spoken about all the questions that would arise in succeeding years. But the basic role of the concrete teaching of Jesus was established, and the guidance of the Spirit would interpret that teaching and lead the church to apply it as it faced new situations.

4. Jesus Christ is the church's Lord and Head. Overemphasis on the ministry and teaching of Jesus has bad results. It leads his church to think of him only in terms of that past earthly ministry. The main point of our entire presentation of the New Testament message is that for the writers of these books the present role of Christ as the risen, exalted, active Lord of his church holds a central place (Phil. 2:11). Once he had been crucified, had risen, and had assumed the exalted leadership of his people on behalf of the Father, the church could never again think of him merely as the prophet, teacher, friend, healer, and example of Galilee. They could never think of him as a dead martyr. He was alive; he was the authoritative Lord of his people.

To describe this living relation a widespread tendency today prefers to call Christ the "Head" and the church his "Body." There is New Testament basis for this (Eph. 1:22-23; 4:15-16). But it is not the central New Testament theme. The reference to the church as the body of Christ is a figure of speech, and the modern tendency to ignore that fact is regrettable.[19] A Christian has more of an individual will and responsibility than does a finger or toe in a body. (The figure of the vine and its branches, in John 15:1-6, has the same limitation.) The illustration of the body and its members, or of the body and its head, is therefore not completely adapted to describe the relation between the Christians and their Lord. Each Christian is a responsible individual, but he is answerable to Christ and subject to him.

That is why the New Testament uses "Lord" so widely for Christ.[20]

[18] See my *Origins of the Gospels* (New York and Nashville: Abingdon Press, 1938), ch. iv.

[19] The church is also referred to as a building or temple or city or wife or bride (Eph. 2:21; 5:32; Rev. 21:9). On the church as the body of Christ, see Nelson, op. cit., pp. 67-84.

[20] See Hermann Sasse, "Jesus Christ, the Lord," in *Mysterium Christi*, ed. by G. K. A. Bell and A. Deissmann (New York: Longmans, Green & Co., 1930).

As we have said, every New Testament writer uses it, as did both the Aramaic-speaking and Greek-speaking circles of the church. It was early in origin and universal in use. It expresses the power and authority of Christ, who is authorized to act for the Father. It avoids all suggestion of an automatic relation to the Head of the church, and gives a clear place to responsible faith and loyalty. It avoids any suggestion that Jesus' followers are freed from the demand for intelligent decision and living.

Christ is the active, authoritative Lord of his church. As such he receives reverence such as no human leader rightly receives. The worship of the church is directed to God, and the relation of the Lord of the church to the Father is so close that the worship addresses them both.

5. Jesus Christ is the Shepherd of his flock. It is worth while to note this New Testament title because "Lord" may suggest a forbidding sternness and severity which it did not have for believers. When we see how the "friend of tax collectors and sinners" (Matt. 11:19) was moved by a pastoral concern for the people of God, we place his lordship in the true light.

This shepherd theme occurs in the teaching of Jesus. His friendship for the despised and the outcasts expressed his concern and his seeking love for all conditions of men; he is the shepherd seeking his lost sheep, and he was sent to the lost sheep of the house of Israel (Matt. 15:24; 18:12-14; Luke 15:3-7). In the Gospel of John he is the Good Shepherd who lays down his life for his sheep rather than let them suffer harm (10:11-18). He is "the great shepherd of the sheep" (Heb. 13:20), "the Shepherd and Guardian of your souls" (I Pet. 2:25).[21]

Wherever the church is mentioned as a flock, this idea of Jesus as shepherd is probably in the background (Luke 12:32; I Pet. 5:2). It expresses the fact of his kindly, active, constant pastoral care for his people.

6. Jesus Christ is the giver of the Holy Spirit to the church.[22] The Spirit is the gift of the Father and the exalted Lord; he brings the

---

[21] It is a reversal of the figure to call him the "Lamb of God" in John 1:29, 36, and "the Lamb" in Rev. 5:6; 14:1; here the sacrificial offering of himself and the traditional image of the lamb as leader are involved.

[22] See ch. viii.

presence and power of God to the church and to individuals as they share the church's faith and fellowship; he is given to all believers, and particularly to those with specific tasks and responsibilities. He is God's eschatological gift, the first payment and guarantee of the series of eschatological blessings which God will give to the church (II Cor. 1:22; 5:5; Eph. 1:14).

Through the Spirit, Christ's work is carried forward. He interprets Christ's teaching and ministry, witnesses to Christ and continues the work of Jesus among men. He effects regeneration in men. He creates unity and community fellowship among believers. He gives joy, guidance in prayer, interpretation of prophecy, guidance in decisions. He qualifies leaders to assure men of the forgiveness or continued guilt of sins. He gives power to witness to Christ, bestows various spiritual gifts which enable all to take a mutually helpful part in the life of the church, produces the fruit of the Spirit in daily life, gives endurance in hardship, and fosters hope.

These results are the work of God in the church. We may say, and the New Testament says of many of them, that they are the work of Christ. We may also say, and the New Testament does say, that they are the work of the Holy Spirit in the church and in the Christian. At its origin and at every stage, the church is completely indebted to God for all that it has and achieves. Christ has done all that is needed to make possible the existence, life, and work of the church. The Holy Spirit is active to make this work of Christ effective in the faith, worship, fellowship, witness, and life of the church.

"All Who Believe"

Who then may be members of Christ's church? The full answer to this question was not clear at first. It is characteristic of biblical revelation that the full meaning of God's actions is not always completely understood at the start. It becomes clear in the course of his dealings with his people. This was the case with the question of the range of membership in the church. Jesus did not make clear the later form or extent of the church; he spoke of the failure of some in Israel to take advantage of God's offer to them, and he said that men from all points of the compass would finally have a place in the Kingdom (Matt. 8:11-12). But his primary appeal was to Israel. The apostles after Pentecost likewise appealed first to their own people. Only through the guidance of unfolding events did the full scope of the church become clear to them.

One thing, however, was clear from the beginning. The church was the covenant people of God, and it was God's call, not man's brilliance or goodness, which gave men their place in the church. This church was no human creation or achievement. God's action was its basis. Men came into it because God in his goodness offered the privilege to them. And as God's covenant people, the church was the successor to the Israel of the Old Testament story. It was the new form of the people of God into which Jesus was born.

Naturally, therefore, the gospel came "to the Jew first" (Rom. 1:16). This idea was no invention of Paul; it was plain historical fact. Jesus was born a Jew, worked among Jews, had almost no contacts with Gentiles during his ministry, and aimed basically at winning Israel to accept God's newly revealed will and so become his loyal servant.

The apostles continued this appeal to Israel. It took persecution to scatter them into other regions, where, much to their surprise, the gospel began to win adherents among Gentiles. Even Paul made it his practice to preach first in every city to the Jews. The curious idea that after he turned to the Gentiles at Antioch in Pisidia (Acts 13:46) he thereafter concerned himself only with Gentiles is wrong. He later continued his fixed practice of going first to the Jews in every city (e.g., Acts 14:1). Some of the first Christians refused to recognize Gentiles as Christians unless they accepted the Jewish Law and became Jews before they sought admission to the church. Such stagnant narrowness was wrong, but it reminds us that the gospel came "to the Jew first."

But it came "also to the Greek." In the Hellenistic cultural setting of the Mediterranean world in the Apostolic Age the word "Greek" was widely used, as it is in this phrase of Paul, to mean "Gentile." The gospel was for Gentiles as well as Jews. The early church was slow to recognize that Gentiles could believe in Christ and enter the church without prior conversion to Judaism. The Apostles stayed in

Jerusalem—even when persecution scattered the Greek-speaking wing of the Jerusalem church (Acts 8:1). The scattered disciples at first did not preach to Gentiles; humanly speaking, it was almost by accident that they began to preach to non-Jews; it was a step they had not planned (Acts 11:19-20). The much later legend that the apostles divided the world into twelve parts and went out to conduct a systematic world mission is pure fiction. The church haltingly and through the scattered Greek-speaking survivors of the Jerusalem persecution was pushed out into wider work.

The steps sketched by the Book of Acts are entirely credible.[23] First, proselytes were accepted without question, for their full acceptance of the Mosaic Law and customs made them Jews (6:5). Then the Samaritans, who shared the Law with the Jews, were received (8:6). God-fearers, Gentiles who had an interest in Judaism and partially conformed to its practices, were accepted after hesitation (11:18). Finally, the church decided after debate to include Gentiles who had no previous tie with Judaism (Acts 15:1-35; Gal. 2:1-10). This was the decisive step—to accept such Gentiles without requiring them to observe the Jewish ceremonies and Law.

This final decision followed a violent protest from those who held that the people of God were permanently subject to the legal and ceremonial precepts of the Mosaic Law. These conservatives saw that through such missions as that of Paul and Barnabas the number of Gentiles was becoming so large that the church would soon be predominantly Gentile. Their protest led to conference between the Jerusalem leaders and the missionaries to the Gentiles.[24] The accounts of that conference raise difficulties; if we identify the conference of Acts 15 with that which Gal. 2:1-10 describes—and this seems most likely—the two versions differ in details. But on the basic point they are at one. The Jewish-Christian leaders at Jerusalem agreed with Paul and Barnabas

[23] An able critical but constructive study of developments is that of Maurice Goguel, *The Birth of Christianity*, tr. H. C. Snape (New York: The Macmillan Co., 1953), with which one can agree on most points. See also Gregory Dix, *Jew and Greek* (New York: Harper & Bros., 1953), and J. Munck, *Paulus und die Heilsgeschichte* (Copenhagen, 1954).

[24] See Kirsopp Lake's note on "The Apostolic Council of Jerusalem" in *The Beginnings of Christianity, Part I, The Acts of the Apostles*, Vol. V (London, 1933), pp. 195-212.

that Gentiles did not need to keep the Mosaic Law to be Christians. The entrance into the church was not by way of a prior conversion to Judaism. Gospel preaching henceforth was not subject to Jewish restrictions. The Christian faith has world-wide scope; it is open to all men on the same terms.

Those terms ignore the physical accidents of racial origin, the ritual factors of Mosaic Law, the external conditions in which the gospel finds a person. They focus upon the spiritual and moral aspects, the universal aspects; they require the hearer to repent for past sin, to accept in grateful faith the gospel's offer of salvation, and to dedicate life to the worship of God through Christ and to the service of men in love. The completeness and the immense significance of Paul's victory over Jewish narrowness is reflected in the later books of the New Testament. They simply take for granted these universal aspects of the faith. The violent struggle of Paul's days is past. The gospel is for all who will truly believe.

This message not only ignores henceforth the racial, national, and ceremonial limits that Judaism had known; it also speaks to all classes of men. Jesus included in his sympathy and appeal all the poor and despised members of Israel (Luke 15:1), and on rare occasions, when special need drew his attention, he went outside of Israel to give specific help to Gentiles (Matt. 8:5-13; Mark 7:24-30).

The same kindly concern for all classes—the poor, the underprivileged, and even the slaves—is prominent in the apostolic ministry. Persons of means and influence are mentioned, in Acts and in the letters of Paul, but they are the small minority. All the evidence supports the picture of I Cor. 1:26; the overwhelming majority of the early Christians came from humble social situations. The early church had sensitive sympathy and concern for just those persons and classes who most needed a message of friendship.

The Role of the Family

The discarding of racial ties left a need for other ties to hold the church together. When race, nation, class, and cultural standing are no longer the basis of unity, a strong new bond is greatly needed. The essential new bond was of course the common faith in Christ and the common life which shared faith created. In addition, a social tie which had held a vital role throughout the history of Israel now took on even greater importance. The family became the one natural center of Christian fellowship.[25]

Particularly in the first decades of the church, when there were no church buildings, the homes of hospitable Christians became centers of worship, fellowship, common meals, planning, and instruction (Rom. 16:5, 14-15; I Cor. 16:19; Philem. 2). The family was a unit in Christian faith, worship, and action. The fact that each new family had to come into the fellowship of the church by the definite conversion of at least one of the parents gives great prominence in the New Testament period to personal adult decision. Nevertheless, we find that with a converted parent all the household comes into the church (Acts 16:15, 33; I Cor. 1:16). We encounter instructions for parents and children to heed in their family and community life (Eph. 5:22–6:9; Col. 3:18–4:1).

Thus the family as a social unit becomes prominent and effective in the life of the church. Both by its unity in the faith and by its hospitality to other believers it becomes a church in the home. "The church in thy house" of which several passages tell us was a definite worshiping group larger than the family, but the family was its nucleus, and it recognized the family as practically a small church in itself. Certainly the Christian family was the natural social unit which most supported the growth and nurture of Christians in the church. It recognized that God's will calls for purity of life, love in the home, and Christian witness by the home.

The Leadership of the Church

From the beginning, and by the initiative of Jesus himself, the church had special leaders. Now and then a student of the New Testament has argued that the original church had no legitimate leadership; its form was anarchistic. This contention is certainly wrong. The church arose within the framework of Judaism, and so in its first years did not require a complete new organization independent of Judaism. The patterns

[25] See Cecil John Cadoux, *The Early Church and the World* (New York: Charles Scribner's Sons, 1925), pp. 122-27, 191-94; see also my article, "The Significance of the Early House Churches," in *Journal of Biblical Literature*, LXIII (1939), 105-12.

of Judaism provided a general framework. Until the official leaders and the great majority of the Jews rejected the claims of Christ, the disciples witnessed and worked essentially within the framework of ancestral Judaism. Once separated clearly from Judaism, the need of appropriate forms for the community life of the separate community was more strongly felt. But the community of believers already had the beginnings of leadership and organization. The setting within Judaism and the actions of Jesus himself had provided them.

The forms of leadership took definite shape only gradually. They were not rigid and fixed. This illustrates again the method of biblical revelation. God's will emerges as his people go forward. His full intent becomes clear not merely through decisive historical actions, but also through working out and thinking out their meaning. We need not expect the New Testament to give formal legislation about the constitution, officers, and procedures of the church. Denominations have searched for legal basis in the Bible, but they have erred by introducing the legalistic note into the discussion. We should rather ask: What was God teaching the church about its leadership as the Apostolic Age went on?

The central and constant fact is the key role of Jesus Christ. Not simply as the prophet, leader, example, and martyr, but supremely through his death, resurrection, and active present lordship over his church, he is the Head of the church. Any way of organizing and administering the life of the Christian community must keep this lordship of Christ central and be consistent with it.[26] This principle his disciples recognized. During his ministry they were obligated to accept and do his will and to follow his lead. After his exaltation they gave even fuller recognition to his decisive role as their head and leader. Christ the Lord was the Head of their church; his will and leadership must control.

No inherited pattern of leadership determined the form of the life of the newly emerging church. Continuity with Israel was a fact, and the Scriptures of Israel were accepted without question as the Scriptures of the church. But the prophetic message of the Old Testament replaced the priestly ministry of the law as the central feature of Old Testament

---

[26] Cf. T. W. Manson, *The Church's Ministry* (London: Hodder & Stoughton, 1948); Daniel T. Jenkins, *The Nature of Catholicity* (London: Faber & Faber, 1942).

content, and the leadership of Jesus stepped into the center and replaced the current priestly leadership of the Jews.

It was solid historical fact which the Epistle to the Hebrews expressed when it declared that the priestly ministry of the Old Testament pointed to Christ, but had now been replaced by Christ's sacrificial and interceding ministry. The church did not see this clearly at first. But from the start its center was in Christ and in a form of human leadership which was independent of the traditional Jewish priesthood. The Epistle to the Hebrews is a clear statement of what was implicit in the Christian movement from its first day.

Whenever Christians have used typological, allegorical, or baldly literalistic methods of interpretation to make the priestly system of the Old Testament normative for the pattern of church organization, they have ignored the decisive role of Christ. They have obscured the way in which the church re-interpreted the Old Testament to give the central role to Christ and to do justice to his prophetic and redemptive ministry. Figurative use of Old Testament levitical regulations to describe what Jesus did has a limited role, but to use those regulations to introduce into the church the priestly system of the Mosaic Law, to use them to justify a hierarchy and to channel grace through a priestly class, is to abandon central New Testament truths.[27]

Two basic facts stand out in the New Testament picture. Historically, no fixed pattern of leadership appears. Theologically, no evidence warrants division of the church into two classes of Christians, with two different ways of access to God.

No Fixed Pattern of Leadership

Historically, the New Testament reflects no fixed pattern of leadership.[28] Leadership existed from the first. But it fell into no fixed pattern, and no legislation determines the organizational form of the church. The vivid expectation of the end of the world, which governed so much of early Christian thinking, stood in the way of making plans for centuries

[27] I fear that this is a tendency in the position of Phythian-Adams, op. cit., and in the works of A. G. Hebert, such as The Form of the Church (London: Faber & Faber, 1944).

[28] Burnett Hillmann Streeter, The Primitive Church (New York: The Macmillan Co., 1929), represents this view.

to come. At the most the stages and aspects of New Testament leadership can furnish pointers for the later church.

The church is a definite body of believers. Jesus called disciples. (The word means "learners," "pupils," "followers," and does not in itself indicate a special office as leader in the church.) He gathered a definite group of followers. Similarly the earliest church gathered its converts into a fellowship of faith, worship, and common life. In this respect the church has definite form. It consists of those who have confessed Jesus Christ as their Lord, have received through him the divine gifts which they could not have earned but could only receive through God's grace, and have joined in worship and life with others who have made the same confession and received the same undeserved privilege.

The Twelve—The Apostles

Within this group of disciples, Jesus chose twelve to receive special training and take special responsibility (Matt. 10:2-4; Mark 3:13-19; Luke 6:13-16). Luke says that Jesus also chose a larger group of seventy for a special mission (10:1). The Seventy, however, play no role in the life of the emerging church. The Twelve were to be with Jesus and to go out to teach and to heal. They went out on one such mission of teaching and healing, and reported success. They continued with Jesus to the end of his life, and were the nucleus of his followers.

Either during Jesus' lifetime, or at the beginning of the Apostolic Church, the Twelve began to be called apostles. This word means "one sent forth" on a mission. It could have been given to the Twelve when Jesus sent them out during his lifetime, but it may have been given to them when the risen Christ sent them out to witness to him and to lead his followers. In favor of this latter view is the fact that the word apostle had a wider meaning than the Twelve. Not only was Paul accepted as an apostle, but other leaders of the Apostolic Age were so called—Barnabas (Acts 14:14), Andronicus and Junias (Rom. 16:7), and James the brother of the Lord (Gal. 1:19) are examples.

The Twelve were filled out after the defection of Judas by the election of Matthias (Acts 1:26). But as far as we can tell, this was the last time the church acted to fill a vacancy in the ranks of the Twelve. As time passed, the Twelve ceased to hold a place as the central leaders of the church. For a time they tended to take this leading place. But the emergence of James the brother of the Lord as leader in Jerusalem and the rise of Paul and other men to leadership in the gentile churches illustrate the process by which the Twelve ceased to head the church.

Some, indeed, claim that the apostles continued to be the recognized heads; they hold that all later church organization derives from them and has apostolic character only through an unbroken line of leaders descending from them.[29] The later church is certainly apostolic; it carries on the apostolic witness and preserves the faith which the apostles preached. But the idea of successors to the apostles is open to question. The essential task of the apostles was to witness to the Resurrection. (Acts 1:21-22; I Cor. 9:1.) Their essential role was a first-century witness to what they had seen and heard and therefore could attest.

It may be replied that an unbroken succession of leaders ordained by the apostles and by their legitimate successors gives the necessary guarantee of the purity and truth of the gospel message. This apostolic witness is certainly basic, but it is better preserved in the canon of Scripture than in a succession which now announces as an essential item of the apostolic faith that the Virgin Mary ascended bodily to heaven. The task of the apostles was a unique first-century task; they gave witness and initial guidance to the church; their witness is better preserved in the New Testament than in the numerous curious ecclesiastical developments of later centuries.

The Role of Peter

Among the Twelve, Peter held a special role, both during Jesus' lifetime and in the first years of the church.[30] In fact, he was the "key man" in the first years of the Jerusalem and Palestinian church. But in less

[29] On the ministry of the church, and especially the Apostolate, see Maurice Goguel, L'Église Primitive, Paris, 1947, Part Two. For the Anglican view see K. E. Kirk (ed.) The Apostolic Ministry (London: Hodder & Stoughton, 1946). See also Roderic Dunkerley, The Ministry and the Sacraments (London, 1937), and R. Bultmann, Theology of the New Testament, tr. from the German, Vol. II (1955), 95-111. The newly discovered Dead Sea Scrolls of the Qumrân area apparently come from Essenes. They had a group of twelve leaders and three priests, who may have been included in the twelve (cf. the three "pillars" of Gal. 2:9).

[30] For a comprehensive and up-to-date study of Peter's role, see Oscar Cullmann, Peter: Disciple—Apostle—Martyr, tr. Floyd V. Filson (Philadelphia: Westminster Press, 1953).

than a generation he ceased to be the effective leader of the Jerusalem church; James the brother of the Lord took that place of influence. He was never the real leader of the gentile mission and gentile churches, although Acts 10 and later tradition show that he accepted Gentiles as Christians and visited churches that were partly gentile. Paul says clearly that the leadership of Peter was among Jewish Christians (Gal. 2:7-8). In his one New Testament appearance in a mixed Jew-Gentile church, he sided with divisive Jewish Christians and broke the unity of the group (Gal. 2:11-13).

The New Testament evidence, frankly faced, does not permit us to recognize Peter as the first pope. He was a great Christian and a great leader. His role in the first years of the church was unique and unequalled. Jesus had expected him to carry out such a role, and regarded him as the key man to give the infant church momentum and initial guidance. We must not minimize this immense contribution of Peter. But the New Testament makes it clear that this role did not mean continuing leadership of the whole developing church.

In what we have said we have accepted as genuine words of Jesus the much disputed passage Matt. 16:17-19.[31] Whether they were spoken at the time Peter confessed Jesus to be the Messiah of Jewish expectation is not certain, and is not essential. Were we to give the words the interpretation which many give to them, that they establish a hierarchical priestly succession, we could not make sense either of the message of Jesus or of the history of the Apostolic Age, for no hint occurs elsewhere that Peter was to be the permanent, official, authoritative head of the entire church. But we must give the words their setting in the lifetime of Jesus; we must pay more attention than is often done to what they really say.

Jesus expects Peter to take a leading role, and Peter actually does. He promises Peter that his work will be basic for all the subsequent life of the church, and Peter richly deserves the honor we give to all who carry out their Lord's will in key positions. He assures Peter that he can act with authority, and Peter does act with initiative after the Resurrection; he gives the church leadership of intelligent authority.

[31] Part Two of Cullmann's book on Peter (see note 30) traces the history of the study of this passage and defends its essential authenticity, while dating it at the end of Jesus' life.

But three points deserve more attention than they often receive. First of all, not a word in this passage or in any other saying of Jesus speaks of formal successors to Peter. Jesus never told Peter to appoint successors. He gave him a unique task to do, but said nothing about later generations. This passage gives no support to apostolic succession.

In the second place, the power to bind and loose, whether it means to act in discipline of Christians or to teach with authority what is forbidden or permitted, was not given to Peter alone. According to Matt. 18:18, it was given to the disciples as a group.

In the third place, to regard this authority as a legal function, valid regardless of the intelligence and spirit in which it is exercised, would abandon the whole spirit and intent of Jesus' teaching. It is amazing how Christians can take Matt. 18:18 as literal legislation, valid regardless of the spirit or manner in which it is exercised, when the very next verse contains a promise which every Christian knows is conditioned by spiritual loyalty to Jesus.

In Matt. 18:19 Jesus promises that the prayer of any two Christians will be answered. No condition is mentioned; the prayer will be granted. We know instinctively that God will not grant unwise or selfish or vindictive requests. We must ask in the spirit of Christ, with the reverent desire to know and carry out God's will; we expect to be thwarted when our request is not in accord with God's will. Yet people who know this is true still take the preceding verse as rigid legislation without spiritual or moral conditions. In this they err. Leaders have the approval of God, and Christians as a group have the approval of God, when they ask and act in accordance with his will. Otherwise neither a group decision nor a leader's action can claim authority in Christ's church.

Since, then, Jesus never envisioned successors of the apostles or of Peter, since he gave other disciples the same authority to act for him that he gave to Peter, and since this authority depends basically upon spiritual and moral loyalty to God rather than upon official position, the theory of apostolic succession has no basis in the teaching of Jesus.

New Leaders Emerge

Let us look further at the leadership which emerged in the Apostolic Church. When the needy Hellenistic widows in the church at Jerusalem were not receiving the fair share of relief which their friends thought they deserved, the Seven were chosen (Acts 6:1-6).[32] They are not called deacons, though they were chosen for a task much like that of modern deacons. They did not limit themselves to relief work. All later mention of them shows that they were active in evangelism. In effect, if not in formal recognition, they were the leaders of the Hellenistic Jewish Christians at Jerusalem, a fact which limits the role of Peter and the Twelve even in that city. Stephen soon was martyred for his vigorous preaching, and the rest were scattered in the ensuing persecution (Acts 6:8–8:1). Philip's active preaching in other places is reported (Acts 8:5-40), and the others probably scattered on similar missions.

No successors to the Seven are ever mentioned. They are of great importance in the spread of the church; it was the Greek-speaking Jewish Christians, among whom the Seven were prominent, who spearheaded the spread of the gospel to gentile lands, first among the Jews, and then—somewhat to the surprise of these preachers—among the Gentiles (Acts 8:4; 11:19-21). This epochal development was the work primarily of these Greek-speaking Christians rather than of the Twelve.

James the brother of the Lord was not a believer and follower of Jesus during his ministry (John 7:5). He could not have been entirely unaffected by Jesus' message and work, however, for he was one of those whom the risen Christ confronted and claimed for Christian life. He soon became prominent at Jerusalem, not by any known official action, but by force of personality, earnestness of life, and position in the family of Jesus. He was present from the first (Acts 1:14), had plainly become a leader by the time of Peter's escape from prison (Acts 12:17), and presided at the Council of Acts 15. When Paul went to Jerusalem on his last visit, James was the leader there; Paul "went in" to see him, as one goes into the office of the chief executive of an organization (Acts 21:18). His upright life and strength of character are attested by the Jewish historian Josephus, as well as by ancient Christian writers, and his martyrdom at the instigation of Jewish leaders about A.D. 62 caused even many Jewish leaders to protest. He was the authoritative leader of the Jerusalem church and exercised great influence outside of Palestine

---

[32] On the Seven and Stephen, see Goguel, *The Birth of Christianity*, pp. 167-76.

(Gal. 2:12).[33] Other relatives of Jesus later held leadership at Jerusalem and in Palestine; a tendency emerged to regard physical relation to the family of Jesus as ground for authoritative leadership. This tendency, however, never gained ground outside of Palestine; it had no lasting importance for church polity.

A great and prominent leader, though not one of the Twelve, was Barnabas. A doubtful, later tradition says that he was one of the Seventy. His authoritative role in the church suggests that he probably had been a disciple of Jesus, and since Acts 14:14 calls him an apostle, he probably had seen the risen Christ. Wholly devoted to the church, he even sacrificed his land to feed the poor among the Christians (Acts 4:37). He was the man who gave Paul and John Mark their chance to redeem themselves and serve the church after initial failures (Acts 9:27; 15:39). After leading the important Antioch church for a time, he led Paul out on a missionary program, in which Paul soon proved the more forceful and effective leader (Acts 11:22-26; 13:1 ff.). He illustrates the lack of fixity in early church organization and shows the great contribution which one not of the Twelve could make.

Barnabas was one of the "prophets and teachers" of the church (cf. Acts 13:1). They had a wide and important role. They fit no neat scheme of church officers, but their place in the Apostolic Church must not be ignored in order to find in Acts the outline of some later polity.

Paul likewise fails to fit into any formal scheme of church organization.[34] He was a rank intruder, ecclesiastically speaking, but he established himself in a role equal to that of Peter and the Twelve. He was the leader of most of the gentile churches of which Acts tells us. He claimed, exercised, and was conceded to have authority in preaching, teaching, discipline, and general church leadership. The claims for any scheme of rigid succession which runs through Peter and the Twelve collapse in the fact of the actual role which Paul played. He is the living expression of the principle which Amos illustrates in the Old Testament: God does not have to follow a line of formal succession; he raises up leaders when it pleases him to do so. Those leaders have full authority from God,

[33] On "James and dynastic Christianity," see Goguel, op. cit., pp. 110-18.
[34] He comes in on a broad conception of the Apostolate which is later narrowed to fit the Twelve and Paul only.

and their authority does not depend on formally transmitted, ecclesiastical position.

Local Church Leaders

The leadership of traveling apostles, whether Peter, Paul, or Barnabas, was not enough for the local church. There had to be local leaders.[35] They emerge rather early.

Elders appear at Jerusalem, though we are not told how soon or how appointed (Acts 11:30; 15:2; 21:18). Acts 14:23 mentions elders in churches of Asia Minor. This tradition has been challenged, because Paul in his letters never refers to elders. He does mention local leaders, both those who exercise spiritual gifts without any suggestion that they have been elected or installed to take such leadership (I Cor. 12:28), and those in a more formal position of leadership (Phil. 1:1; I Thess. 5:12). But he never calls them elders. The importance of elders in Judaism, the practice in the church at Jerusalem, and the universal later practice of having elders in the local church (cf. I Pet. 5:1) give good reason to assume that Acts 14:23 has historical basis. In the Pastoral Epistles, which in their present form probably represent a later revision of a Pauline nucleus, the role of elders is clearly defined and their qualifications stated (I Tim. 5:17-22; Tit. 1:5-6).

Closely linked with elders are the bishops. In Phil. 1:1 the term evidently is used of elders, for there are a number of them in the one church of Philippi. In Acts 20:28 they plainly are elders, for they have already been called such in Acts 20:17. In Tit. 1:7 the word "for" clearly implies that the bishop is an elder, one of the group of elders just mentioned. At the most this passage may suggest that one elder is emerging to take a special role of leadership among his fellow elders. The bishop in the New Testament is an officer of the local church; he is an elder in such a church. The New Testament use of the word bishop gives no support to modern episcopal polity.

The other local church officer mentioned is the deacon (Phil. 1:1;

---

[35] In addition to books already mentioned, see the famous essay by J. B. Lightfoot on "The Christian Ministry," in *St. Paul's Epistle to the Philippians* (London: Macmillan & Co., 1868), pp. 179-267. See also Burton Scott Easton, *The Pastoral Epistles* (New York: Charles Scribner's Sons, 1947), pp. 173-79 (bishop), 181-85 (deacon), 185-86 (deaconess), 188-96 (elder).

I Tim. 3:8-13). These deacons were leaders in church life and cared for their fellow Christians in need. We hear also of Phoebe, a deaconess of Cenchreae (Rom. 16:1). This is the one New Testament suggestion that a woman held a formal church office. The deacons of the Pastoral Epistles were all men.

The Role of Traveling Leaders

The argument that the New Testament supports an episcopal and hierarchical system of organization must rest on two main facts. It has no basis in explicit statements of the New Testament, in the use of the word bishop, or in the commission which Jesus gave to Peter. It must rest upon the role of traveling leaders of the church, and upon the fact that they took care to train helpers to continue their work.

In the early days of the expanding church, traveling apostles, prophets, and teachers gave leadership to emerging local congregations and supervised young churches.[36] The church was the total church. The local congregation took its place in the larger fellowship of believers, and was not an independent body. The oneness of the church was expressed not only in the one message which all believed, and in the bonds of friendship which traveling leaders and church members fostered, but also in the supervision which great leaders exercised over more than one local church. The oneness of the church was the primary fact. The "elder" of II John 1 and III John 1 was one expression of this situation; he appears to be a survival of the traveling leadership of the Apostolic Age, and he maintained the bond between local congregations in his region.

What happened when the original traveling leaders died? There is no one simple answer to this question. We know that traveling prophets continued to work in the church even into the second century. These were rather independent leaders.

Another tendency was to turn from traveling leadership and rely on resident, local leadership. Occasional visits gave but temporary help, even when supplemented by letters, as we know was done by Paul. Diotrephes in III John 9 may represent this tendency to rely more on

[36] Cf. H. Greeven, Propheten, Lehrer, Vorsteher, in Zeitschrift für die neutestamentliche Wissenschaft, XL (1952-1953), 1-43.

local leaders. A steady local leader might seem to promise more spiritual help and strength than even the most brilliant occasional visitor.

But a third tendency offered the line along which the idea of apostolic succession was to develop. The Pastoral Epistles, whether Pauline as they stand or only in their nucleus, reflect the conviction that after the apostles were gone, leadership should be taken up by trustworthy disciples who would assume responsibility for a large district. This is the nearest New Testament approach to the later idea of a diocese in which a bishop presides over a group of churches. Nothing, however, indicates that such leaders had the hierarchical ordination and authority of later diocesan bishops. Timothy, we are told, was set apart by the laying on of the hands of the presbytery or body of elders (I Tim. 4:14). This obviously was not the pattern of later episcopal succession.

This discussion of the historical development of leadership in the Apostolic Church shows that there was no fixed pattern. There was leadership, and the church assumed authority when cases of discipline came up. But there was freedom, variety, and development.

The Gospel Excludes Rigid Form

We come now to the second question. What is the theological basis of New Testament thought concerning the form of the church? The church was founded by Christ and serves the risen Christ. It is a redeemed and redemptive society. It is a fellowship of the Spirit, and the power and guidance of the Spirit work freely to adapt the life of the church to the developing situation.

It became clear in time that the church is a universal fellowship of equals, who have a common need, gratefully accept in faith a common redemption, and live in loyalty to a common Lord. They are all members of his church and have a part to play in the one church.

It is a free fellowship; where two or three—any two or three—are gathered together, there is Christ in the midst of his people (Matt. 18:20). This freedom, however, is not selfish or irresponsible; it is freedom in the life of the Spirit and in the responsible fellowship of Christ's people.

It is a prophetic fellowship; the essential thing is not fixed form but attention to the contemporary word of God to his people. Judas can drop out; Paul can come in; nothing in the form of the church stands in the way of such changes. Leaders can be rebuked, as Peter was at Antioch (Gal. 2:14). New ways of doing the tasks of the fellowship can be found and used, as we see when the Seven are appointed. The form is not rigid. Moreover, the Old Testament ritual and pattern of priestly ritual and sacrifice is not normative.

There is no fixed form of government or worship. There is continuity reaching back to Christ and even back to the people of God in the Old Testament period; there is unity in the Spirit; there are order and discipline. But Christ is the Lord, the Spirit can lead into new ways, and the church is free to turn to new methods when life so requires.

There is no hierarchy and no guarantee of formal or legal succession.[37] The guarantee of the church's life and message does not come from human leaders, who are all fallible and so are subject to judgment and rejection when their conduct warrants it. It comes rather from the Lordship of Christ, the guiding power of the Spirit, and the resulting unity of spirit and vital loyalty in the church.

The Worship of the Church

New Testament theology is always tempted to concentrate on the thinking of the New Testament writers. To do so, however, would be to neglect the primary role of worship.[38] The church is first of all a worshiping fellowship of believers, and its formal thinking expresses the convictions and life view implicit in its faith and worship. Clear thinking may correct faulty worship, but in the Christian life worship precedes explicit theology.

It is important to grasp the nature and spirit of New Testament worship. It was vital and fruitful, but this was not because of a pragmatic attitude which judged it by immediate practical results in life. It was an irrepressible outpouring of faith and devotion, without primary regard for its efficiency in gaining benefits for the worshiper.

This worship was not fixed in form. Much of recent talk about "liturgical" patterns in the New Testament is misleading, for it suggests fixed

[37] For the Roman Catholic view see Charles Journet, The Primacy of Peter, tr. John Chapin (Westminster, Md.: Newman Press, 1954).
[38] On early Christian worship see Macdonald, op. cit.; Maurice Goguel, L'Église Primitive (Paris, 1947), Part III, pp. 266-440.

liturgies such as only took set form after considerable time had passed. The riotous variety and spontaneity of worship at Corinth was probably an extreme case (I Cor. 12, 14), but there is abundant evidence that variety and spontaneous freedom characterized the worship of the Apostolic Church. No evidence outside of the Lord's Prayer indicates a fixed pattern of words, and even this Prayer occurs in two divergent forms (Matt. 6:9-13; Luke 11:2-4).

The worship is addressed to God the Father and the Lord Jesus Christ. The opening prayers of Paul's letters illustrate this attitude to Christ in acts of worship; Paul prays that the divine gifts of grace and peace may be given jointly by "God the Father and our Lord Jesus Christ" (e.g., Gal. 1:3). Prayer to Christ occurs. Stephen in his dying moments prays to the Lord Jesus (Acts 7:59). This is possible because the resurrection and active lordship of Christ lead believers to look to him as the present source of divine blessings. This view does not ignore the Father, but it includes Christ.

Such worship is Spirit-inspired (Gal. 4:6). Many modern Christians think that worship is something man does. But the Spirit is present and active in all of the life of the church; its worship as well as its decisions and actions are inspired and directed by the Spirit.

The spirit of this worship is reverent response. It is not the groping quest for God which marks much modern thought. God has come to men, given them what they could not find or earn, and so helped them in their deep need. Man responds to God's initiative and gifts; his worship is not an overture but a reverent response.

The spirit of that response is gratitude (II Cor. 9:15). Numerous passages in the New Testament take the form of prayer and most of them breathe the note of gratitude. This grateful spirit is a continual note of New Testament worship.

Closely coupled with gratitude of response is joy (Acts 2:46-47). The Christians know how deeply indebted they are to God and Christ, and this sense of privilege finds in joy its spontaneous expression.

The sense of immense privilege already received creates also a mood of expectancy and hope. "He who did not spare his own Son but gave him up for us all, will he not also give us all things with him?" (Rom. 8:32.) The New Testament church is often persecuted, but it is not despondent. It looks forward to the victory of God's cause and the vindication of his church, because it has already received great gifts and knows that the future is in the hands of God who has abundantly proved his power and his gracious concern for his people.

There is no magical note about this worship. The worshiper whose brother has something against him is to interrupt his gift and go and do what he can to right the wrong he has done. (Matt. 5:23-24.) The sacraments cannot save; just as Israel had their equivalents but perished in the wilderness (I Cor. 10:1-5), so Christians who are disloyal to Christ will not be protected by sacramental observance. The spiritual and moral always take precedence over form and ritual. It is the attitude of the worshiper and his spirit of obedience to God which count. Far from being a help, insincere worship can be a damaging thing (I Cor. 11:29). Faith, sincerity, love—these are central, and worship has value only as it springs from these and leads to their expression in life.

Private and Public Worship

The New Testament recognizes the place of private worship. Jesus went off alone for times of private prayer (Mark 1:35). He speaks of entering into one's own room and praying (Matt. 6:6). This does not exclude common prayer, but it does give a test of faith and sincerity. One may pray in public because it is the thing to do or because it gives a good public impression. One can pray even in private as a matter of habit and form, but private prayer is free from some temptations to formalism and hypocrisy, and the believer who is deeply grateful for all that God has done for him will be moved to personal expression of reverence, praise, petition, and dedication. Paul speaks of remembering the churches "in my prayers" (e.g., Rom. 1:9; Phil. 1:4). Private worship has its place.

Yet its place in the New Testament is small. Most of the references to worship mean public worship, shared with other Christians. The modern stress on individual devotional techniques sometimes obscures this fact. Jesus set the pattern by going to the synagogue, "as his custom was" (Luke 4:16). He taught his disciples the Lord's Prayer, in which "our" and "we" and "us" remind us that one Christian cannot pray this Prayer unless at least in spirit and outreach he prays as one of the church. The early Christians went to the temple at the hour of prayer (Acts 3:1), worshiped in the Synagogue in the consciousness that they were the true Israel (Acts 13:5, 14), and gathered in houses when they had no other place to assemble for worship (Philem. 2). Common worship was the prevailing New Testament pattern. The hymns of the Book of Revelation both reflect the church's practice of common worship and henceforth further such worship (e.g., 4:8, 11; 15:3-4; 19:1-8).

Aspects of Public Worship

The church's worship had no rigid pattern, but as far as it had discernible roots other than Jesus' career and teaching, they were in the synagogue worship rather than in the temple worship of the Jews or in the varied worship patterns of gentile faiths.[39] Great variety was the constant fact. Freedom was axiomatic. But we can note that prominent features of New Testament worship reflect the synagogue pattern.

The inherited Scriptures were continually used. The church immediately accepted Israel's scriptures, and abundant evidence shows that Christians continually searched and quoted and taught them.[40] The pattern of the synagogue, where Scripture was regularly read and taught, set the pattern for the church. Nor was this only among the strictly Jewish-Christian churches. For all Christians, regardless of origin, the Scriptures were authoritative. Paul unhesitatingly quotes them to gentile churches. They were regularly read in public, for none but a few rich Christians could own a copy. Public reading was therefore necessary. One other fact needs renewed emphasis. All of this reading and study was in the light of the career and work and lordship of Christ. The Scriptures were a witness to Christ, and were interpreted in the light of what God had done in Christ.

Preaching with its explanation of Scripture and life duty was a con-

---

[39] Cf. W. O. E. Oesterley and G. H. Box, *The Religion and Worship of the Synagogue* (London, 1907); George Foot Moore, *Judaism* (Cambridge: Harvard University Press, 1927), II, 3-15.

[40] So Adolf von Harnack, *Bible Reading in the Early Church*, Eng. tr. from the German (New York, 1912), pp. 32-37. This book deals mainly with private reading.

stant feature of worship. This preaching and teaching took different forms according to the situation. Evangelistic preaching and answering of inquirers would meet the needs of those not in the church; further explorations of the meaning of the gospel and application of it to the life of the church was what believers needed. The church followed the synagogue in continually explaining the Scripture and applying it to life. But the church always did this in the light of the fact of Christ.

Just how extensively the first Christians used hymns is hard to say. But evidence proves that they did use them. Such hymns probably included both the well-known Psalms of Israel known from Scripture, and other traditional Jewish hymns. Soon hymns appeared which spoke more directly of God's work in Christ. The hymns of Luke's infancy story (1, 2) and of the Book of Revelation (e.g., chs. 4:8, 11; 5:9-10), with other snatches that seem to come from church usage (e.g., Eph. 5:14; I Tim. 3:16), illustrate this aspect of Christian worship. Gratitude and joy find better expression in hymns than in prosaic treatment. The New Testament church was a singing church.

Prayer was of course the heart of Christian worship.[41] It could never be omitted. It was earnest, humble, grateful, and in spirit if not always in specific wording it was offered in the name of Christ—through whom all the gracious gifts of God had been given to the church (cf. John 14:13-14). The sense of reverent adoration breathes through this prayer. Gratitude permeates it. Humble recognition of human need is expressed. Earnest petition for needed gifts for daily life is offered. Intercession for others—most of all for other Christians, with whom the believer is closely bound—is a necessary part of Christian prayer. (Jas. 5:16.) A spirit of dedication to God and his will is likewise essential.

The only fixed prayer of which we have any knowledge is the Lord's Prayer (Matt. 6:9-13; Luke 11:2-4).[42] Even here we cannot determine the exact form. The form in Luke is much shorter than in

[41] See Gerhard Delling, Der Gottesdienst im Neuen Testament (Göttingen, 1952), ch. viii.
[42] See Alfred Plummer, An Exegetical Commentary on the Gospel According to St. Matthew (New York: Charles Scribner's Sons, 1910), pp. 93-104.

Matthew, which shows that the exact words have no magic even in this prayer. Yet both forms contain essentially the same parts.

This pattern prayer reverently recognizes God as both mighty and fatherly; it voices concern that God, who has made himself known to men, may be reverently acknowledged and honored on earth. Its great petition is that God's kingdom may come, that the divine purpose and will may be fully realized on earth and among men as well as in heaven and among God's heavenly hosts. It is proper to ask God for the real needs of daily life, and because of men's weakness and failure, even in the fellowship of the church, they must make honest confession of sin, pray for forgiveness, and always remember that the worshiper who asks forgiveness must first forgive others who wrong him. The stern seriousness of life's moral struggle warrants the request not only to be spared too great a trial, but also to be given divine help and protection in meeting the inevitable tempations of life.

There was no concluding liturgical formula in this prayer which Jesus gave his disciples. Protestants are widely accustomed to use the doxology which concludes the Lord's Prayer in the King James Version (Matt. 6:13b). This doxology, however, is not found in Luke, and it is absent from the earliest and most reliable manuscripts of Matthew. The most likely explanation of its origin is that when the prayer began to be used in public worship, the doxology was added to give a reverent ending. It probably was composed of words and ideas taken from I Chron. 29:11: "Thine, O Lord, is the greatness, and the power, and the glory, and the victory, and the majesty; for all that is in the heavens and in the earth is thine; thine is the kingdom, O Lord, and thou art exalted as head above all."

Worship in the Sacraments

In addition to the use of Scripture, preaching, hymns, and prayer, Christian worship includes also the sacraments: baptism and the Lord's Supper.[43] They express the basic attitudes of other Christian worship. In them God gives, and man receives with gratitude and responds with

[43] On the sacraments, see Nelson, op. cit., pp. 120-41; H. H. Rowley, The Unity of the Bible (London: Kingsgate Press, 1953), ch. vi.

dedication. They put Christ at the center, and base worship on what God has done for believers through Christ. In the sacraments as in all worship the risen Christ—not merely the human Jesus, the dead leader—is in mind. They promise no magical blessing or automatic gift regardless of the attitude of the worshipers. And the New Testament never suggests that they are controlled or administered by a priestly class or hierarchy.

Christian Baptism

Baptism was not a complete innovation.[44] Even before John the Baptist appeared, the Jews probably were already baptizing Gentiles received as proselytes. But they did not baptize Jews. That innovation apparently was due to John the Baptist. In expectation of the imminent Kingdom, John baptized all Jews who repented and wanted to prepare for its coming.

The method of Jesus, however, was different. In the Synoptic Gospels he never baptizes. Only two verses in the Gospel of John suggest that he had anything to do with baptism, but a correction follows which ascribes the practice exclusively to his disciples (3:22; 4:1-2). Paul also subordinated baptism to preaching (I Cor. 1:17). Such facts warn against overemphasis on sacramental means of grace. But it may well be that Jesus' disciples continued a practice which the Baptist had begun. Certainly the church practiced baptism from the first and understood it to be in accord with the intent of Jesus.

The church baptized "in the name of Jesus Christ" (Acts 2:38). Only once is the trinitarian formula mentioned (Matt. 28:19); the prevailing practice was to use the simpler formula.

The mode of baptism, over which so many verbal wars have been waged, is never made completely clear. There is evidence for immersion; Rom. 6:4 seems to imply it. But other evidence indicates that the church did not always practice immersion. More important were the conditions—repentance and faith. The setting was the fellowship of the

---

[44] See Macdonald, op. cit., ch. xiv; Goguel, L'Église Primitive, pp. 295-342; Franz J. Leenhardt, Le Baptême Chrétien (Neuchatel, 1946); W. F. Flemington, The New Testament Doctrine of Baptism (London, 1948); Karl Barth, The Teaching of the Church Regarding Baptism, Eng. tr. from the German (London, 1948); Oscar Cullmann, Baptism in the New Testament, Eng. tr. from the German (London, 1950); G. W. H. Lampe, The Seal of the Spirit (London, 1951).

church. Baptism was not a private or merely family matter; it was part of the worship and life of the church. It marked the entrance of the baptized person into the church, and therefore was a once-for-all experience.

To one who came to baptism in repentance and faith, the benefits promised were first of all forgiveness for sins, and then the gift of the Spirit (Acts 2:38). This gift was not rigorously tied to the exact moment of baptism; it was received before, or at the time of, or after the baptism (cf. Acts 2:38; 8:14-17; 10:44, 47). Later the rite of confirmation was regarded as the time when the Spirit was given. In the Apostolic Age, however, Christian thought and expectation usually connected that great gift with baptism. The baptized person received the benefits of the death of Christ, entered into the church, and received the Holy Spirit—who henceforth gave direction, power, and joy to the Christian in his worship and life. The sacrament reminded the Christians present of what God had done for them all, and as they welcomed the new member of the church, they were stirred to renewed gratitude for their own privilege.

Infant Baptism?

The church has long disputed whether the New Testament attests infant baptism.[45] Adult conversion was necessarily the means by which the church arose and spread. In the first years, emphasis on the faith and the decision of the adult was common and basic. This may explain why no specific mention of the baptism of a child occurs.

The background, however, would lead us to expect that children were baptized. The importance of the family as a unit in Judaism, the practice of circumcision as a rite marking the place of the boy in the ancestral faith, and the practice of proselyte baptism, in which the family was apparently baptized when the gentile father was converted to Judaism, argue for this conclusion. Gentile cults also initiated families.

The concern for children expressed in such sayings as Mark 10:13-16 proves nothing, though it is in harmony with such a conclusion. More significant are the statements that whole households were baptized

---

[45] In addition to the works mentioned in Note 44, see Pierre Ch. Marcel, *The Biblical Doctrine of Infant Baptism*, Eng. tr. from the French (London, 1953).

at one time (e.g., Acts 16:15, 33). They render it highly probable that small children were included in such groups. In Tit. 1:6 children are addressed as members of the Christian circle. Justin Martyr in the second century speaks of persons who had been in the church from childhood, and Polycarp says that he himself had been. The first protest against infant baptism, by Tertullian, assumes that it had been established practice long before his time. The covenant relation of God with his people, and the vital place of the family in the people of God, imply that the family takes its place in the church and that children are within the covenant. Their baptism attests that fact.

The baptized person receives the undeserved grace of God. Such complete dependence on God is expressed in infant baptism. This was not a primary New Testament idea, but since so much has been made of the necessity of faith as a condition for baptism, it may be pointed out that the role of the family and the place of children within the covenant are likewise basic ideas of the Bible, and so is the complete dependence of men on God for salvation.

The Lord's Supper

The Lord's Supper recalls the Last Supper which Jesus ate with his disciples the evening before his death.[46] All four Gospels tell of that occasion, but only Matt. 26:26-29; Mark 14:22-25; Luke 22:17-20; and I Cor. 11:23-26 tell of Jesus' symbolic action with the bread and wine. The Book of Acts mentions "the breaking of bread" (2:42, 46; 20:7, 11), which is presumably the same type of observance; it is also a special instance of the common practice of breaking bread at every meal.

It is impossible to determine precisely just what Jesus did and said at the Last Supper. The accounts differ in details; the church evidently did not find it necessary to have a rigidly controlled account even of the words of Jesus on that significant occasion. But the essential things are clear. Jesus broke bread (and passed the cup) to call to mind his

[46] See H. Lietzmann, Messe und Abendmahl (Bonn, 1926); Macdonald, op. cit., chs. x, xi, xii; Goguel, L'Église Primitive, pp. 343-62; Franz J. Leenhardt, Le Sacrament de la sainte Cène (Paris, 1948); A. J. B. Higgins, The Lord's Supper in the New Testament (Chicago: Henry Regnery Co., 1952); Joachim Jeremias, The Eucharistic Words of Jesus, Eng. tr. from the German (New York: The Macmillan Co., 1955).

impending death and to interpret it as a benefit to his cause and his followers. He thus gave positive meaning to his death and promised his followers that it would yield them positive benefits. He looked forward to victory in spite of the apparent defeat which he and his cause were facing. He acted in hope. And whether he asked his disciples to repeat this rite or not, he certainly did this symbolic act so that in time to come they would remember what he had done and the meaning he had attached to it, and thus would benefit from his death.

The church did remember and hold to the promise which Jesus gave them. From the references in Acts to the breaking of the bread, as well as from what Paul says of eating and drinking at Corinth in I Cor. 11:21, it is clear that this remembrance took place at a real meal. Paul suggests that those who are too hungry and hurried to recall the meaning of the event, and so may fail to keep the spirit of fellowship, should eat at home before coming to the service. This marks the beginning of the separate rite as now practiced. In many ways, however, the church supper is a better setting for the apostolic type of Lord's Supper than is the rite as we now practice it in our churches.

The Supper did much more for the church than point backward to the death of Jesus and its benefits. That alone would not be a Christian Lord's Supper. Christ had risen; he was the exalted Lord of the church; he was destined to put all enemies under his feet and complete the purpose of God. Therefore, with the Resurrection and Exaltation as the background, the Supper was a time when the risen Christ was with his people. It was a time of fellowship in Christian faith and friendship; therefore the cliques which Paul attacked had no place (I Cor. 11:17-22). It was a time of hope, for the risen Christ was the Lord who would bring the future triumph. The idea of the messianic banquet, in which God's people would feast with Christ in his kingdom, was no doubt often in the minds of the Christians who took part in the Lord's Supper (Luke 22:16). And so the mood was not a time of mourning, but of reverence and gratitude. The Supper rightly came to be called a Eucharist, a thanksgiving service celebrated in joy and hope.[47]

[47] Whether every Christian service of worship had as an integral part the celebration of the Lord's Supper is doubtful to me, but Oscar Cullmann asserts it in *Early Christian Worship*, Eng. tr. from the German (London: SCM Press, 1953). At the December,

Other special practices marked the worship of the church. Fasting and the taking of vows are examples (I Cor. 7:5; Acts 13:2; 18:18). But Christian worship centered in services in which the Scriptures were read, preaching was heard, hymns were sung, and prayer offered, and in special occasions when baptism was administered and the Lord's Supper celebrated. In such worship the faith and convictions of the church came to maximum expression.

The Task of the Church

It belongs to the very nature of the church to worship "the God and Father of our Lord Jesus Christ" (Rom. 15:6; II Cor. 1:3; Eph. 1:3; I Pet. 1:3). It is also its constant duty to care for its members and to develop mutual concern and helpfulness, so that physical needs are met and each member receives the teaching, guidance, and encouragement which every Christian needs. But these duties are not what the New Testament considers the essential task of the church. That essential task is to witness to Jesus Christ and make known what God has done through him, in order that more and more people may come to Christian faith and find their loyal place in the worship and fellowship of the church. The basic task was evangelistic and missionary.[48]

The church may give its witness in more than one way. Whenever Christians live a good and true life, they commend their faith to alert observers. Much as we stress this method today, however, it was rarely emphasized by New Testament writers. The writer of First Peter points out how by loyal lives, the Christian wives of pagan husbands may win their respect and attention to the gospel (3:1).

The church also gives an effective witness when its members live together in loyal Christian friendship. Their relations to one another commend their faith to the outside world (John 13:35). Quarrelsome-

1954, meeting of the Society of Biblical Literature and Exegesis the similarities between the group life, common meals, and eschatological expectation of the Qumrân Essene sect and the early Jerusalem church were pointed out. See now Burrows, op. cit., and on the Messianic Supper, see *Discoveries in the Judaean Desert. I. Qumrân Cave I.* Ed. D. Barthélemy and J. T. Milik (Oxford, 1955), pp. 108-18.

[48] See C. H. Dodd, *The Apostolic Preaching and Its Developments* (Chicago, 1937). Some books which discuss the New Testament doctrine of the church do not consider its mission.

ness repels observers, but mutual friendship and helpfulness win respect and demonstrate the power and worth of the faith which Christians profess.

Patient endurance of wrong was no doubt an effective witness to bystanders. In view of the great amount of ill treatment which the early Christians received, we might have expected repeated emphasis on this point, but in fact it is almost never mentioned. We may infer it from the course of events, and we may surmise that men like the persecutor Saul did not escape the effect of the courageous loyalty of men like Stephen (Acts 8:1). But none of the above three views dominated New Testament thinking.

The one witness which the New Testament almost continually has in mind is the witness to Christ by preaching the gospel and patiently teaching the Christian message to all who will listen. The task is evangelistic. The apostles were to witness to the Resurrection and to the meaning this great event has for faith and commitment to Christ (Acts 1:22; 4:33). All prophets and teachers continually brought the same message to men; first among the Jews, and then in wider circles, they preached and taught and called men to faith. This was what the Spirit prompted men to do. Paul could think of no higher privilege and duty than to preach the gospel, and so he left baptizing to his helpers and concentrated on presenting the gospel to men and pressing them to put their faith in Christ (I Cor. 1:17).

The scope of that witness was the world. The task is a missionary witness. This was not clearly seen at first. The apostles began at Jerusalem; they stubbornly stayed there (Acts 8:1); only the rough hand of persecution scattered the church and taught it that Gentiles too would receive the gospel. It was not the Twelve but the Greek-speaking Jewish Christians who traveled the way to the gentile lands and peoples. Even they had to be scattered by persecution, and even then it was, humanly speaking, almost by accident that they found Gentiles equally open to the gospel message (Acts 11:19-26). But they took the step, and they followed it up.

The apostle Paul emerged as the master statesman of the gentile mission and became the supreme theological and literary defender of that step. Once he had fought out to a successful conclusion his claim that Gentiles, on the simple basis of repentance, faith, and Spirit-led living, had equal rights in the church, the issue soon dropped from sight. The later books of the New Testament are not concerned with it. They can take it for granted that the gospel is for the world. They have understood finally the logic and the clues implicit in the life and teaching of Jesus.

And so we can read in the New Testament the clear statement of the full task of the church. "This gospel of the kingdom will be preached throughout the whole world, as a testimony to all nations" (Matt. 24:14). "For God so loved the world that he gave his only Son, that whoever believes in him should not perish but have eternal life" (John 3:16). "You shall receive power when the Holy Spirit has come upon you; and you shall be my witnesses in Jerusalem and in all Judea and Samaria and to the end of the earth" (Acts 1:8). "Go therefore and make disciples of all nations" (Matt. 28:19).

After this I looked, and behold, a great multitude which no man could number, from every nation, from all tribes and peoples and tongues, standing before the throne and before the Lamb, clothed in white robes, with palm branches in their hands, and crying out with a loud voice, "Salvation belongs to our God who sits upon the throne, and to the Lamb!" (Rev. 7:9-10.)

CHAPTER X

Christ and the Christian

THE NEW TESTAMENT SAYS LITTLE CONCERNING THE origin of man. Its interest centers in the present situation and the future prospect. What it does say about the past is deeply rooted in the Old Testament. There the story begins by telling that God created the heavens and the earth, the world and man. In the light of the lordship of the risen Christ, the church tended to think that even in the divine work of creation, the Father acted through the Son or Logos. But this conviction took no prominent place in the total New Testament content. Christians were keenly aware that their central message was the coming of the Son of God into human life and the radically new work of Jesus Christ. The Son of God had indeed acted throughout the whole sweep of God's work with his world; this the church soon asserted. But they preserved a wholesome sense of the decisively new action of God in the historical life and work of Jesus Christ.

Back of the entire New Testament witness is the deep certainty that God had made man in his own image.[1] He had made man to worship and serve his Maker. He had made man to do the will of God, and man was to do that divine will in all of his life. Since God created the entire man, body as well as spirit, the whole life of man is a unity and must express loyalty to his Maker. For the Creator is also the Preserver and the Lord of man, and so rightly and always claims man's reverent obedience. This basic view, which puts all of human life under the Creator, Preserver, and Lord of mankind, is the unquestioned axiom of New Testament faith and thinking.

[1] See Gösta Lindeskog, *Studien zum neutestamentlichen Schöpfungsgedanken*, vol. I (Uppsala, 1952).

The Fact of Sin

Against this background of God's role as Creator and Lord, the terrible unnaturalness of human sin stands out with startling clarity.[2] Man does not live as he should. The trouble is not that he is finite and dependent, and so limited in life and abilities. This is true, and it continues to be true even of the Christian at every stage of his life on this earth. But it is not the real problem. Finite, dependent man can have a good and happy life.

But such good life exists only where man obeys God's will. Man is so made that he is not himself, he cannot find happiness, unless he accepts God as his Lord and lives in obedience to the divine will. But, as the New Testament sees, man has not yielded this acceptance and obedience. He is a sinner. His need roots in this fact. And this need is universal.

The biblical basis of democracy is quite different from that which we so often hear today. We speak much of the native rights and abilities of men; the Bible speaks of their common lack, their common failure, their common need of help.

This view is often thought to derive from the apostle Paul. He certainly shared it.[3] He definitely and emphatically states the sinfulness of man. "All have sinned." They all "fall short" of the great privilege of a good life with God (Rom. 3:23). This is not merely the fault of a few, nor is it the defect only of those outside the reach of the Jewish Law. All mankind, Jew and Gentile, cultured or illiterate, are sinners (Rom. 3:9). Throughout his letters Paul reflects this conviction, and he argues it in detail and with urgency in Rom. 1:18–3:20.

Since Paul is often accused of blaming the entire problem of sin on Adam, it is worth noting that in these three chapters Paul never mentions Adam. He builds upon his own observation that both Jews and Gentiles sin, and he confirms that picture by the repeated testimony of Scripture. It is true that Paul gave a place to Adam's original sin and

---

[2] See the study of the word "Sin," by Gottfried Quell, Georg Bertram, Gustav Stählin, and Walter Grundmann, in Bible Key Words (New York: Harper & Bros., 1951). This is an English translation from Gerhard Kittel's Theologisches Wörterbuch zum Neuen Testament.

[3] See Andrews, op. cit., pp. 41-43; Rudolf Bultmann, Theology of the New Testament, Eng. tr. from the German, Kendrick Grobel, Vol. I (New York: Scribner's, 1951), pp. 239-53.

its effects. This appears in two passages which contrast the damaging effects of Adam's sin with the redemptive and renewing results of the work of Christ, who thus begins a new humanity (Rom. 5:12-21; I Cor. 15:21-22).

Paul emphasizes the present need, which he plainly sees in the life around him. Moreover, he sees this sin not merely in individual wicked acts, but in the permeation of man's whole life and outlook. The attitudes, desires, strivings, and thoughts of men are corrupted by his evil choices. The whole man is degraded by sin; the whole man needs redemption; the remedy must reach the roots and every branch of human life.

Jesus on Sin

It is true, then, that Paul does teach this universal sinfulness and need of men. But this is not an original invention of Paul. From the beginning the Christian message was an answer to man's spiritual and moral failure. It was so in the preaching of Jesus.[4] He came preaching Israel's need of sincere and radical repentance (Mark 1:15). Their great heritage and special privileges had not saved them from sin; they needed forgiveness from God.

We must not think that Jesus thought many to be sinless when he said: "I came not to call the righteous, but sinners" (Mark 2:17). This clearly was irony. Precisely those complacently satisfied with their spiritual condition were the people in whom Jesus saw the most tenacious sin. How axiomatic he regarded this general need of men to be comes out in one brief thrust: "If you then, who are evil" (Matt. 7:11); he knows that men are not what they ought to be.

Jesus teaches even his disciples to pray regularly, "forgive us our debts, as we also have forgiven our debtors" (Matt. 6:12). They must forgive others; the people they meet will be sinful; the disciples must forgive them all. And they themselves must ask for forgiveness; the taint of sin leaves its mark even on them; they need God's grace continually.

[4] For a study of the word "sin," including its use in the Gospels, see the special note by Ernest De Witt Burton in the I. C. C. on *The Epistle to the Galatians* (New York, 1920), pp. 436-43.

As if to vindicate this view, the disciples repeatedly showed lack of understanding and failed to live in the spirit of Jesus. They *did* need forgiveness; their behavior in the gospel story confirms the teaching of Jesus. It is not only his enemies who need forgiveness (Luke 23:34); so do his friends and followers.

Sin in Apostolic Preaching

The Apostolic Church continued this note.[5] The earliest preaching comes to a climax in its appeal to repent and believe (Acts 2:38). Whether it is Peter speaking to the Jews at Jerusalem, or Paul addressing the cynical Greeks at Athens (Acts 17:30), the apostles preach to sinners, and their aim is to get them to turn from sin and believe in Christ, who offers the answer to their spiritual need.

How soon the apostles clearly and explicitly formulated the tradition that "Christ died for our sins," we cannot say. The original disciples knew from experience, however, that the faithfulness and costly death of Jesus had done something for them. It had given them the open door to a new life and a new opportunity to serve God. When Paul was converted, less than six years after the death of Jesus, he received this tradition: "Christ died for our sins" (I Cor. 15:3).

No evidence exists that the Jewish Christian church ever objected to this message. All available evidence indicates that the church was convinced from the first that sin was the problem which all men had to face; that men could not meet that problem; and that Christ's work provided, as a gift of God, a redemption men could not win for themselves. Paul did not invent the idea of universal sinfulness; he continued with emphasis the attitude of Jesus and the common conviction of the earliest church.

The later New Testament writers share this conviction. It underlies the entire argument of the Epistle to the Hebrews,[6] whose concern is to show that God through his Son has dealt effectively once for all with the problem of sin. We find in I Pet. 2:24 the confident statement that Christ "himself bore our sins"; they were man's pressing problem. In the Book of Revelation the main interest is on deliverance from

[5] See ch. ii.
[6] See C. Spicq, op. cit., I, 284-87.

persecution, but the fact that the Lamb had been slain and had ransomed men of every nation is the background of the further deliverance for which the Christians hope (5:9); salvation both from sin and from the enemies of God is in mind; even Christians had need of redemption from sin. In the Gospel of John the emphasis is on the sin of unbelief (16:9), but the Lamb of God has taken away the sin of the world (1:29).

In other words, all New Testament preaching is fully aware of the sin of all men. The gospel is the answer to that dilemma; the universality of the need is matched by the gospel offer to all.

This sin may be viewed in various ways. Basically it is disobedience to God, who as man's Creator and Lord rightly claims man's worship and loyal obedience. It expresses itself in acts of wrongdoing, and the word sin often applies to such acts. But from the heart "flow the springs of life" (Prov. 4:23). Sin corrupts the whole life of the wrongdoer. The remedy calls for more than outward forgiveness or release from penalty; it calls for cleansing of the mind and heart; it calls for renewal and redirection of the will. Thus sin brings guilt, since man is responsible for his wrong actions, but it brings an inward damage that is even more ominous. To Paul especially sin is an evil power, an almost personal tyrant, which seizes the life of the wrongdoer and enslaves it to evil desires and purposes (Rom. 7:13-20).[7]

It is part of the strength and truth of the Christian message that it takes seriously the fact and corrupting results of sin. Man cannot choose wrong and remain unharmed by his choice. Sin is not merely a personal failure with harmful social effects; it is also and centrally a wrong against God the Lord. It is rejection of God's claim and rebellion against the divine will.

This is the climax of man's dilemma. Man sins; he is in the wrong before God; he loses the ability to right his life and he cannot make good what he has done. Above all, he has no right to expect help from God, whom he has rejected and wronged.

Men's hope lies outside himself, and no other man can help him meet the central problem. Only God can act effectively to meet it. The

---

[7] The best detailed study of this famous passage is by Werner Georg Kümmel, *Römer 7 und die Bekehrung des Paulus* (Leipzig, 1929).

gospel is the story of the answer which God has provided to the problem of human sin, the problem man cannot meet but which must be met if man is to have life and hope.

The Gift of Redemption

What has God done to meet this urgent and universal need of man? We may summarize the amazing variety of the New Testament answers in six statements:

1. Through Christ, God has come to man in his need. The initiative was on God's side. He "sent forth his Son" (Gal. 4:4). The entire ministry of Jesus is an action to find man in his need and bring him God's challenge and help. Jesus used parables to emphasize this outreach of his ministry.[8] He told of the shepherd who searched for his lost sheep, of the woman who searched for her lost coin, and of the father whose love led him to look down the road for the returning prodigal and to plead with the elder brother to show a kindly spirit (Matt. 18:12-14; Luke 15).

What Jesus did during his ministry, the apostles did during the Apostolic Age. They were led by the Spirit to speak first to their countrymen, but before long the church was led, beyond their original understanding and intention, to preach to other peoples. They knew that the responsibility of bringing others into the Christian fellowship lay not with outsiders, but with those already committed to Christ. God was acting through them by his Spirit. He was reaching out to find others and lead them to take their place within the church. "All this is from God" (II Cor. 5:18); he came to man in his need through the sending of Christ and the work of the Holy Spirit.

2. Through Christ, God has provided a costly redemption for sinners. The basic fact is not the later theological formulation of this truth; it is the ministry and death of Jesus. They show how hard it was to deal with human sin and what a price the reclaiming of sinners required. This truth Jesus put vividly when he said that the Son of man came not only "to serve" but even "to give his life as a ransom

[8] On this "new, original, and historic feature in his teaching" see C. G. Montefiore, *The Synoptic Gospels* (2nd ed.; London, 1927), I, cxvii-cxviii.

for many" (Mark 10:45).[9] There is no reason to deny that Jesus said this, especially since it agrees with the implications of the Last Supper, where Jesus promised that his impending death would give positive benefit to his followers.

The theme of redemption finds clearer expression in the letters of Paul; in Christ "we have redemption" (Eph. 1:7; Col. 1:14), a fact which the writer of Hebrews likewise attests (9:12). It is clear to Paul as to other Christians that in a sense this redemption is still incomplete; in the full and final realization, "the day of redemption" is still to come (Eph. 4:30; Rom. 8:23). But the basic redemption from sin has been effected. Through the work of Jesus Christ, God has provided a way to gain release from the guilt and the grip of sin.

3. This redemption from sin through Christ is a free gift which God offers to men who do not deserve it. The gospel is a message of forgiveness. To persons who thought their main need was physical, Jesus first gave assurance that their sins were forgiven (Mark 2:5). "Forgiveness of sins" was what Peter in early sermons promised to Israel (Acts 5:31). It was also the message of Paul: "God in Christ forgave you" (Eph. 4:32; Acts 13:38; 26:18). The Spirit-led disciples can assure men of divine forgiveness (John 20:23). The word grace, a key New Testament term, carries this thought of the free, undeserved outreaching, continual forgiving work of God which comes to men through Jesus Christ.[10]

Another prominent New Testament word which carries this central truth is justification.[11] It is a bold figure. Taken from the law court, it would naturally suggest that the accused person is acquitted, declared innocent, and freed because he deserves it. But Paul seizes upon this word to express the paradoxical fact that God in Christ has acquitted the guilty sinner, who deserved condemnation and punishment. Man stands before the tribunal of God. He is guilty, and cannot conceal that fact from God. He has no right to demand or expect anything but the condemnation he knows he deserves. Yet the miracle of God's

[9] On the authenticity of this saying see Vincent Taylor, *Jesus and His Sacrifice* (London, 1937), pp. 99-105.

[10] See James Moffatt, *Grace in the New Testament* (New York: Harper & Bros., 1932).

[11] Gottfried Quell and Gottlob Schrenk study the word "Righteousness" (and Justification) in *Bible Key Words*; see n. 2 above. See also Ernest De Witt Burton, *The Epistle to the Galatians*, pp. 460-74.

grace is that he acquits the sinner, frees him, and opens to him a new life. Perhaps only a condemned man freed after being strapped into the electric chair could fully appreciate this miracle.

This startling way of putting the fact of God's grace was Paul's emphasis, but he did not originate the idea. The original disciples found that Jesus treated them far better than their dullness and their fumbling lives deserved. Jesus let them see, in the parable which told of the Prodigal Son, that forgiveness is not earned but freely given (Luke 15:21). The publican praying in the temple expresses the need of a forgiveness which is sheer miracle (Luke 18:9-14). Thus the truth to which Paul gave vivid expression roots in the action and the teaching of Jesus. The figure of speech of the guilty criminal acquitted by his judge protects this central truth of the gospel: man deserves condemnation, but in Christ God freely forgives.

4. Through Christ God reconciles men to himself.[12] It is not enough to deal with the guilt of sin. Nor is it enough to break its grip on human life. Man was made in the image of God, and his destiny is to live an obedient life of reverent fellowship with God. Until the fellowship broken by sin is restored, until man is effectively reconciled with his Father, redemption is not a realized fact. For this reason the figure of justification, though vital and meaningful, cannot express the full range of the gospel of grace. The real gift to the Prodigal Son was not merely forgiveness, but restoration to the family fellowship and life with his father.

Jesus was concerned to bring men back into a living fellowship with God which would include loyalty to God's will. Similarly, when Paul speaks of redemption in terms of personal relations, saying that God reconciled us to himself through Christ, he is expressing in a vital way the depths of the privilege of forgiveness (II Cor. 5:14-20; Col. 1:19-23). "We were reconciled to God by the death of his Son" (Rom. 5:10).

The meaning of this reconciliation Paul also expresses by the illustration of adoption. To much modern thought we are all sons of God, regardless of how we live. There is truth in this. God is our Maker, and

---

[12] On the theme of reconciliation in New Testament theology see Vincent Taylor, *Forgiveness and Reconciliation* (London: Macmillan & Co., 1941), especially pp. 83-129.

we belong to him no matter how wayward our life may be. But the New Testament rarely suggests that God is the Father of all men. To early Christian writers, sonship to God is a relation based on spiritual kinship; it requires a response of man to God's goodness and demand, and the prodigal knows that he does not deserve to be called the son of his father (Luke 15:21). Sonship is not a natural right on which the sinner can insist; it is a gift which only God in his grace can give to undeserving man.

This is why Paul uses the figure of adoption. He uses it seldom (Rom. 8:23; Gal. 4:5), and other New Testament writers do not parallel his usage. Yet they agree with his basic attitude, his awareness that it is not natural for a sinner to come into living fellowship with the holy God; such sonship is a miraculously new relationship for one who has been a sinner to enter.

The figure of adoption also dramatizes the deep difference between the relation which Christ the Son holds to the Father and the relation in which redeemed sinners stand to God. They receive what is not their natural right; they are "adopted" into the very family of God, and are given rich privileges which they could never claim as their just due.

This gift of reconciliation and adoption, this establishment of vital personal relations between God and the forgiven sinner, finds a characteristic Christian expression in the theme of union with Christ. In Christian thinking, God's gift of grace, forgiveness, and reconciliation comes through Christ. It is in Christ that the redeemed man finds God dealing with him graciously and authoritatively. So the disciples are called to join their lives with Jesus. "Follow me." (Mark 1:17; 8:34.) This bond, which grew in meaning through the public ministry, was portrayed and deepened in the Last Supper; the benefits which God would give in days ahead would come from what Christ does for them. Apparently broken by the death of Jesus, the bond was clearly reestablished through the Resurrection. It continued in accented form through the exalted lordship of the risen Christ, who through the Spirit was with them to guide, empower, and cheer their lives.

Paul expresses this fact when he declares that it is "Christ who lives in me" (Gal. 2:20). We Christians are "united with him" and as Christians, "Christ is in you" (Rom. 6:5; 8:10). This living bond finds expression in the figure of Christ as the head of the church (Eph. 1:22; Col. 1:18); he is in living touch with all of his people. The Gospel of John expresses this vital relation by the figure of the vine and the branches (ch. 15), and the Book of Revelation presents it in the picture of the Lamb with his people (14:1).

Through Christ, God brings his sinful people back into personal relations with himself; he reconciles them to himself, adopts them into his family, and gives them through their life union with Christ a living fellowship with himself even during the difficult days of this earthly life.

5. Through Christ, God renews sinners and gives them a new and wholesome quality of life. The life of sin is at best a living death. To live is to accept and do the will of God as one lives in fellowship with him. So Jesus tells of a returned prodigal of whom it could be said that he had been dead, but in returning to the father had found life again (Luke 15:24, 32).

Paul put this even more vividly when he spoke of the effect of God's redemptive work in Christ as a resurrection. He implies in Rom. 6:1-4 that the Christian has already experienced a transformation so radical that it can be called a resurrection. Because he still expects the great resurrection at the final day (vs. 5), Paul does not speak quite clearly here of the present state, but he plainly means that the redeemed sinner has undergone a radical renewal. So it is not surprising when he says in Col. 3:1 that the Christian has already been "raised with Christ." This confident assertion was misunderstood (II Tim. 2:18); it led some to say that the Resurrection was already past. Paul still expected the great final resurrection of the body, but the sinner had been raised from the death of sin to "newness of life."

Another figure which expressed the same thing was regeneration. The idea of rebirth in the dialogue with Nicodemus (John 3:3-8) and the assertion of regeneration in Tit. 3:5 illustrate this view. It is implied in other passages, such as I Pet. 2:2, where the writer speaks of new believers as "newborn babes."

Back of this idea is the conviction that sin is a deep, deadly, permeating corruption, which requires a radical renewal if the sinner is to find salvation. A real change in heart, attitude, and life is needed, and

233

God effects it through Christ. A "new nature" comes into being (Col. 3:9-10). The Christian is not the old man he was before; something radical has been effected by God through Christ, not merely on the Cross but also in the very life of the believer.

It is not surprising, therefore, that the New Testament expresses so strongly the theme of sanctification. Divine grace and redemption really change a man. They do more than write off his guilt or give him an outwardly good position; they renew him. And so New Testament writers insist that forgiven persons cannot live in the old ways. These writers think of God as the Redeemer whose redemptive work has transforming power, and so they expect to see changes in the lives of converted Christians. "Newness of life" is the natural way for Christians to live. Struggle they must face, but defeat they need not know.

The apostles see that Christians sin, but they preserve the healthy sense that such sin is abnormal in Christians, and so they refuse to make with it an easy peace. They talk confidently of sanctification;[13] they look for "the fruit of the Spirit" in the lives of followers of Christ (Gal. 5:22-23). This is not an optional or secondary feature of the Christian life; it is an inherent and essential expression of a really Christian life (Jas. 2:14-26). The high ethical demands of Jesus are matched in I Cor. 1:30; I Thess. 4:3; II Thess. 2:13; and I Pet. 1:2, by the demands for sanctification through the work of God's Spirit. The Christian life is a new life of loyalty to the will of God. "This is the will of God, your sanctification." This work of God through Christ and the Spirit is an integral part of the work of redemption.

6. Through Christ, God gives full and eternal life to men. The message of redemption is not a negative message. It has that aspect; salvation suggests first of all being saved from danger and damage and ruin. But the term in the New Testament thought includes being saved to a priceless privilege. This privilege is life, life with God—life which fulfills the deepest needs of man and realizes his full possibilities.

All of the Gospels and many other New Testament passages speak of this gift of life, but none more often or more vigorously than the Gospel of John.[14] This life is open to believers now (e.g., 3:36); it

[13] Cf. Vincent Taylor, op. cit., pp. 172-225.
[14] See Wilbert Francis Howard, Christianity According to St. John (Philadelphia: Westminster Press, 1946), ch. viii.

will endure and its quality and privilege make it endlessly desirable. The heart of it is not harmonious inner adjustment, although it will bring that with it. Nor is the heart of it congenial relations with others, although they will be included. Its essential privilege is stated in John 17:3: "This is eternal life, that they know thee the only true God, and Jesus Christ whom thou hast sent."

Golden streets, gates of pearl, harps and crowns—these images may suggest the beauty and privilege of that life. But they can mislead unless they point us to what the New Testament puts at the center as the real meaning of life—full, unmarred, and unbroken fellowship with God through Jesus Christ.

All this is the gift of redemption. It is God's free gift; man does not deserve it or even partly earn it. It is all the doing of God, who planned it and brought it to pass. It comes through the work of Christ—his life, death, resurrection, and living power; the Christian knows no redemption or word of hope except this message of redemption effected and given through Christ. The Holy Spirit makes it effective in human lives. And since the need is universal, the gift is offered to all men, and on a basis equally open to all men. To the terms of man's response we now must turn.

The Response of Faith

No stress on the initiative and work of God excludes or obscures the responsibility of man to make the right response. To recognize the primacy and completeness of God's work through Christ puts the focus where it belongs, and gives the credit where it is due. But God has made man as a person, responsible for right decision and action. The gift of redemption does not relieve man of responsibility, but rather creates the urgent responsibility to respond promptly in the way which God intends.

1. Man must respond in honesty. He is not what he should be. He has sinned. His life has not expressed reverent loyalty to his Creator and Lord. He needs help, for he cannot help himself. And only God, against whom he has sinned, can give that help. The first thing a man must do is to recognize and face the facts. He must not play the hypocrite. He must be honest before God and with himself.

2. Man must respond with repentance.[15] God gives the gift of redemption and new life only to those who regret their failure and desire the right relation to God and his people. Therefore Jesus came preaching the need of repentance (Mark 1:15), and the apostles took up this appeal (Acts 2:38; 17:30).

The Greek word for repentance, *metanoia*, means a change of mind. It refers primarily to an alteration of mental attitude. This is included in what the New Testament means by repentance. But it is too intellectual a description. When we ask what Aramaic word Jesus and the first apostolic preachers used, we learn that it probably was the word *tûb*, equivalent to the Hebrew word *shûb*, which means "turn." This Aramaic word describes a complete turning about, a change of life direction—a change which affects the whole life and not merely the mental attitude. The sinner turns from the wrong way; he repudiates and turns his back on his wrong purposes and acts; he turns to God and to the right way in which God wants him to walk.

3. Man must respond with faith.[16] Jesus opened his preaching ministry with a call to "repent, and believe in the gospel" (Mark 1:15). He lived in faith; he taught and urged the necessity of faith, even if at first it was as small as a mustard seed (Matt. 17:20; Luke 17:6). Faith men must have; and it must be sincere.

As Jesus won men, and taught and led them, their faith in God became linked with their trust in him and loyalty to him. Even during his ministry, the basis for the later demand for faith in Christ was laid. Once the church began to realize the meaning of the death, resurrection, exaltation, and living lordship of Christ, its message became a clear call to believe in Jesus Christ and acknowledge him as Christ and Lord. "Believe in the Lord Jesus, and you will be saved, you and your household" (Acts 16:31). At every stage of the Apostolic Age and for every New Testament writer, faith meant faith in Christ and through him faith in God.

This faith was more than mere belief. It always included belief—

[15] See William Douglas Chamberlain, *The Meaning of Repentance* (Philadelphia: Westminster Press, 1943).

[16] See Ernest De Witt Burton, *The Epistle to the Galatians*, pp. 475-85. On the Old Testament background see C. H. Dodd, *The Bible and the Greeks* (London: Hodder & Stoughton 1935), pp. 66-70.

firm and confident belief. It included belief in God and in the truth and meaning of the events of the gospel story. But it was never mere belief. The Epistle of James gives the caustic reminder that "even the demons believe—and shudder" (2:19), but they do not reform and cease their demonic actions. It is possible to know certain facts and be aware of the existence of God, and yet do nothing in response. Faith includes an active personal response which accepts the gift God offers in the gospel.

This faith includes trust in the person through whom this gift is given. It is trust in Christ, the Lord of the Christian and the church. This active attitude was what Jesus wanted in response to his preaching, and it was explicitly demanded in the preaching of the Apostolic Age. Faith at its deepest, as we see in Paul's letters, is a commitment of mind and life, a response of the whole person to Christ.

This full faith, as we shall note later, is the basis of Christian ethics. Christian living is not what man does by himself; it grows out of his vital relation with Christ through belief, trust, and commitment of the whole life to Christ as Lord. Since this is true, it is natural that the word faith sometimes takes on the meaning of faithfulness (e.g., Gal. 5:22). Especially when life is hard and opposition arises to the Christian gospel and witness, to believe in Christ and commit life to him may involve standing firm against all danger and all temptations to give up the faith. Faith and faithfulness are not two separate things but one.

This faith is not a good deed which earns man's new relation to God. It is nothing for which to claim praise or credit. It is the sinner's wholehearted acceptance of God's great gift of forgiveness and renewal through Christ. The sinner does not deserve this free gift. He receives it in spite of his character and record. To introduce the element of personal pride and credit would blur the complete credit due to God; it would bar the way to the blessing which all may receive if they accept it with regret for all past failure and with dedication to do God's will in the days ahead.

This seems to be what Paul says in Eph. 2:8-9: "By grace you have been saved through faith; and this is not your own doing, it is the gift of God—not because of works, lest any man should boast." If the word "this" refers back to the word "faith," the sentence means that even the faith with which one accepts God's grace and gifts is prompted by God; it is not an unaided human achievement or expression. Possibly, however, "this" refers to "you have been saved."

The idea, however, does not rest on one uncertain passage. The whole tenor of New Testament teaching about salvation is that it is God's doing; at every stage the work of God anticipates and precedes man's response. Faith is a response; it is not an original pioneer quest which finds a passive or inactive God. It is called forth by what God has done and by the working of his Spirit. So regardless of the meaning of Eph. 2:8, human pride and credit are excluded from the experience of faith. The believer is repentant, not proud; receptive, not the creator of his own salvation; indebted, not rich by his own independent action. As James S. Stewart has said in stating the meaning of Paul, "No man who is too proud to be infinitely in debt will ever be a Christian." [17] Faith receives what God in his goodness freely gives to the undeserving.

4. Man must respond in gratitude. When he grasps the full, deep meaning of faith, and senses even dimly the immensity of the gift of God, the response of gratitude is inevitable. "Thanks be to God for his inexpressible gift!" (II Cor. 9:15). Through New Testament worship and prayer runs the continual note of grateful thanks to God for giving in Christ so rich a privilege. True Christian faith, worship, and living are never grudging, complacent, or indifferent. The New Testament writings sing their witness of gratitude. Faith breaks forth into grateful praise both to God, who gave the gift of salvation in Christ, and to Christ, who at great cost won the victory over sin and death and made it available to all who truly believe.

This note of gratitude, as well as the commitment inherent in faith, must be kept in mind when we face the duty of the Christian in daily life. The Christian is not under a hard rule to which he regretfully bows. His whole life expresses his faith and his gratitude for what God has given him.

[17] A Man in Christ, p. 224.

The Christian's Daily Duty

The gospel makes grace central; it emphasizes forgiveness. This raises for some an ethical problem: Can such a message be morally vital? What will be its effects in daily life? Paul's opponents in Galatia brought up that issue. Salvation by free grace, accepted through simple faith, seemed to open the door to moral laxity or perversion. Is not something else needed? Is not some law necessary to give moral vitality to life?

The New Testament answer is that only through grace can man become and continue morally vital. There is no separate Christian ethics, independent of the gospel message and supplementing it.[18] To become a Christian means to enter into vital relation to God, to receive release from sin, and to be given through the Spirit the resources with which good living becomes possible. Real faith, as we have said, includes trust and commitment. It leads to grateful worship and willing dedication of the life to God. It opens the life to the divine gift of the Holy Spirit whom the Lord Christ gives to God's people.

The Christian life, therefore, is shaped by loyalty to Christ; it is given guidance and power by the Spirit. The whole life is involved in this dedication. Every phase of life is included in this loyalty. It is no wonder that the Epistle of James says, "Faith apart from works is dead" (2:26); idle faith is not real Christian faith; it has not yielded the life to Christ. Nor would Paul object to this assertion. He was quite different in temperament from the writer of the Epistle of James, and he dealt with different problems, but he says essentially the same thing; he tells the Galatians that what counts is "faith working through love" (5:6). The solid moral fiber of the Old Testament law and prophetic teaching continued to sound forth in the teaching of Jesus, "You will know them by their fruits" (Matt. 7:16, 20), and it echoes with vigor in the writings of the Apostolic Age. The gospel is a morally vital and fruitful message.

[18] Cf. T. W. Manson, *The Teaching of Jesus*, ch. ix; L. H. Marshall, *The Challenge of New Testament Ethics* (London, 1946), pp. 15-25, 232-43; Lindsay Dewar, *An Outline of New Testament Ethics* (Philadelphia: Westminster Press, 1949), pp. 1-2, 99 ff.

False Interpretations of New Testament Ethics

False interpretation of key passages and key ideas has sometimes obscured this healthy moral vigor of the New Testament gospel. To clear up misunderstanding and to bring out the character of the ethical teaching in the New Testament we must examine these interpretations.

1. For some interpreters the seventh chapter of Romans bars the way to a healthy ethical message.[19] It seems to them to deny the possibility of good living in obedience to God. The speaker says that he cannot do the good which he knows he should do, and cannot keep from doing the evil which he knows full well is evil and wrong. Therefore, if Paul is speaking of his Christian life, the Christian life appears morally impotent. A Christian must believe, but he cannot do anything good or keep from doing evil.

A right interpretation of this passage is of crucial importance for our study of the New Testament. In the first place, the sixth and eighth chapters of Romans plainly speak in terms of moral vigor and victory. The Christian obviously can walk in "newness of life" (6:4). He has broken with sin (6:2). Paul flatly denies that sin must rule over the man who has received God's grace in Christ (6:12-14). Real sanctification is a fact in the Christian life. The Christian can now fulfill the requirements of the Law (8:4), though formerly, before conversion, he could not do so. Man lives in the body, but he lives by the power of the Spirit, and he lives a victorious life (8:2, 5, 13).

All this Paul says too plainly for us to deny. If then in the seventh chapter he says he cannot do good and cannot keep from doing evil, he has hopelessly contradicted himself. Indeed, he has acted foolishly in giving long sections of ethical teaching and exhortation in his letters, for on this view, men cannot do anything good at all. We ought to be forced to such an interpretation before we ascribe to Paul so glaring a contradiction.

In fact, however, Paul is not describing his Christian life in the seventh chapter of Romans. He writes, of course, from the Christian

[19] See Kümmel, cited above in n. 7. For the view that Paul is describing the Christian life, see Anders Nygren, *Commentary on Romans*, tr. Carl C. Rasmussen (Philadelphia: Muhlenberg Press, 1949), pp. 284-303.

standpoint. He understands the rise and power of sin in the light not only of his experience under the Law, but also of his later Christian insight. Before his conversion he could not have written as he does. He now sees the issue as never before. But he is describing *life under the Law*, and the Christian is not under Law, as Paul had been before conversion (Rom. 6:14; 10:4). He is explaining the helplessness of a life which is lived under God's demand but lacks the redeeming, renewing power which God gives in the gospel of grace.

This dismal picture of moral failure ends with the gift of grace and the gift of the Spirit. Man is changed—but not by his own merit or act. His moral fiber is renewed by God's grace and power. The Spirit of God gives him direction and power for living. He can avoid evil and do good (Rom. 6:6, 13; 8:4). The credit belongs to God, but the change is real. Struggle continues; a Christian may slip and sin; but life is no longer a slavery to sin; it is freedom in Christ and under the Spirit; the Christian can produce in his life the "fruit of the Spirit"; he can walk in "newness of life"; he can take part in the struggle of life without defeatism, for moral victory occurs in his life as the work of God.

2. For other scholars the eschatological emphasis in the New Testament makes its ethical teaching of little importance. Albert Schweitzer has made this problem acute for many Christians.[20] He insisted that Jesus thought the end of the age was close at hand—perhaps only a few weeks off. He sent out the disciples two by two, and thought that the end would come before they returned. When that did not happen, he determined to go to Jerusalem and force the leaders to put him to death, believing that this sacrifice of himself would set in motion the final drama of world history.

All that Jesus said to men, Schweitzer interprets in the light of this vivid expectation. Jesus did not teach men how to live in normal circumstances, but only how to behave in the very brief time until the end of the age. As soon as it became clear that his expectation was unfounded, and that life would continue on this earth, his specific ethical teaching—which was only an "interim ethic" for the brief period of crisis—was no longer valid or important.

[20] In *The Quest of the Historical Jesus* and other writings.

Schweitzer thought that the early Christians lived at first in this same mood of vivid expectation, and so had no ethical message by which later times could guide their life. Prior to Paul, on this view, the church had not faced the problems of continuing life. Paul began to do so, or to prepare the way for doing so, when his mystical idea of union with Christ introduced a new way of conceiving the relation to Christ.[21] All in all, the ethical teaching of Jesus, the first generation, and even Paul is largely useless for us because of its interim accent.

Jesus and the apostles did summon people to face the impending judgment of God. In an occasional passage, such as Paul's advice not to marry because the end of the world was at hand (I Cor. 7:26-31), we can trace influence of such views on specific teaching. But the view of Schweitzer distorts the basic New Testament evidence.

In the first place, we have seen that for Jesus the Kingdom was not entirely future.[22] It had begun in his own work and movement. He was not teaching his followers what to do in a brief time until the Kingdom began, but how to live in the Kingdom they already had begun to share.

In the second place, though he had a vivid expectation of the coming judgment of God, he did not know the time of the end (Mark 13:32). Moreover, he allowed for the continuance of his movement after his death.[23] So his teaching looked to a longer period of continuing history than Schweitzer allowed.

In the third place, as Rudolph Otto pointed out,[24] the great bulk of Jesus' teaching was not determined by the thought that the end was near. It was teaching valid for a sincere and earnest believer regardless of the actual time of the end of history.

In the fourth place, as Oscar Cullmann has emphasized,[25] Jesus saw the decisive action of God taking place in his work, and so he did not ground his claim merely on a future divine action and judgment—as Schweitzer thinks—but on God's decisive acts already known and now

---

[21] Albert Schweitzer, *The Mysticism of Paul the Apostle*, tr. William Montgomery (New York: Henry Holt & Co., 1931).

[22] See ch. v.

[23] See Karl Wilhelm Heinrich Michaelis, *Der Herr Verzieht Nicht die Verheissung* (Bern, 1942).

[24] *The Kingdom of God and the Son of Man*, pp. 59-63.

[25] *Christ and Time*, especially pp. 81-93.

occurring. Man's duty grows out of what God has done and is doing in Christ; it does not have to look to the future to find a basis. The ethical demand grows out of God's action in Christ and calls men to share in the common life and mission which Jesus began.

Finally, as Amos N. Wilder has underlined,[26] the eschatological emphasis in the Gospels is not so lacking in ethical point as some have thought. The thought of facing God's judgment gives urgency and depth to the ethical demand; it expresses the immediacy and completeness of God's claim on man's life, and reminds man that now— without delay—man should face that claim, do God's will, and do it in all of his life. The eschatological teaching of Jesus and of the early church may make it necessary to re-think the application of the teaching in our changed circumstances, but it does not affect the substance of that teaching. It rather adds urgency to it.

3. At times the New Testament shows a tendency to dualism and asceticism. This would leave the physical life out of the range of the Christian's loyalty to God. In the ancient world dualism was widely accepted. In this view, matter is inherently evil and spirit is naturally good; therefore, the physical aspects of life have no essential place in the good life. They may be considered indifferent; then with libertine laxity one may indulge in all manner of gluttony and sexual excess without harming the spiritual life. Or they may be considered things to suppress; then, with ascetic severity, the flesh is treated harshly to keep it subject to the spirit of man. In this latter way of thinking the less we pamper the body and indulge in natural impulses, the better it is for our spiritual life.[27]

This dualism had no real influence in the New Testament. When Paul or any other Christian leader found the libertine tendency, he denounced it as inconsistent with Christian faith (I Cor. 6:12-20; Gal. 5:13). Moreover, he rejected the ascetic position on principle.

The great protection against error here was the Old Testament doc-

---

[26] A. N. Wilder, *Eschatology and Ethics in the Teaching of Jesus* (revised ed.; New York: Harper & Bros., 1950).

[27] Such ascetic concern tacitly admits, however, that there is a life connection between body and spirit. Another point is also worth noting. Ascetic dualists rarely took the consistent step which logically would follow, namely, suicide. That would seem to be the quick, effective way for a dualist to get rid of the evil, degrading influence of his body.

trine that God created man and the world, and saw that it was good (Gen. 1:31). The whole man, in all of his life, is under the lordship of the Creator. In fact, the Old Testament view makes no such sharp distinction between the physical and spiritual sides of man as later thought has tended to do. Man is a unity; he is created by God to live in obedience to God and to exercise both his physical and his spiritual functions in a wholesome way under divine direction. "The earth is the Lord's and the fulness thereof." (Ps. 24:1.) The body is "a temple of the Holy Spirit." (I Cor. 6:19.) The physical, intellectual, and spiritual phases of life are all one life under God.

What confuses many people is the vividness of Paul's warnings against the flesh (e.g., Rom. 7:18, 25; Gal. 5:13, 16 ff.).[28] But by flesh Paul does not mean the physical being of man as such. He means the lower side of man, degraded by sin and subject to sinful impulses. He knew that the body can become the seat and center of sinful living, and that it needs discipline (I Cor. 9:27). But the best way to see the real meaning of flesh for Paul is to read his list of "the works of the flesh" in Gal. 5:19-21. They include "immorality, impurity, licentiousness, idolatry, sorcery, enmity, strife, jealousy, anger, selfishness, dissension, party spirit, envy, drunkenness, carousing, and the like." They thus include not only physical immorality and excess, but also expressions of selfishness and base living which come from the mind and will.

Paul thinks, not in dualistic terms, but rather in terms of disobedience to the will of God. On occasion he speaks disparagingly of marriage, partly because he vividly anticipates the impending end of the age (I Cor. 7:25-31). But he does not condemn marriage; he rather insists that it is legitimate and according to the will of God (I Cor. 7:1-16; Eph. 5:22-23)). He is no dualist.

Outside of Paul the New Testament has little suggestion of dualism. In Rev. 14:4 we see reference to "virgins," meaning "chaste" men. The passage asserts their complete loyalty to Christ, so it is not certain that it carries an ascetic note. Quite possibly it does. If so, it is a rare note in the New Testament, which accepts all of God's creation as

[28] See Burton, *The Epistle to the Galatians*, pp. 492-95.

244

the sphere of man's obedience, and insists that body and spirit are both to be subject to the divine will.

4. Christians of later generations have sometimes tried to find in the teaching of Jesus and the apostles a legal code. There are those who think that the writer of the Gospel of Matthew had a tendency in this direction. He arranges most of the teaching of Jesus in five great discourses, each closing with a formal conclusion (5:1–7:29; 10:5–11:1; 13:1-53; 18:1–19:1; 24:1–26:1). Is he suggesting, as B. W. Bacon thought,[29] that Jesus has thus given the New Law in five books to replace the five books of Moses? This theory is too subtle to be convincing. But the codification of teaching can reflect, or at least easily foster, a legalistic tendency.

The codes of household duties (Eph. 5:22–6:9; Col. 3:18–4:1; I Pet. 2:18–3:7)[30] and the tone of the Pastoral Epistles[31] suggest a tendency to specific rules and instructions, but they do not lay down formal laws.

In any case, the entire trend of Jesus' teaching was antilegalistic. He pressed home the will of God upon man's conscience, but he did not issue a code of law, or seek to define a fixed tradition which would govern the lives of his followers. E. F. Scott thought that the prohibition of divorce was one exception;[32] in this one case Jesus, who everywhere else avoided the legal note, gave a law legally binding on every disciple. This seems doubtful; if Jesus avoided legalism everywhere else, it is hard to believe that this once he lapsed into rigid legislation. Certainly the general tenor of his teaching was against putting life under an external code of rigid law.

The nonlegalistic attitude permeates the New Testament. It puts man's obligation at its maximum, but the setting of life is "the law of liberty" (Jas. 1:25). The good life springs out of faith and dedication to Christ. It is an expression of gratitude. It is the disciple's answer to the immediate situation—an intelligent, personal, Spirit-guided an-

[29] B. W. Bacon, *Studies in Matthew* (New York: Henry Holt & Co., 1930), pp. 81-82.
[30] See Karl Weidinger, *Die Haustafeln* (Leipzig, 1928).
[31] Cf. Burton Scott Easton, *The Pastoral Epistles* (New York: Charles Scribner's Sons, 1947), p. 24.
[32] E. F. Scott, *The Ethical Teaching of Jesus* (New York: The Macmillan Co., 1924), p. 98.

245

swer. For law by its very nature cannot anticipate the infinitely varied situations of life.

The Marks of Christian Living

The Christian ethics will seem vague and weak to those who want everything prescribed in legal form. But to the Christian, God's moral demand does not seem vague and weak. It claims his whole life. What then is the spirit of that life? What are the marks of the Christian response to God in daily life?

1. Christian living is grateful living. It is an expression of gratitude to God who has done so much for sinful man. This truth bars the idea that the Christian earns his salvation by the way he lives. He owes everything to God, and his loyal obedience in daily life expresses his gratitude to his Maker, Savior, and Lord.

2. Christian living is humble living. The disciple of Christ knows his past; he had nothing to boast of. He knows his weakness; in the struggle of life he himself is not strong enough to win the victory. He does not know the future; he can face it intelligently and steadily only through trust in God. But he does not draw back in despair. What he cannot do by himself, God can do for him and through him. He humbly trusts in God, yields his life to the leading and power of the Spirit, and earnestly gives all his energy to the loyal service of his Redeemer and Lord.

3. Christian living springs from inward acceptance of God's will and sincere purpose to do it. Such living is never living by rule; it is marked by continual intelligent response to God's guidance. It is not living by whim, for man's inward decisions are in response to the will of God rather than to human impulse. Good living expresses inward loyalty and outward obedience to God.

4. Christian living is a life of love.[33] Prominent among Old Testament Scripture quotations is the command, "You shall love your neighbor as yourself" (Lev. 19:18). Love to God and love to neighbor (Mark 12:29-31), love of enemies (Matt. 5:44), faith working through

---

[33] See James Moffatt, *Love in the New Testament* (New York: Harper & Bros., 1930); Anders Nygren, *Agape and Eros*, tr. Philip E. Watson (revised ed.; Philadelphia: Westminster Press, 1953).

love (Gal. 5:6), love for one another (John 13:34-35; I John 4:7-21)—the theme of love runs through the New Testament, and the spirit of love is to permeate Christian living (I Pet. 1:22). It means sympathy with those in need (I John 3:17). It means humane living rather than callous indifference to the needs of others (Luke 10:29-37). It means unselfish living, thinking of the good of others (Phil. 2:4). It means readiness to give up things for the sake of others or to avoid offending others (I Cor. 8:13). It means generous giving to help those in need (II Cor. 8:1-7).

Love is patient and kind; love is not jealous or boastful; it is not arrogant or rude. Love does not insist on its own way; it is not irritable or resentful; it does not rejoice at wrong, but rejoices in the right. Love bears all things, believes all things, hopes all things, endures all things. Love never ends. (I Cor. 13:4-8.)

It is a warm, intelligent, persistent, kindly, resourceful, patient, friendly, sacrificial good will, which finds active expression in a life that seeks to help others and do them good.

5. Christian living is a life of purity. It gives an honored place to marriage, and honors the loyal love of husband and wife (Mark 10:2-12). It shuns the perversion and excesses which have marked the sex life of mankind, and it emphatically stands for pure life on the part of both unmarried and married people (Heb. 13:4). This purity is not merely the avoidance of fornication or adultery, though that is included (I Cor. 6:18; I Thess. 4:3). It is a purity of mind and desire as well as of act (Matt. 5:27-28).

6. Christian living is honest living. Integrity in word, intention, and action is essential to the life of Christian discipleship. This excludes stealing and lying and the desire to defraud others of their rights or belongings (Eph. 4:28; Col. 3:9); it also excludes all pretense and false parade. The hypocrite who pretends before God and men is an object of condemnation (Luke 18:9-14). Man must be honest before God, and honest in dealings with men; he must not pretend to a goodness or a friendly purpose which he knows he does not have. And he must avoid any way of life which would involve him in dishonesty in dealing with others.

7. Christian living is faithful living. This was especially clear in the early church, where ridicule, opposition, and active persecution were so frequent; Paul could even insist that such ill-treatment was a normal part of Christian living (Rom. 8:17; cf. II Tim. 3:12). The only way to be a Christian was to stand steady in the face of distracting and threatening situations. Patient endurance of wrong, loyal persistence in the Christian witness, fearless friendship toward other Christians who were under fire, daily steadiness which does God's will in gratitude and love—this was what Christian living meant to the Apostolic Age (Mark 13:13; Heb. 12:7; Jas. 1:12).

This calls for positive living. There are important negative teachings in the New Testament. But the prevailing note is positive— believe, love, serve, help, be faithful. To fail to do what is right is serious. "Whoever knows what is right to do and fails to do it, for him it is sin" (Jas. 4:17; cf. 2:14-26). Christian living is a continuous expression of faith in action. "Whatever does not proceed from faith is sin" (Rom. 14:23).

Faults Condemned

To supplement this survey of the spirit of Christian living, we may look at the dangers and faults which the New Testament mentions. Unbelief is the sin perhaps most frequently mentioned (John 16:9). God has sent Jesus Christ to redeem men and give them life; to ignore or reject him is an immeasurable wrong and failure. Complacency which senses no personal need of divine help is a fault which Jesus condemns (Luke 18:11). Pride in personal worth and achievement, instead of humility in the face of personal need and failure, is a barrier to spiritual renewal and benefit. The callous or cruel spirit calls forth some of the most vigorous rebuke Jesus gave; whatever hurts people draws emphatic condemnation from Jesus and his followers (Matt. 25:41-43; Jas. 2:15-16). The love of money is condemned because it closes the eyes to one's need of God and to the claim of others on us; it fosters both selfishness of spirit and covetousness of attitude (I Tim. 6:10). Selfishness in any form, whether in lust for physical possession of another in illicit intercourse (I Thess. 4:6), or in desire for personal or financial advantage (Jas. 5:4), calls forth unhesitating condemnation. Selfishness is the opposite of the spirit of Christ, the spirit of Christian love.

The Christian's Social Duty

We have spoken of the Christian's daily duty mainly in personal terms, to discern the spirit and attitudes which must find expression in a truly Christian life. But serious living true to the gospel message always involves the believer in relations with others both within and outside of the church. In fact, there can be no loyalty and obedience to Christ which does not find expression in the varied social relations of life. We need to study more directly the Christian's social situation and responsibility.

The Lack of a Social Program

At first sight, the New Testament disappoints those who are looking for a vital social message.[34] It did not anticipate a steady development which will gradually realize a perfect human society. The parables of growth do suggest that there will be a growth in the advance of Christ's cause (Mark 4:1-32). But the stubbornness of evil in the world was too clearly seen, and its power was too well known, to permit easy optimism about the victory of the gospel. Human resources could not bring about a perfect order. Active service, even with the power of God behind it, could not eliminate all evil and wrong from social life.

Moreover, the New Testament has no detailed plan for social reform or revolution. Since the world was a sinful world, and sin found expression in both personal actions and social movements, the kingdom of God would differ radically from the existing world order. But the New Testament writers and teachers did not urge planned action to alter the outward form of social life.

[34] Among older works from the period of emphasis on the "social gospel," see Samuel Dickey, *The Constructive Revolution of Jesus* (New York: Doubleday, Doran & Co., 1923); Shailer Mathews, *Jesus on Social Institutions* (New York: The Macmillan Co., 1928). Of special value for its historical survey is Cecil John Cadoux, *The Early Church and the World* (Edinburgh, 1925). Recent discussion of such subjects usually recognizes the eschatological note in the New Testament and writes with a solid theological emphasis; e.g. John C. Bennett, *Social Salvation* (New York: Charles Scribner's Sons, 1935); Reinhold Niebuhr, *The Nature and Destiny of Man*, Vol. II (New York: Charles Scribner's Sons, 1943); Paul Ramsey, *Basic Christian Ethics* (New York: Charles Scribner's Sons, 1950). See also Holmes Rolston, *The Social Message of the Apostle Paul* (Richmond, 1942).

There was no revolt against pagan government, even when it persecuted the church. Jesus refused to countenance revolt by Israel and advised paying tribute to pagan Rome (Mark 12:13-17). Paul likewise, sensing the order and other benefits which Rome gave, urged acceptance of that government which God in his wisdom had given its position (Rom. 13:1-7). The writer of the Book of Revelation spoke hard words about the persecuting Empire, and called it Babylon in condemnation (17:1–19:8); but it was God, not the church, who would give deliverance and victory to Christ's cause.

Just as there was no political revolt, but rather prayer for all in authority (I Tim. 2:1-2), so also there was no antislavery agitation (Col. 3:22-25). Nor was there a compulsory share-the-wealth program; even in Jerusalem, in the early days of the church, the sharing was voluntary (Acts 5:4). There was no class war; men of every kind and class lived together in the church (Gal. 3:28; Col. 3:11). The church had no program of political action to alter the form of society.

What then was the New Testament social program or message? It all centered in and derived from the gospel message and the life of faith. The basic need of all men was spiritual; therefore they needed first of all to hear the gospel and believe. Conversion and spiritual renewal were the hope of the world and of society as well as of individuals. Thus the New Testament never departs from a fully justified individualism, which seeks first of all to spread the gospel and win individuals to faith in Christ.

Coupled with this basic need of individual conversion and faith was the need of fellowship with other Christians. The spiritual tie between Christ's followers was the basic tie of all. Jesus had taught that those who did the will of God had the real family tie (Mark 3:35). Nothing superseded that bond between believers. The church, with its common faith, its common worship, its mutual helpfulness, and its friendly care for all its members, was the supreme social unit. Every other social tie had to be subordinated or, if necessary, broken to preserve and strengthen that central tie with Christ and Christians in the church (Luke 14:26).

Beyond this social fellowship in the church, the social responsibility was felt first as the duty to give clear witness to the gospel message and so to win others to Christ. A minor theme of the early church was the withdrawal from society, insofar as it was pagan and morally unworthy (II Cor. 6:17; Rev. 18:4). But the pressing obligation to witness to Christ before all men kept the church from becoming a closed society or a group of recluses (Matt. 28:19; Acts 1:8). The Christians recognized that their main concern was not only to be Christian in their relations with one another, but also to give the gospel to as many others as possible.

The Social Aspects of New Testament Life

It was, of course, a fact that the Christians lived in the world and shared in social relations of various kinds. The nature of their faith and their witness, and the form which that witness took, will become clearer if we examine briefly the part Christians took in the main social groups of the day.

1. The clearest Christian witness occurred in family life.[35] It was the one social group which the church gave an essential and constant role in the Christian life and fellowship. God had made man, male and female; marriage and the home were of divine institution (Mark 10:6-8). But the marriage must be built on faith. No attempt was made to break up a home in which one partner became a Christian while the other did not (I Cor. 7:12-14); this is the only kind of "mixed marriages" which the New Testament knows. But it was clear teaching that a Christian was to marry only a Christian (I Cor. 7:39). Faith must be central in the life of a Christian; all life must be lived on the basis of faith in Christ and as a service to Christ. Marriage, too, is a demanding loyalty, and if the married partner does not share the Christian faith, an inevitable clash of central interests will occur. So the Christian is to marry a Christian.

This Christian marriage rests on love, purity, and faithfulness. Divorce has no place in a fully Christian life (Mark 10:2-12; Luke 16:18; I Cor. 7:10-11). Matthew gives one exception, fornication (5:32; 19:9), but Mark, Luke, and Paul know of no such exception, and it appears that Matthew attempts to adapt the basic principle which

[35] Cf. E. F. Scott, *The Ethical Teaching of Jesus*, ch. xiv; C. J. Cadoux, *The Early Church and the World*, pp. 58-60, 122-27, 191-94.

251

Jesus stated. This principle is that marriage is the permanent life union of one man and one woman, and any breaking of that bond is a failure to realize the will of God for the marriage.

In the home, parents are to care for their children and train them in the life of faith and wholesome living. The children in turn are to honor their parents, and later provide for them when they are in any need. (Eph. 6:1-4; Col. 3:20-21.) Thus in every respect the home is to be a center of Christian faith and love, and a school of Christian teaching.

The New Testament exaltation of the home is subject to two limitations. For one thing, Jesus makes it clear that should a clash arise between family loyalty and loyalty to the cause of Christ, first claim belongs to the cause of Christ, since it is the cause of God, and so is God's will for all men (Mark 3:31-35; Luke 14:26). Family love and loyalty are blessed and disciplined by the dominant loyalty to God's cause and people.

In the second place, Paul advises against marriage in cases where a helpful and wholesome life is possible without it (I Cor 7:1). He is moved largely by his conviction that the end of the age is near (I Cor. 7:25-31); the continuance of the family through many generations and centuries was not in his mind.

The limitation which Jesus placed on family loyalty to prevent it from crowding out God's call is of permanent validity. The advice of Paul, however, in view of the long duration of the church and the prominent role the family has held in preserving and enriching the Christian heritage, has proved to be a transient feature of our New Testament heritage. Even for Paul it was only a preference; he did not deny the rightful place of marriage or condemn those who did get married. In general, the family was for him, as for the entire New Testament, the most important social unit outside of the church, and it deserved honor and support from all Christians (Heb. 13:4).

2. The church met the division of society into classes not by a program of legislation, but by a program of brotherly action. Jesus welcomed the tax collectors and the outcastes of Judaism (Matt. 10:6; Luke 5:29-30; 15:1). He befriended them, aroused in them a desire for better things, gave them a respect they were not accustomed

to receive, and opened to them a future which they had not expected or perhaps desired. Paul's hearers in Corinth were mainly the "foolish," the "weak," the "low and despised," and his converts came mostly from the lowest classes (I Cor. 1:26-31). Partiality to the rich was condemned by both Jesus and the early church (Mark 10:25; Luke 16:19-26; Jas. 2:1-4).

The early church offered the gospel to the slave as well as to his master,[36] to the uncultured as well as to the intellectual. The slave was made worthy of equality; he became a "beloved brother" (Philem. 16). The master must treat his slave as a brother, and the slave was to serve his master willingly and faithfully. We need not claim that snobbishness was unknown, but brotherhood was the aim and the widely realized fact. In essence the program of the church disregarded the social divisions of society; it made the church a home for all classes; its democratic basis was a common repentance, a common faith, a common worship and fellowship, and mutual love.

3. The Apostolic Church had no program to transform the economic order.[37] It was a minority group, which numbered less than one per cent of the population of the Roman Empire. Christians were few; they lacked the rights of representative government; they had little opportunity to effect sweeping alterations in existing economic conditions.

The church taught honesty (I Cor. 6:10; Eph. 4:28). It pointed out the dangers of wealth and even of the lust for wealth. Jesus had warned that loyalty to God and to wealth (mammon) could not be reconciled (Matt. 6:24). He even warned against the consuming desire for possessions. His parable about the rich fool, who was so concerned about material prosperity and security that he forgot his spiritual need, warned men not to misplace life's center (Luke 12:16-21). His encounter with the Rich Young Ruler brought out the fact that to follow him was the first and great demand; to meet it every hindrance, even great wealth, must be put aside (Mark 10:17-22). The readiness of so many of the early church in Jerusalem to share their goods with the needy in the church (Acts 2:44; 4:32, 36-37), the warning to the rich in I Tim. 6:10, and the vigorous denunciation of

[36] See C. J. Cadoux, op. cit., pp. 131-36, 199-201.
[37] See S. Dickey, op. cit., ch. v; C. J. Cadoux, op. cit., pp. 61-66, 127-31, 195-99.

the callous rich who do not care for the workmen they exploit (Jas. 5:1-6), are echoes of this attitude of Jesus.

In warning against consuming concern for possessions the New Testament interest is mainly with their effect on faith and character. When the workman is wronged or deprived of prompt payment of his wages, the injustice is denounced (Jas. 5:4). But the main point is that wealth, or even the desire for it, distracts attention from God's claim, leads man to a fatal callousness to the needs of others, and so is spiritually ruinous. No program of social reform is promoted. The gospel is for poor and rich alike. Yet it has a special tenderness for the poor (Luke 6:20; Acts 6:1). When the disciples have means, they are to be generous and to use their possessions to help the church and other men (Matt. 6:2-4; II Cor. 9:6-7).

4. Racial questions as such did not play so great a role in the first century as they do today. We often think that the issue between Jews and Gentiles in the church was a race issue. Essentially, however, the problem was not racial.

The basic question was whether the covenant privilege which Israel had long possessed should be shared with Gentiles without first requiring them to become converts to Judaism and accept the Jewish Law. The Jews were quite willing to receive proselytes from other races. They sometimes looked down on such proselytes, but in principle these converts became full members of the covenant people. Jesus limited his efforts to his own people, and instructed his disciples to preach only to Jews (Matt. 10:5-6; 15:24), because of his conviction that he was sent to the covenant people and must concentrate on winning their response to his gospel. His attitude was not due to race feeling. It was the Law and the covenant privilege which divided the Jews from the Gentiles, and constituted "the dividing wall of hostility" of which Paul speaks (Eph. 2:14).[38]

There was undoubtedly race feeling. The Jews may not have been a pure race—scholars correctly insist they were not—but they felt their difference from other peoples, and racial background contributed to that feeling. Other races felt contempt for the Jews, and while this was mainly due to their special faith and practices, the feeling rested

[38] See Gregory Dix, Jew and Greek (New York: Harper & Bros., 1953).

in part on racial difference. Between other races, race feeling no doubt existed. But it was not the decisive thing in the first century. The Law and covenant divided Jews from Gentiles; Greek culture divided the Hellenistic world from the "barbarians."

In the Apostolic Church, except for the dispute whether Gentiles could come into the church without accepting and keeping the Jewish Law, there is no evidence of division on the basis of race or color. The Jew, the Ethiopian, the Cyrenians, the Syrians, the Galatians, the Greeks, the Romans—all found their place in the church, and we discover no trace of race prejudice, no trace of division on racial lines. That is the important fact.

5. Participation in the life of the pagan world could not be entirely avoided, especially since the church's basic duty was to witness for Christ before all men. But Christians were keenly aware that they could not share some features of pagan life.[39] This problem did not emerge prominently so long as the Christian movement was limited to Jews, for non-Christian Jews shared with the Christians faith in one God and respect for the Scriptures as well as high standards of spiritual worship and moral life.

In the pagan world, however, the missionaries found much idolatry, immorality, laxity of life, and a general framework of life uncongenial to the Christian faith. From specifically idolatrous and immoral practices, the Christian had to keep aloof. Where his presence did not clearly approve or support pagan beliefs, however, he might accept the social situation and say nothing, withdrawing only when his friendliness was misunderstood (I Cor. 8:9-12; 10:28-29).

In general, the Christians found their center of life in the little Christian group and in the Christian homes of church members; they kept away from the pagan observances and amusements of people around them. They had to maintain a delicate balance between friendship and contact with all kinds of people on the one hand, and separation from clearly pagan and cheap aspects of social life on the other. With their lack of numbers and social influence they could hardly have done otherwise. They were contributing to social change by the vitality of their faith, their wholesome worship and fellowship, and

[39] Cf. C. J. Cadoux, op. cit., pp. 92-96, 135-36, 141-50, 201-202.

their moral life. But it was a slow and indirect method of change; it offered no formal program for direct action.

6. The rightful place of government was assumed, and the right of the Roman Empire to govern was accepted.[40] Jesus set the pattern for this attitude of acceptance (Mark 12:13-17); the church continued it. Even when Jesus was put to death and the apostles were imprisoned, the disciples did not think of revolting or plotting to set up a new government. They were a small and often persecuted minority in a totalitarian empire, and they had no such avenues of influence on legislation and administration as are open to citizens today. They accepted the situation, and Paul particularly was aware of the benefits of Roman rule (Rom. 13:1-7). Whether Christians could take part in imperial administration was rarely a question at first for these politically unimportant people, but Erastus was the city treasurer at Corinth (Rom. 16:23), and it appears that soldiers could be Christians (Acts 10). All could and should pray for the rulers (I Tim. 2:1 ff.), and payment of taxes was a duty that Christians did not seek to evade.

The Christian acceptance of the existing government was subject to two limitations. One was that the Christians did not think that the Empire was a direct agent of God to spread the gospel or give Christian training. The witness and educational work of the church were independent of the government's task, which was to keep order and administer the general social life.

The second limitation was that when the government made decisions which definitely challenged the right of the church to exist and to worship God through Christ, the church could only refuse to yield to that claim of the State (Rev. 13:15). Emperor worship was impossible for Christians who acknowledged only "one God, the Father, from whom are all things and for whom we exist, and one Lord, Jesus Christ, through whom are all things and through whom we exist" (I Cor. 8:6). Yet even in the face of the demand for emperor worship the Christians did not revolt; they refused to compromise their faith, and trusted their souls "to a faithful creator" (I Pet. 4:19). It was

[40] See S. Dickey, op. cit., ch. iv; E. F. Scott, op. cit., chs. x, xi; C. J. Cadoux, op. cit., pp. 34-57, 97-122, 166-90.

not their task to determine who should rule on earth, but no matter who ruled, they had to keep their Christian witness pure.

The above survey shows that Christians were keenly conscious of their social duty to their fellow Christians, and were bound to help them in every spiritual and physical need. Christians were also aware of their obligation toward all other men. This obligation they discharged by friendship and by clear witness to Christ, for their aim was to win as many as possible to believe in Christ and enter the Christian fellowship. They were quite aware that they must express their faith in their social relationships, but their small numbers, their lowly social position, their expectation that this world would not last long, and their position in a totalitarian empire where they had no political influence help to explain why they did not instantly present and promote a definite political and social program.

The Social Relevance of the Gospel

It is not our purpose in this book to discuss the application of these views to modern life. We may avoid misunderstanding, however, if we indicate briefly how far the changed conditions of modern life warrant or demand a change in the views we have sketched.

Basically the Christian has no reason to alter those views. If the gospel is true, then faith, fellowship in faith, life in Christian love, and persuasive witness to the gospel in the world are continuing aspects of essential Christian living. Moreover, since the early church's clear insight that evil is tenacious still proves true, we cannot expect or promise that skillful legislation and social planning will create a new and perfect social order. Without radical, redemptive, God-wrought changes in human nature, without the wide acceptance of the gospel, we have no reason to expect a good and stable society. Christians deceive themselves, fail to give their witness, and do others no good, if they ignore the basic and universal need of the gospel.

It would be tragic, however, if this central emphasis concealed the changed conditions and increased social responsibility of Christians in our day. There are vastly more Christians now than there were in the days of the apostles. In countries such as ours those Christians are citizens, with avenues of influence and action open to them which never were open to first-century disciples. The large-scale operations of modern social and economic life, illustrated in the activities of capital, labor, and Communism, make it clear that Christians need to express their convictions in the social groups of our day.[41]

There is a place for social teaching and action to protect human life, to thwart evil forces (which sometimes are organized in mammoth conspiracies for vicious purposes), and to create conditions as favorable as possible for good living. The church and the Christian must be careful first of all to be Christian in their own participation in social relations, but then in human sympathy and concern they must throw their influence on the side of the wholesome and constructive programs in government and society. They can and should utter a prophetic warning against whatever damages human life and happiness. A callous church would no longer be a Christian church. A callous Christian is unworthy of the name.

But when all of this is said, it must be reiterated that the main social program of the church is twofold: It must first of all witness to all men that the gospel contains the central answer to their need. It must also demonstrate the socially beneficial effects of Christian faith by the quality of its own life and by the high quality of its dealings with other social groups. Without that demonstration in action, any verbal witness to social ideals is futile and obviously hypocritical. But given that demonstration in action, the social witness of the church can hope to be heard with respect.

---

[41] On the social relevance of the gospel, see Amos N. Wilder, *New Testament Faith for Today* (New York, 1955).

CHAPTER XI

Christ and the Final Goal

IN RECENT DECADES THE PLACE OF ESCHATOLOGY IN
the gospel message has been hotly disputed. Fruitful discussion has
become difficult, however, because some have drained the word eschatology of any reference to the future, and used it to express in a time-
less sense the ultimate issues of life. This is a definition which Webster's 1939 New International Dictionary had never heard, but it is
used as though it were both biblical and deeply rooted in history.
We respect the future note in Webster's definition; eschatology is
"the doctrine of the last or final things, as death, resurrection, immortality, the end of the age, the second advent of Christ, judgment,
and the future state." [1]

To more than one spokesman of current Christian thinking, true
eschatology is a topic better ignored than emphasized. In many ways attention has been drawn from the future to the present.[2] Concern for the
practical social effect of the gospel in current society governs the interest
of many. The existentialist philosophy of Bultmann and the Platonic
tinge of Dodd's thinking put a strong accent upon the present. Those
who hold such views can point out that the recurrent predictions of the
impending end of the age have continually been proved wrong; they
can argue that we have no solid basis for charting the future; and so
they can conclude that wisdom dictates attention to the present.

---

[1] Webster's *New International Dictionary of the English Language* (2nd ed.; Spring-
field, 1939), *sub voce.*

[2] The recent Second Assembly of the World Council of Churches (Evanston, 1954)
represented a renewed interest in the vital role of eschatology. Its theme, "Jesus Christ,
the Hope of the World," included a strong eschatological aspect. Those who follow
Rudolf Bultmann in regarding all this as mythology reinterpret such eschatological
language.

Such views can appeal to New Testament notes which at first glance are impressive. The kingdom of God, as we have seen in ch. v, had already begun to come in the person, work, and movement of Jesus. This present reality that "the kingdom of God has come upon you" (Matt. 12:28) has impressed the writer of the Gospel of John so much that he lays remarkable emphasis on the fact that "he who believes *has* eternal life" (John 3:36). God has "transferred us to the kingdom of his beloved Son" (Col. 1:13).

The modern Christian may also be influenced unconsciously by another fact. Nineteen centuries have passed since Jesus lived and the church emerged. The world still goes on; we have a long church history to read and it influences our thinking. We unconsciously expect the church to continue and the world to go on as usual. The urgent message of the transiency of things does not impress us so much when we think how long the history of the church has been. The past is long and significant. The present is the crucial time of our life and duty. The future is veiled. Why bother with eschatology?

Why Eschatology?

Sound Christian thinking, however, sees at least three important meanings in eschatology. First of all, eschatology says something essential about God. In the present world the purpose and justice of God are not clearly apparent. A Christian will not question God's justice, but conditions in the world do not demonstrate it. Faith cannot escape the conviction that in the end God will vindicate his justice, manifest his fairness and goodness, and show his power to achieve his purpose. To regard this present tangled world situation as our last word about God would be fatal to New Testament faith. Eschatology is necessary to a satisfying faith in God.

It is also necessary to a sound faith in human destiny. It is not now obvious that life deals out fair treatment and offers wholesome fulfillment to all who seek it. Yet this is clear to Christian faith. Those who put their trust in God and seek to find and do his will are certain in the end to receive a rich, full answer to their prayer for true life. They will receive perfectly fair dealing at the hands of God. Eschatology is necessary to a satisfying faith about the meaning of life for each human being.

It is also necessary to set the world conflict in perspective. The good so often seems weak or even doomed to defeat. Evil appears powerful and threatens to win triumph after triumph until it completely controls the field. My Christian conscience cannot rest satisfied with the faith that I will gain happiness no matter what happens to the cause of God. The weakness of much thinking about the future is right here; it is too easily content with assurance of isolated personal salvation. The New Testament breathes continually the conviction that the cause of God, the cause of human justice, will win out over every force of evil. The final issue of history will be the triumph of God's cause; that victory will vindicate all who share the Christian faith in his goodness, justice, and power. Eschatology says something necessary about the outcome of the world struggle.

It is not surprising, therefore, to find that eschatology holds so prominent a role in New Testament faith and thought. The New Testament is concerned first of all with the work and purpose of God; it could never rest content with the assurance to individuals that they at least will not be dragged down in the general defeat that may overtake God's cause. It has to assert that God is just; that his good and gracious purpose will be fulfilled; that individuals find their assurance as they find their place in that work of God which is moving to certain victory; that every hostile person and power will be defeated and eliminated; and that a Kingdom which wholly achieves God's purpose will stand eternally as the final result of his work in history. This eschatological note pervades the New Testament.

Present Fact and Coming Completion

Our modern thinking, however, may easily misunderstand the extent of the eschatological outlook in the New Testament. For us the work of Christ is far away in the past. Centuries have elapsed since the church arose and took up its mission. Eschatology for us now means things that will happen in the time that is yet to come. But unless we escape this manner of thinking, we can never understand the New Testament. In it eschatology is not a purely future thing,

261

whether near or far away. The final, climactic, decisive action of God has already begun. The eschatological order invades the present. The eye of faith can see it.

This vivid sense that eschatology is no longer purely future but already present leads some scholars to say that the New Testament teaches "realized eschatology." [3] What God has promised has come to pass. The kingdom of God has come. The promises have been fulfilled. Did not Jesus announce at the opening of his ministry that "the kingdom of God is at hand" (Mark 1:15)? Did he not say that "the kingdom of God has come upon you" (Matt. 12:28)? Did not the writer of the Gospel of John see this clearly and say that by faith we now enter into and enjoy eternal life (e.g., 3:36)? Did not Paul say that God has "transferred us to the kingdom of his beloved Son" (Col. 1:13)? Does not the New Testament emphasize the fact that God has acted and fulfilled his promises?

To this pardonable overemphasis we must say two things. The New Testament does indeed say that the final action of God has begun in Jesus Christ. The Kingdom has begun to come. The eternal order is breaking into the historical order, and men of faith can and do already enter it and know its privileges. This means that the entire New Testament gospel is eschatology. The work of Christ, the gift of the Spirit, the victory of the gospel—all this is part of the final action of God to fulfill his divine purpose; to the New Testament writers this is all eschatology. We have lost the sense of amazing newness, of decisive action, of crucial victory already won and made basic for all eternity. But that sense thrills the New Testament writers. The present chapter, therefore, does not begin the subject of eschatology. It concludes a presentation which throughout has dealt with eschatological fulfillment.

But what we still have to say is a necessary conclusion of the total eschatological message. The advocates of "realized eschatology" have

---

[3] C. H. Dodd is generally regarded as the leading spokesman of this view. Dodd himself recognizes another aspect of New Testament thought and cites two other "labels" which may avoid misunderstanding: "inaugurated eschatology" (Florovsky's phrase) and "sich realisierende Eschatologie" (Jeremias' phrase, meaning eschatology in process of being realized). Dodd likes the latter best; see his *The Interpretation of the Fourth Gospel* Cambridge, 1953), p. 447, n. 1. A good summary of recent study is given by Nelson, *The Realm of Redemption*, pp. 211-34.

overstated their case. God had acted in Christ, he was acting in the church, but he still had to act to establish completely his final order. The advocates of "realized eschatology" should have spoken instead of "partially realized eschatology." For the New Testament preachers and writers never thought that the complete and final Kingdom had come. The action of God then under way would bring that full Kingdom, which had not yet been completely established. Evil was still at work, God's justice could still be disputed, the victory of God in the world scene was not yet apparent, and personal fulfillment still had far to go before every human being would receive his just and final lot.

This New Testament position, that God has begun his final action but has not yet completed it, has an anchor for faith which some eschatological messages cannot match. God has given a solid basis for faith and hope in the ministry, death, and resurrection of Christ.[4] The believer is not reduced to desperate hope which flies in the face of all the evidence. It takes faith to discern the meaning of these central events of history, but to the one who has that faith, these historical events, these facts of God's work in history, support confidence about the future. "He who did not spare his own Son but gave him up for us all, will he not also give us all things with him?" (Rom. 8:32.)

The decisive battle has occurred. Christ has won the crucial victory.[5] The ultimate crushing and banishing of the forces of evil is assured. Christ is the Lord; the Spirit is given to the church as the first fruits or guarantee of the total victory that is sure to come (Rom. 8:23; II Cor. 1:22; 5:5; Eph. 1:14). The note of hope, therefore, does not defy all facts; it rather discerns the full and final meaning of events already past and actions now in progress. This is eschatology already begun, in process of being realized more fully, and certain to come to complete realization. The essential factor that supports and steadies Christian hope is not a bright promise of impending relief from present evils; it is the fact that in Christ and the Spirit, God has already achieved the decisive beginning of his final victory and thus given the sure promise that all the rest will follow.

[4] Oscar Cullmann stresses this in *Christ and Time*, pp. 81-93.
[5] Oscar Cullmann, op. cit., pp. 87, 141. Cf. also Gustaf Aulén, *Christus Victor*, tr. A. G. Hebert (London, 1931), ch. iv.

The Christian of the Apostolic Age thus lives in the time of continuous fulfillment. He sees God in the process of completing the final plan. This accent marks New Testament eschatology. The final events for which Christian faith looks will bring the completion of the eschatological action of God through Christ; they will lead to his perfect, permanent divine order in which all of God's people will find their eternal home and blessedness.

Did Eschatology Fade or Become Transformed?

Before we sketch the New Testament expectation concerning the great final drama which will establish God's eternal and perfect kingdom, we should first examine an objection. It asserts that the eschatological note, while prominent in the earliest years of the church, soon faded from view or was so transformed that it referred only to the present and the life of this world. This assertion takes many forms. Formerly a number of scholars held that Jesus himself had not shared this strong emphasis on eschatology; it had been added to the gospel tradition by the early Christians, who as Jews were so strongly under the influence of Jewish apocalyptic that they could not keep their inherited views separate from their Christian tradition.[6] It should no longer be necessary to answer this objection. Unless the gospel tradition is quite unreliable, Jesus looked to the future triumph of God's cause and spoke with urgency about the imminence of the Kingdom and the coming of the Son of Man. We hear a cautious note in his words; he disclaimed knowledge of the exact time (Mark 13:32). But his message was framed in an eschatological setting and breathed a strong note of expectancy.

While the strong eschatological note in Jesus' teaching is now all but universally recognized, there are scholars who claim that Paul's thinking about eschatology went through two stages.[7] At first, he held to an immature, strongly eschatological emphasis; he expected the Lord to return quickly to execute final judgment and bring in the

[6] See the able argument by Ernest De Witt Burton, *New Testament Word Studies* (Chicago: University of Chicago Press, 1927), pp. 83-98, where Burton studies "Kingdom of God, Kingdom of Heaven."

[7] See Albert Schweitzer, *Paul and His Interpreters*, tr. W. Montgomery (London, 1912), for various views on Paul's thinking.

eternal Kingdom. But later, it is alleged, Paul gave up such ideas, or let them to recede into obscurity. He then thought in terms of the present privilege of faith, without really expecting a decisive, final drama.

This view involves two separate questions. Did Paul expect to live until the return of the Lord? In his earlier letters, which speak of those still living on this earth when the end comes, he uses "we" of this group (I Thess. 4:15, 17; I Cor. 15:52). He thus implies that he expects to be among those survivors. This is good evidence that for much of his life he expected to be alive and at work in the church at the time of Christ's return. In later writings, however, Paul recognizes at least the possibility that he may die before Christ comes (II Cor. 5:6-8; Phil 1:23). The change seems to trace back to the time in Asia Minor when he faced death, and only by a miracle—as it seemed to him—escaped alive (II Cor. 1:8). Yet even in the passages which speak of the possibility of his death, he is not certain that this will occur at once. In fact, in Phil. 1:25 he rather says the contrary; he expects to live for a time at least, though he is ready to die. But II Tim. 4:6— probably from Paul—speaks of death as near.

This issue, however, is quite separate from the other question, whether Paul gave up his eschatology. There is no evidence that he did. As the years passed, he may have silently adjusted his attitude to allow for a somewhat longer time before the end should come.[8] But even in Philippians, which is probably one of his latest letters, he plainly says, "The Lord is at hand" (Phil. 4:5). And in Romans, the last letter before his Caesarean and Roman imprisonment, he feels the end drawing nearer: "It is full time now for you to wake from sleep. For salvation is nearer to us now than when we first believed; the night is far gone, the day is at hand" (Rom. 13:11-12). In Eph. 4:30 Paul looks forward to "the day of redemption."

Paul never gave up his vivid expectation of the great decisive day which would bring the final condemnation of evil and the full triumph of God's cause. He was gratefully aware of rich gifts already given. But he looked for great victories and gifts still to come.

[8] Albert Schweitzer, The Mysticism of Paul the Apostle, tr. William Montgomery (New York: Henry Holt & Co., 1931), argues that Paul prepared for the abandonment of thoroughgoing eschatology by his vivid mysticism and sense of the present gifts of Christian life.

If any New Testament writing supports the elimination of the eschatological note from the Christian message, it is the Gospel of John.[9] This Gospel accents the present gift of eternal life through Christ to those who will believe (3:36). But it does not ignore the expectation of future resurrection and judgment. "The Father raises the dead," and this cannot mean only a spiritual inward renewal in this life, for "all who are in the tombs will hear his voice and come forth" (John 5:21, 28-29). The fourfold reference to "the last day" in John 6:39, 40, 44, 54 confirms this eschatological meaning. The resurrection of Lazarus and that of Jesus point forward to this final resurrection.

The eschatology of the Gospel of John, then, is not limited to the present gift of eternal life. Nor is it confined to individual rescue by Christ, as 14:3 might be taken to imply. It includes the great final drama in which all men are raised and God's final order is fully established. It is quite wrong, therefore, to let modern distaste for eschatological imagery obscure its importance in all stages of New Testament thought. It was vigorous and central throughout these writings; variations of accent occur, but this forward look continually recurs.

The Final Drama

The great drama will complete God's work; it will not be a totally new action. The coming and work of Christ, and the gift of the Spirit, were initial parts of the great final action of God. The Kingdom had begun to come in the person and work of Jesus. Eternal life was open through faith even in this earthly life (John 3:36). Jesus can say to Zacchaeus, "Today salvation has come to this house." (Luke 19:9.) Paul can say that God has "transferred us to the kingdom of his beloved Son." (Col. 1:13.) Thus radical actions by God have already occurred. They do not give all that God has to give; even the gift of the Spirit which followed the earthly work of Christ was but the first fruits, the guarantee of far greater gifts and works still to come (Rom. 8:23; II Cor. 1:22; 5:5; Eph. 1:14). But they are a part of the eschatological work of God.

Several times the expectation appears that a reward or new privilege

[9] I think that Paul S. Minear overstates this tendency of the Gospel of John; see his study, And Great Shall Be Your Reward (New Haven: Yale University Press, 1941), pp. 67-68. But he has a stimulating study of the meaning of the New Testament hope in Christian Hope and the Second Coming (Philadelphia: Westminster Press, 1954).

will be received at death. But this does not exclude the great final drama. Jesus told the penitent thief, "Today you will be with me in Paradise." (Luke 23:43.) When the poor man Lazarus died, he "was carried by the angels to Abraham's bosom," while the rich man found himself in Hades (Luke 16:22-23). John 14:3, in its promise that Jesus "will come again and will take you to myself," may be referring to this privilege given at death. Paul is sure that if he dies he will depart and be with Christ, which will be a far better life than the Christian privilege he here knows (Phil. 1:23). The martyrs are given honor and comfort while waiting for the end (Rev. 6:11).

But New Testament eschatology was not merely a promise of personal immortality. It assured believers that God's full purpose would triumph throughout his world in the face of all opposition.

This assurance is not presented in a literalistic way; through vivid word pictures the writers seek to make the expectation live for the reader. The writers have little or no interest in speculation about exact details and secrets of God's ways. Their interest centers in the outcome. They reveal not the details and mechanics of the drama, but the fact of victory and the meaning it has for faith.

We do find luxuriant imagery; it is drawn from many ancient sources, and chiefly of course from the Old Testament. If we try to fit all such imagery into a consistent literal picture, we end in confusion. Is Jesus both a priestly figure, a Lamb, a Lion, a Root, and a warrior victorious in fierce battle? Yes, he is all this and more in the Book of Revelation (1:13; 5:5-6; 19:11-16). But to take all these references literally and include them in a visual picture of Christ would be absurd.

So throughout the New Testament we must recognize the figurative and symbolic nature of such references, and yet discern their real meaning: they express God's power, purpose, and victory. With this point of view we must now look at the aspects of the final drama which the New Testament mentions.[10]

Christ Present and to Come

The "coming" or "appearing" of Christ is prominent among the promised events of the end (e.g., I Thess. 2:19; II Thess. 2:8). But a

[10] See the sketch of New Testament teaching on these points in Edward Langton, Good and Evil Spirits (New York: The Macmillan Co., 1942), ch. ix.

curious difficulty besets this expectation. To Christians Christ was the Lord of the church; by the Spirit he led and upheld it. To Paul the relation was even more intimate and vivid; "it is . . . Christ who lives in me" (Gal. 2:20); "we were buried therefore with him by baptism into death," and we are now "alive to God in Christ Jesus" (Rom. 6:4, 11). Christ was not out of touch with his church. The living Christ was really present in the community at the celebration of the Lord's Supper. He had promised every obedient disciple that he would "come to him" (John 14:23); he had promised his disciples that in their witness and ministry he would be with them "always, to the close of the age" (Matt. 28:20).

We cannot say how vivid or widespread this sense of the presence of the living Christ was in the daily life of Christians. However, it plainly was a recurrent note to which we hear frequent testimony. When we couple with it the universal confession of Christ as the living Lord of the church, we know that the church did not think that he was out of touch with his followers.

Yet he had gone away, as had the man in the parable (Matt. 25:15). He had withdrawn from the visible and open fellowship with his people which had marked his ministry. The tie with him was real, but it was incomplete. There existed a limitation which the Christian expected to give way to open, richer, fuller fellowship. The same Paul who could say that it is "Christ who lives in me" (Gal. 2:20) could also say that "to depart and be with Christ" will be "far better" (Phil. 1:23), and he could anticipate as a priceless new privilege the time when "we shall always be with the Lord" (I Thess. 4:17).[11]

So the church which knew Christ as their present Lord still looked for the full, open, final manifestation of Christ to complete his work and establish the final order willed by God. The spatial, pictorial portrayal of this open manifestation is the vehicle of essential truth. Christ will act openly and appear clearly to all; he will prove beyond dispute that he has been and is the Lord; he will bring to climax and completion what God has promised his people.

[11] See James S. Stewart, A Man in Christ, pp. 199-203.

The Full and Final Defeat of Evil

This appearance of Christ will bring deliverance to the church. The New Testament never guarantees to God's people earthly security. Persecution and opposition are considered normal in this world (Rom. 8:17; II Tim. 3:12). The martyrs cry out impatiently, "How long?" (Rev. 6:10), but the church must wait until the end of the struggle for final deliverance from the attacks of evil. But that time of deliverance will come. Christ will free his people from injustice and attacks by foes and oppressors. He will establish an order which will free God's people from all such trouble; every evil person and power will be crushed and banished.

Thus the return of Christ will bring the defeat of evil, the final and complete defeat of every God-opposing power.[12] The mastery of Jesus over the demons who plagued men was for him and his church a first stage of that defeat. It meant that the kingdom of God was already in process of coming (Matt. 12:28). The reign of Christ as Lord was a time of conflict against all the forces of wickedness, "for he must reign until he has put all his enemies under his feet" (I Cor. 15:25).

In the New Testament, evil has terrible reality. It has personal embodiment and Satanic leadership. It does not respond to reason or good teaching. It does not flee at the first sign of opposition; not even Jas. 4:7, "he will flee from you," promises easy victory. It fights the right with fierce, persistent, and desperate violence. It cannot be let alone in the hope that it will go away; it must be defeated, and only Christ the Son of God, exalted Lord, can defeat "every rule and every authority and power" that is evil before "he delivers the kingdom to God the Father" (I Cor. 15:24).

We often tend to think of life as a neutral scene. One may choose to believe in Christ; one may wish that all would do so; but outside of that realm of faith in Christ, we may imagine, is a quiet passive region in which non-Christians may safely live. The New Testament never makes that mistake. Life is a battleground, and it will continue such until evil is finally defeated and banished from the scene.

If we see no evil and have no sense of its tenacity and power, we

---

[12] See Elias Andrews, *The Meaning of Christ for Paul*, ch. v.

may feel no need of eschatology with its pictorial assurance of the complete victory of Christ over all who oppose God and the church. But once we discern how cunning, determined, and resourceful evil really is, the New Testament eschatology becomes much more reasonable. For the New Testament writers it was indispensable, and one reason was that it expressed this conviction that every evil power must and will be defeated.

The Resurrection of the Dead

Another prominent aspect of the final drama is the resurrection of the dead. This expectation, so vivid in New Testament thought, is not a central feature of Old Testament thinking. A few passages there point to a resurrection. Perhaps the most explicit are Isa. 26:19 and Dan. 12:2. Other passages which speak of the life-giving power of God (e.g., Ezek. 37) suggest to Christians more than they explicitly said at the time.

By the first century, however, this small seed of Old Testament thought had produced quite a tree of expectation in Judaism. Jesus spoke with confidence of the resurrection of himself and of others (Mark 8:31; 9:31; 10:34; 12:25-27). His own resurrection placed this expectation in the center of New Testament thinking,[13] and so the idea pervades the New Testament, often finding explicit expression and elsewhere lying behind what is said. Christ is the risen Lord; resurrection is axiomatic to Christian faith. It is a "living hope." (I Pet. 1:3.) Even the Gospel of John shares it, as we have seen; its emphasis on the present gift of eternal life does not exclude the hope of resurrection at the last day.

Was this resurrection to include all men, or only the people of God? A few passages speak explicitly of the resurrection of all. A pictorial account of the final judgment, on all nations, all people, good and bad, is found in Matt. 25:31-46. In Rev. 20:11-15 are depicted the resurrection and judgment of all. John 5:28-29 definitely refers not only to "the resurrection of life" for "those who have done good," but also to "the resurrection of judgment" for "those who have done evil."

Yet most references to resurrection speak only of the resurrection of believers. This does not contradict the passages which point to a uni-

[13] See A. Michael Ramsey, The Resurrection of Christ (Philadelphia: Westminster Press, 1946).

versal resurrection. The attention of Christians normally centered not on the doom of the wicked, but on the positive expectation of what the last day would bring to believers. They could speak often of that side of coming events without denying the fuller picture. The final drama concerned all men, but the privilege of the believer was most often mentioned.

Resurrection meant more than immortality. New Testament Christians came to Christ from the background of the Old Testament, where man was a unity. Body and soul were but aspects of the one person. A man without a body was a mere shade, an incomplete being. So when Christians began to think of a full, rich life in the final Kingdom, they had to conceive of it as life in a body.

Many modern Christians look with condescending scorn on this view. They take the Greek view that life in the body is an inferior way of living; for them the free life of the disembodied spirit is the real hope to cherish.

To this view, two things should be said from the New Testament outlook. For one thing, note the intent of the teaching of the resurrection of the body. It was meant to say that the life of that future time will be rich and full; it will be no partial, unsatisfying existence, but a life in which the whole person fully participates in the joy and privilege of the perfect Kingdom. By God's grace the whole man will take his place in the final order.

A second fact is worth noting. New Testament Christians could not conceive of this full, rich, satisfying life without a body. Can we? Do we in fact do so? Or do we not really conceive that the spirit of man in some way possesses a form, a means of living and having personal ties? Such real personal life has to have for us a conceivable center and means of expression. This is what the apostle Paul was saying in his teaching of the resurrection of the body. He did not expect the revival of the physical body we now have: "flesh and blood cannot inherit the kingdom of God" (I Cor. 15:50). But he held that man must have a body, a form of life, an organ for the expression of personal existence and personal relationships.

It may be doubted whether with our situation in this world, where we never escape anthropomorphic ways of thought, we can get beyond Paul's way of thought.[14] Abstract conceptions of a life free from all the conditions we know yield no picture of real life. A frankly anthropomorphic picture of life, in terms related to, even if not identical with, those we now know is the nearest we can come to expressing Paul's rich content of the life in the age to come.

But even if we think we can do better than Paul, even if we claim that we can adequately picture the future life with God without any idea of resurrection of the body or any provision for a definite form of personal existence, it remains a fact that the New Testament expresses the richness of that life by speaking of the resurrection of the body. God will bring men back to a full and conscious form of existence, where each can answer for his former life and enter into the lot assigned him. The life to come will concern the whole man.

The Final Judgment

This resurrection will be the prelude to the final judgment and give entrance to the permanent life to come. The note of judgment sounds repeatedly throughout the New Testament.[15] Jesus speaks clearly about it (Matt. 25:32; Mark 8:38), the preaching summaries of the Book of Acts include it (10:42; 17:31), and the writers of the various books state it as the common conviction of the church (II Cor. 5:10; Heb. 10:30; Jas. 5:9; Rev. 20:12).

God is the Lord. Men must answer to him. He is good and gracious, but he cannot and will not permit deliberate and persistent rebellion against his righteous rule. He will forgive; he even opens up the way to forgiveness on his own initiative, and provides a way to new life to all who will accept it; but judgment will come, and it will condemn those who stubbornly continue in evil ways. In the end his final order will be free from rebellion, sin, and attacks upon his people. He will judge and condemn the wicked.

[14] On Paul's view see John A. T. Robinson, The Body (London, 1952), especially the latter part of ch. iii.
[15] On the judgment in Jesus' teaching see Amos N. Wilder, Eschatology and Ethics in the Teaching of Jesus (revised ed.; New York: Harper & Bros., 1950), pp. 94 ff. On Paul's teaching cf. James S. Stewart, op. cit., pp. 268-70; Gillis Piton Wetter, Der Vergeltungsgedanke bei Paulus (Göttingen, 1912); and my monograph, St. Paul's Conception of Recompense (Leipzig, 1931).

We may ask: But how will God be able to tell the good from the evil? Is there much difference? The New Testament faith is that God can and will make the separation, and that his decision will be both fair and just. In the face of his manifested wisdom there will then be no justifiable reason to complain (II Thess. 1:5; Heb. 12:23).

Some New Testament passages are content to say that God judges. But others state with equal confidence that Christ will judge. It is before the Son of Man that all nations will be gathered (Matt. 25:32). He will be the judge of the living and the dead (Acts 10:42). "We must all appear before the judgment seat of Christ, so that each one may receive good or evil, according to what he has done in the body." (II Cor. 5:10.) In II Tim. 4:8 "the Lord, the righteous judge" is evidently the risen Christ whose "appearing" Christians await.

The explanation of this apparent contradiction is easy to find. Paul puts it clearly when he refers to "that day when, according to my gospel, God judges the secrets of men by Christ Jesus." (Rom 2:16.) God acts; the entire gospel story is the story of God's action for the salvation of men. But he acts through Christ, and Christ acts with the authority of God. Not only the winning of redemption for men, but also the lordship of the church and the final judgment of the world are God's work through Christ.

This judgment both believers and unbelievers must face. All the passages quoted above assume or state this; II Cor. 5:10, for example, is unmistakably clear. Those who believe in Christ do not escape God's moral demand. They are not released from moral obligation, but they are given new life and the resources of the Spirit by which they can live wholesome and fruitful lives (Gal. 5:22-23). And they must make good use of their privilege and opportunity.

God's Gifts and Rewards to His People

How are reward and salvation described? [16] The usual view is that those who really believe, and in that faith dedicate their lives to God, will hear the words "Well done" and will be welcomed into his kingdom.

---

[16] On rewards in the teaching of Jesus and the early church see Paul S. Minear, *And Great Shall Be Your Reward* (New Haven: Yale University Press, 1941), chs. iv and v.

Occasional hints suggest that even so they will still be receiving the grace of God. Just as Jesus had taught his disciples, "Forgive us our debts, as we also have forgiven our debtors" (Matt. 6:12), so he assured them that the merciful will receive mercy but the servant who will not forgive cannot be forgiven (Matt. 18:21-35). Others make similar statements: "judgment is without mercy to one who has shown no mercy; mercy triumphs over judgment" (Jas. 2:13), and "love covers a multitude of sins" (I Pet. 4:8).

Thus the note recurs that in the end even believers will stand in need of the kindly grace of God (Jude 21). They will receive it if their kindness toward others recommends them. The Judge will examine the Christian's record, but with mercy for all who have shown a merciful spirit to others. The note of grace is still present in the final judgment scene.

The promise of divine welcome goes out to certain groups in particular. Those who have passed through the fire of persecution and faithfully endured it for the sake of Christ will receive a welcome and comfort. "He who endures to the end will be saved." (Mark 13:13.)

It is this promise of tender care and sure honor which explains the picture of the millennium in Rev. 20:4-6. In modern times this passage is often thought to promise an early resurrection and special privilege for all Christians. The passage does not support such a view. It speaks of the martyrs, "those who had been beheaded for their testimony to Jesus and for the word of God." [17] The further reference to persons "who had not worshiped the beast or its image and had not received its mark on their foreheads or their hands" might at first sight seem to refer to others besides martyrs. But the expectation of the writer of the Book of Revelation was that the second beast, which rose out of the earth, would "cause those who will not worship the image of the beast to be slain" (13:15).

In other words, Rev. 20:4 speaks only of martyrs. For their faithfulness and as a special privilege, they will be raised first and live and share Christ's reign for a thousand years. Then will come the final

---

[17] So among others R. H. Charles, *The Revelation of St. John* (New York, 1920), II, 180-86.

defeat of Satan, followed by the final judgment. Thus the honor shown the martyrs precedes the actual judgment.

Here as elsewhere in the New Testament, however, we feel that the Judgment will confirm a status already given the faithful. It will manifest openly the favorable judgment of God on these who have suffered for the cause of Christ. This is an important part of the New Testament idea of the final judgment. It openly manifests the divine approval of the right and condemnation of the wrong. The ambiguity of history gives way to the clear recognition of good and evil, and each receives the open reward or punishment which he deserves.

But it is not only the oppressed and persecuted who will receive special favor. The suffering and needy will also receive welcome and privilege. These needy persons, for whom God has a special concern, are thought to be responsive to his goodness and open to his blessing; there is no intention to cancel the spiritual and moral standards of God's judgment. But we recall that in the Old Testament the widow and orphan were the special concern of God, and the poor likewise evoked his active interest. So also in the New Testament God's mercy and care for those whose lives have known want and suffering is clearly expressed (Luke 16:22), and his people are expected to reflect the divine sympathy for all in need (Matt. 25:40; Jas. 1:27).

In view of this fact, it is not surprising that Jesus speaks with approval of those who show a humane and kindly spirit. The Good Samaritan is mentioned with obvious approval (Luke 10:29-37). In Jesus' picture of the last judgment, the Son of Man approves those who have fed the hungry, befriended the strangers, clothed the needy, and visited the sick and imprisoned (Matt. 25:35-36). This is in keeping with other teachings of Jesus. He spoke with indignation and condemnation of those who were callous or cruel to their fellow men (Matt. 25:41-43; Mark 10:42; 12:40). God's judgment takes into account the way in which we treat our human comrades, especially those in need. Man's fitness to live eternally in fellowship with God comes most clearly to expression in this spirit of compassion.

Are there degrees of reward and privilege in the eternal kingdom? The privilege given the martyrs, the special tenderness to those who have suffered unusual hardship in this life, may suggest that there are.

And the parables of the talents and the pounds may indicate that some will have greater honor than others (Matt. 25:14-30; Luke 19:12-27).

However, we must not overemphasize these passages. The privilege of the Christian life is basically God's free gift to undeserving men. The joy of fellowship with God in the eternal Kingdom is not so graded that class distinctions rule in that final order. God will "make it up" to all who have suffered; this is certainly said. And the parables of the talents and the pounds say that men's task and activity in that future time will be according to each one's demonstrated ability. But this is not class legislation. In Rev. 7:9-10 a "great multitude" stand before the throne of God and praise the Lamb who redeemed them; they all share essentially the same great privilege.

God will comfort the ill-treated and honor the faithful, but this does not obscure the basic equality of all God's people. They had a common need; they received the same grace and salvation; they share in the same eternal Kingdom; and they have the same privilege of eternal life, which is to know and be with the Father and his Son (John 17:3).

What Will Happen to the Wicked?

The final fate of the wicked calls for careful study. There are passages which speak definitely of their exclusion from the final order which Christ will establish. Jesus spoke of the outer darkness, in which there will be weeping and gnashing of teeth to indicate the exclusion from life and privilege (e.g., Matt. 22:13; Luke 13:28).[18] In his picture of the final judgment he clearly divided those judged into two classes, one accepted and one rejected (Matt. 25:31-46). Some would rise to life and some to judgment, that is, to condemnation. (John 5:29.) Paul is as clear as Jesus that divine condemnation will fall on the disobedient and wicked (Rom. 2:5-10). The Book of Revelation is thus stating common Christian conviction when it pictures the great final judgment and the rejection of the wicked (20:11-15).

Certain other passages suggest a more pleasant outcome. To some they justify the conclusion that all men will eventually be saved. Paul in particular speaks in sweeping terms of the world-wide effects of Christ's

[18] This expression occurs five times in Matthew and once in Luke. The use in Luke shows it is not Matthew's invention.

redemptive work. He contrasts the universal effect of Adam's sin with the universal life-giving effect of Christ's work (Rom. 5:18; I Cor. 15:22). He says that Christ died for all (II Cor. 5:14). He speaks of the salvation of all Israel at the end (Rom. 11:25-26).

Upon closer examination, however, these statements do not mean to contradict other passages where Paul, like the other New Testament writers, clearly expects the condemnation of some. He is asserting the universality of the gospel. He is expressing the conviction that at the end all Israel will believe. But he is not saying that each and every human being will be saved and received into the final Kingdom. He found no basis for expecting universal salvation either in the teaching of Jesus, the preaching of the other apostles, the testimony of Scripture, or the facts of life as he observed them. He worked to lead as many people as he could to Christ, and he was active to build up those converts in faith and loyalty. But he was sure that he and all men would face God's test, and he expected that some, by their rejection of God's will and goodness, would fail to receive final salvation.

Many questions which we might ask about the Judgment the New Testament does not answer. What will happen to all the previous generations which have not heard the gospel? Since the New Testament writers think that they are living "in these last days" (Heb. 1:2), we might expect them to take great interest in the lot of earlier generations, for the great majority of mankind, as they supposed, would be from pre-Christian times. But they did not stop to ask the question or demand a clear-cut answer. That issue lay in the hands of God. We may find clues that partly sketch an answer. God will deal with men according to their knowledge and opportunity in their day (Rom. 2:12-16). But the real interest of the New Testament leaders was in the people whom they could reach. Speculation was not their task; they were to give their witness to Christ and reach as many persons as possible. The rest they left to God.

"We Shall Always Be With the Lord"

The New Testament gives no clear or full picture of the final order in which God's people find their permanent home. It has no interest in speculation or in answering questions prompted by curiosity. The

Christian writers are mainly concerned to say what this great privilege will mean to believers.

It is not even clear where believers will live in the end. In this respect I Thess. 4:17 is characteristic. Both the risen Christians and those still living will be caught up into mid-air to meet the Lord. Whether this meeting leads to a life on a renewed earth or in a glorious heaven, the passage never says. Instead, it ends with the assurance, "and so we shall always be with the Lord." This is the one thing which is important. The place is secondary.

Certain suggestions point to a new order on a transformed earth. Paul looks forward to a time when "the creation itself will be set free from its bondage to decay" (Rom. 8:21), presumably to furnish the scene of life for God's people in the eternal Kingdom. In the Book of Rev. 21:1-2, the holy city descends from heaven, and God dwells with men; the scene appears to be a new earth which, centered in the holy city, becomes the fit home of the faithful. That the new earth is in part at least the scene of the future life is suggested by the "new heavens and a *new earth*" mentioned in II Pet. 3:13. The statement that the Son of Man will come to judge (Matt. 25:31) also implies that the earth is the scene of the final judgment and may be the scene of the perfect life which follows.

Other passages, however, suggest that the perfect order will not be on this earth but elsewhere, presumably in heaven. In Rev. 7:9-10 the multitudes stand before the throne of God and praise him and the Lamb for giving them salvation. In John 14:2-3 Jesus promises to take his own to live with him "in my Father's house."

This uncertainty shows that the geography of eternity is not the central interest of New Testament Christians. They use imagery familiar to them. It points now to a perfect life on a renewed earth, and now to a blessed life in heaven.[19] The place and the details of the setting are not important. The one central fact is that in God's perfect order they will have the inexpressible privilege of permanent fellowship with God and Christ. With all hostile forces defeated and banished, Christ will yield up his kingship to the Father (I Cor. 15:24-28). His work

[19] God's whole created order will be redeemed. This is somewhat of a cosmic parallel to the New Testament idea of the resurrection of the body.

will be complete; the salvation of God's people will be won and their complete and lasting happiness assured. They will be with the Lord Christ, to whom their debt is infinite and their gratitude gladly expressed (I Thess. 4:17). They will be with God, for in that final order "the dwelling of God is with men" (Rev. 21:3). This is the real meaning of the eternal life which is God's gift to faith: "this is eternal life, that they know thee the only true God, and Jesus Christ whom thou hast sent" (John 17:3). With this privilege in prospect, the place and outward setting may be described in vivid traditional imagery, but the point is never the details but the central relation to God and Christ.

This life with God is life in a fellowship of worshipers. In both the Old and New Testaments the people of God furnish the setting of individual faith and worship. So, too, in the final order it is not as hermits, but as sharers in a human fellowship that men know and worship and serve God. Abraham had "looked to the city which has foundations, whose builder and maker is God." (Heb. 11:10.) All those who live and die in faith "are seeking a homeland." "Therefore God is not ashamed to be called their God, for he has prepared for them a city" (Heb. 11:14, 16). "The holy city" comes down to be the home of those who have this concern and promise (Rev. 21:10). God's people share together the eternal life that he gives to those who believe.

To every Christian who looked for this great day, it was axiomatic that the future country—the city to come—would be a place "in which righteousness dwells" (II Pet. 3:13). They will live in an order where God's kingdom has fully come and his will is fully done (I Cor. 15:24-25). They will find their joy in their salvation, in the triumph of God's cause, and in the fact that the confused conflicts of this age have given way to the holy God's righteous order, which Christ "the Holy and Righteous One" (Acts 3:14) has established. With the law of God written in their hearts, they will live in willing and glad obedience and in rich fellowship with God and Christ. Their life will be wholesome and happy and given to the worship and service of God. In this hope, born of faith, built upon the historical work of Jesus Christ, and attested by the Spirit in their hearts and common worship, the Apostolic Church lived and worked and suffered and died, telling each other that "in the Lord your labor is not in vain" (I Cor. 15:58).

INDEX OF PASSAGES

OLD TESTAMENT

APOCRYPHA

PSEUDEPIGRAPHA

NEW TESTAMENT

APOSTOLIC FATHERS

Epistle of Barnabas

INDEX OF PERSONS AND SUBJECTS